The Lion Within

RANDALL J.
BREWER

THE LION WITHIN

CONTENTS

INTRODUCTION

There is something inside you that refuses to stay quiet. It has been buried under comfort, dulled by distraction, and silenced by fear but it has never died. It is the strength God placed within you from the beginning. It is the call to stand, to lead, to fight, to build, and to endure. It is the lion within.

Too many men today have been taught to shrink back instead of rise up. They have been conditioned to choose ease over purpose, silence over conviction, and passivity over responsibility. But you were not created for a life of retreat - you were created for a life of impact. Deep within you is a God-given fire that was never meant to be extinguished.

Scripture reveals a powerful image of strength, authority, and unshakable presence - the lion. Jesus Himself is called the Lion of Judah. This is not a symbol of reckless aggression, but of controlled power, fearless leadership, and unwavering truth. And as men created in His image, we are called to reflect that same strength not in pride, but in purpose. Not in domination, but in devotion.

This book is a call to awaken what has been asleep. It is a call to confront fear, reject passivity, and rise into the man God designed you to be. It will challenge you. It will sharpen you. It will stretch you beyond what is comfortable. But on the other side of that stretching is strength - real strength - the kind that cannot be shaken by storms, opposition, or doubt.

You were never meant to live half awake. You were never meant to blend in with a culture that has forgotten what true manhood looks like. You were created to stand out. To stand firm. To stand strong. So let this be the moment everything changes. Let this be the moment you stop silencing the voice within you. Let this be the moment the lion within you begins to rise.

| 1 |

"THE CALL TO AWAKEN"

There is a call that echoes deep within every man - a quiet but unrelenting voice that refuses to be ignored. It stirs in moments of stillness and in times when life feels too small for what you sense inside. This is the awakening of purpose, the stirring of God-given strength that cannot be satisfied with passivity or complacency. It is the reminder that you were not created to drift through life, but to rise with intention, to stand with conviction, and to carry a calling that is greater than yourself. This call is an invitation to move beyond fear and into faith, and to become the man God designed you to be. It will challenge you, refine you, and stretch you, but it will also strengthen you in ways nothing else can. When you answer it, you begin to walk in alignment with your true identity - not shaped by the world but forged by God. And in that place, you will discover that the life you were meant to live is not found in ease, but in obedience, courage, and a relentless pursuit of the purpose placed within you.

Too many men underestimate what God has placed inside them because they have grown accustomed to measuring their lives by comfort instead of calling. Ease has become their standard, but God never designed you for a life of ease - He designed you for a life of purpose. What is inside you was not meant to remain dormant; it was meant to be developed, stretched, and proven. The truth is, there is more in you than you have allowed yourself to believe. More strength to stand, more discipline to endure, more faith to press forward when others quit. You are not limited by your past, your fears, or your current circumstances - you are limited only by what you are willing to step into. When you stop measuring your life by comfort and start aligning it with your calling, everything changes. You begin to see pressure as preparation and difficulty as development. Rise to the level God has already placed within you, because the man you are becoming is far greater than the man you have settled for.

Dormant strength does not disappear - it waits beneath the surface, quiet but unbroken. It watches as a man drifts through distraction, settles into passivity, and trades purpose for comfort. Yet even in those seasons, it does not fade. God placed it there intentionally - strength to lead, to endure, to stand when others fall. It is not erased by delay or dulled by misuse; it is simply waiting for the moment a man decides he has had enough of living beneath who he was created to be. That awakening begins with a decision. The moment a man chooses discipline over ease, courage over fear, and obedience over hesitation, that buried strength rises to meet him. It responds to action. It grows through resistance. And what once felt distant suddenly becomes alive and active within him. God has not withdrawn what He placed inside - you have simply not called it forward yet. But when you do, you will discover that the strength you thought was gone was never gone at all - it was waiting for you to rise.

The tragedy is not that a man lacks strength - it is that he never awakens it. God has already placed within him the capacity to endure, to lead, to stand firm, and to rise when life presses hard against him. But when a man chooses comfort over calling, ease over growth, and passivity over purpose, that strength remains buried. He begins to settle into a life that demands little and produces even less. Over time, he grows disconnected from the fire that once stirred within him. What was meant to be a life of impact becomes a life far beneath what God intended. But something inside him knows this is not who he was created to be. Awakening begins the moment a man starts responding to that call. It requires him to rise, to confront complacency, and to step into the responsibility he has been avoiding. When he does, strength that once seemed absent begins to surface, and purpose becomes clear again. The man he was meant to become has not disappeared - he has simply been waiting to be awakened.

A man does not have to run from God to drift from Him; he only has to stop pursuing. The fire that once burned with conviction becomes a flicker when it is not fed, and urgency fades into indifference. What once stirred his spirit now barely moves him, and he begins to settle into a life that requires little faith, little sacrifice, and little awareness of God's voice. This is the danger of complacency - it numbs without warning and convinces a man he is fine when he is slowly losing ground. But God does not call men to a passive existence - He calls them to rise, to seek, to burn with purpose again. The remedy for spiritual sleep is intentional pursuit. Fire is not sustained by emotion - it is sustained by discipline and devotion. And when a man chooses to lean in instead of pull back, to pursue instead of coast, what once felt distant begins to reignite. The presence of God becomes real again, and the man who was once spiritually absent steps fully back into the life he was created to live.

When a man is asleep spiritually, he reacts instead of leads, responds instead of prepares, and slowly surrenders ground he was meant to hold. Without awareness of God's voice and direction, life begins to shape him instead of him shaping his life through faith and conviction. What once required strength becomes compromised by convenience, and what once stirred purpose becomes dulled by distraction. But a man who awakens refuses to drift any longer. He becomes intentional again - grounded in truth, steady in identity, and anchored in purpose. He no longer allows circumstances to define him; instead, he stands firm in who God created him to be. With renewed clarity, he takes responsibility for his direction, his decisions, and his discipline. Where there was passivity, there is now action. Where there was confusion, there is now conviction. Awakening is not just a moment - it is a decision to rise, to engage, and to live fully aligned with the calling God has placed on his life.

Comfort becomes his hiding place, not because he chose weakness, but because he slowly stopped choosing strength. What once stirred his spirit now sits untouched, buried beneath routines that require nothing and distractions that demand little. Days pass, and what felt like rest becomes avoidance, what felt like relief becomes retreat. He convinces himself that he's waiting for the right moment, but in truth, he's drifting from the very calling that once burned inside him. The tragedy is not that the fire was extinguished - it's that it was ignored. A neglected fire does not rage; it fades quietly, leaving behind the illusion that nothing was ever there. But the fire is not gone - it is waiting for a man who will step out of comfort, silence the distractions, and return to what God placed within him. God has not withdrawn what He placed inside him - He is waiting for him to awaken it. And the moment he does, he will realize that what once felt distant was never lost - it was simply waiting for him to return and carry it forward.

God does not call men to drift through life in comfort or remain hidden in passivity. From the beginning, His voice has carried a clear command: awaken, stand up, and take your place. This is not a gentle suggestion, but a divine summons to step out of spiritual sleep and into purpose. A man who hears this call begins to see that he was created to stand, to lead, and to engage in what truly matters. This call is not reserved for the exceptional - it is extended to every man willing to respond. It does not require perfection, but it does require surrender. God is not searching for the most qualified; He is calling the most willing. The man who chooses to rise may feel unprepared, but obedience will shape him, and faith will sustain him. When he stands up, he steps into alignment with something far greater than himself. He becomes part of God's purpose, a vessel of strength, and a force for good in a world that desperately needs men who are awake, alert, and willing to take their place.

To awaken is to step out of the fog of passivity and into the clarity of purpose. It is the moment a man realizes his life is not accidental, his strength is not random, and his presence is not insignificant. Awareness ignites responsibility. He no longer drifts with culture, comfort, or convenience; he begins to think, to evaluate, and to take ownership of his path. What once felt ordinary now feels intentional, and what once felt optional now feels necessary. And with that awareness comes a decision. A man who is awakened does not wait for life to shape him - he rises and begins to shape his life. He chooses discipline over distraction, purpose over passivity, and calling over comfort. He understands that becoming who God designed him to be will require effort, courage, and consistency. But he also knows that within him is everything needed to begin. So he stands up, sets his direction, and moves forward with conviction. No longer drifting, he becomes deliberate. No longer asleep, he becomes alive.

Awakening requires the kind of honesty that refuses to hide behind excuses or distractions. A man must be willing to stand still long enough to truly examine where he is, not where he pretends to be. He must acknowledge the places where he has settled for comfort instead of calling, where passivity has replaced purpose, and where distraction has dulled his focus. This kind of honesty is not meant to tear him down, but to wake him up. It strips away illusion and brings him face to face with reality, not as a sentence of defeat, but as an invitation to rise. When he confronts his passivity, he regains his power to act. When he recognizes his distractions, he can reclaim his direction. And when he admits where he has disengaged, he can choose to reenter the fight with renewed purpose. Honesty becomes the doorway to growth, and clarity becomes the foundation for change. A man who is willing to see clearly is a man who is ready to live differently.

Once a man truly sees, comfort loses its grip on him. The illusions that once kept him passive begin to fall away, and he can no longer pretend that drifting through life is enough. There is a holy disturbance that rises within - a quiet but persistent voice that says, "You were made for more than this." What once satisfied him now feels shallow. What once distracted him now feels like delay. This awakening is not chaos; it is clarity. It is the moment a man realizes that staying the same is no longer an option. With that clarity comes a new weight - a sense of responsibility that cannot be ignored. He begins to feel the call to rise, to lead, to build, and to stand with intention. It is not that he suddenly has all the answers, but he now knows he cannot go back to living small. There is purpose in his bones and fire in his spirit. And though the path forward may require discipline, courage, and sacrifice, something inside him has already decided - it would rather struggle toward purpose than settle for comfort.

Awareness is only the beginning, not the destination. When God calls, He calls a man out of passivity and into purpose, out of comfort and into responsibility. There is always movement attached to His voice. To hear Him clearly is to feel the weight of action stirring within. A man who truly awakens cannot remain still - he begins to rise, to step forward, to take ownership of what has been entrusted to him. The call of God demands more than agreement; it demands response. Strength is not formed in what a man intends to do - it is formed in what he chooses to obey. Obedience activates what potential alone cannot. Each step taken in faith builds resolve, sharpens character, and awakens the strength that was lying dormant. It is in the doing, not just the knowing, that a man becomes who he was created to be. God does not reveal purpose so it can be admired - He reveals it so it can be lived. And the man who answers that call with action will discover that strength rises to meet him with every step forward.

To take your place is to step out of passivity and into ownership. It is the moment a man stops shifting responsibility and begins carrying it with purpose, when he understands that growth begins the moment he decides to act. His life is no longer something that happens to him, but something he builds with intention. He accepts responsibility not only for where he is, but for who he is becoming. In that decision, strength awakens, clarity sharpens, and purpose begins to take form. God's call does not echo from a distant future; it speaks into the present. The opportunity before you is not accidental - it is appointed. To delay is to drift, but to respond is to rise. When a man embraces this truth, he stops hesitating and starts moving. He becomes faithful with what is in his hands, knowing that obedience today prepares him for what is ahead. Taking your place is not about having everything figured out - it is about being willing to step forward when called, trusting that God meets a man in motion.

There will always be resistance when a man begins to awaken. Comfort will pull at him, urging him to stay where things are easy, predictable, and safe. But growth never happens in the place of ease - it happens in the place of decision. Rising requires effort. And taking your place demands courage to move forward even when fear whispers and doubt tries to linger. The path forward may feel heavy, but it is the weight of purpose, not the burden of emptiness. The greater danger is not the struggle - it is remaining asleep. When a man chooses comfort over calling, he slowly trades strength for stagnation and potential for regret. But when he steps forward despite the difficulty something within him comes alive. Courage grows. Clarity sharpens. Strength awakens. The cost of rising may be real, but the cost of staying where you are is far greater. So step forward. Embrace the resistance. And take your place with boldness, knowing that what lies ahead is worth every ounce of faith it requires.

The man who truly awakens lives differently. His days are no longer left to chance or driven by impulse. He becomes intentional with his time, recognizing that every moment carries weight and purpose. What once slipped through his hands unnoticed is now stewarded with care. Discipline begins to shape his habits, not as a burden, but as a pathway to strength. He understands that growth is built through consistent, deliberate choices. Grounded in purpose, he is no longer searching for direction; he is walking in it. Where he once drifted, he now directs. Where he once avoided responsibility, he now steps into it with courage. He engages with life fully, knowing that his calling requires presence, effort, and faith. This awakening produces a quiet confidence, not rooted in himself, but in the God who has called him forward. And as he continues to rise, his life becomes a reflection of intentional living - steady, focused, and aligned with something far greater than comfort.

As a man rises into the life God has called him to live, something unmistakable begins to take shape. His strength becomes visible in how he carries himself, how he speaks, and how he stands firm when pressure comes. His presence begins to carry weight because it is anchored in truth. His words carry conviction because they are forged through obedience, tested in difficulty, and aligned with God's purpose. People recognize that there is something different about him - something steady, something real. Without striving for attention, he influences those around him simply by the way he lives. His consistency speaks. His integrity teaches. His courage challenges others to rise as well. He becomes proof that responding to the call of God produces transformation - not just in private, but in every area of life. And in that transformation, he reflects a greater reality: that a man fully surrendered to God becomes a force for good, a pillar of strength, and a light that points others toward truth.

This is the call to awaken - a call that does not echo once and fade, but one that meets you every morning with fresh urgency. It is the quiet yet persistent voice that reminds you that your choices matter, and that your purpose is worth pursuing. Awakening is a daily surrender to becoming who God designed you to be. It is choosing discipline when comfort calls, choosing obedience when resistance rises, and choosing growth when stagnation feels easier. The man who answers this call understands that greatness is not built in a moment, but in consistent decisions over time. He refuses to drift back into passivity, knowing that every step forward strengthens his character and sharpens his purpose. Even when he stumbles, he rises again because awakening has changed his direction. He is no longer content with merely existing haphazardly. And as he continues to answer the call, day after day, he steps more fully into the man he was created to be: steady, purposeful, and alive with conviction.

There is something inside you that refuses to stay buried forever. It stirs in moments of conviction, whispers in seasons of stillness, and rises when you are faced with the choice to remain comfortable or become who you were designed to be. That strength is not accidental. That purpose is not optional. And the place you are meant to stand cannot be filled by anyone else. To ignore it is to live beneath your calling, but to awaken to it is to step into the life God intended for you all along. The call has already gone out. It is here, now, pressing on your spirit, inviting you to rise. The question is not whether you are capable, but whether you are willing. Will you leave behind passivity and step into responsibility? Will you exchange comfort for calling? Every day presents the decision to remain asleep or to awaken fully and move forward with purpose. And the man who answers that call will discover that the strength he needs was already placed within him waiting for the moment he chose to rise.

| 2 |

"CREATED WITH POWER"

Manhood is not something a man stumbles into - it is something he steps into with intention. Before a man ever tries to define himself, he must understand that he has already been defined by the One who created him. Strength, responsibility, leadership, and purpose are embedded within him by divine design. When a man begins to see himself through God's perspective, confusion fades and clarity takes its place. He no longer asks, "Who am I supposed to be?" but instead, "Am I becoming who God designed me to be?" A man must turn his attention away from the noise of the world and toward the voice of God. It is in that place of surrender and obedience that his true identity is formed and strengthened. The more he aligns his life with God's truth, the more solid and unshakable he becomes. He stops being shaped by circumstance and starts being guided by purpose. And in that alignment, he does not just find himself - he becomes the man he was created to be.

From the very beginning, man was marked by intention. God formed him with care, breathed life into him, and placed purpose within him from the start. Before there was struggle, before there was failure, there was assignment. Man was given responsibility in the garden, entrusted with stewardship, leadership, and dominion. You were not designed to drift through life without direction; you were created to build, to protect, and to lead with purpose that originates from God

Himself. When a man understands that his identity is rooted in divine intention, everything begins to change. He no longer asks, "What should I do with my life?" but instead, "Am I walking in what I was created to carry?" True manhood awakens when a man embraces his assignment with courage and conviction. He realizes that he was not just given life - he was given responsibility. And when he chooses to rise into that calling, he reflects the strength, authority, and purpose that were placed in him from the very beginning.

When God created man, He did not design him to live timid, passive, or uncertain. He formed him with strength woven into his spirit - a strength that endures pressure, stands firm in truth, and carries responsibility with conviction. This strength is steady, anchored, and purposeful. It shows up when life becomes difficult. It remains when others walk away. A man walking in God-given strength does not need to prove himself to the world, because he is already established in his identity and assignment. This strength was given so a man could lead with clarity, protect with courage, and build with intention. True strength does not seek power for itself - it seeks purpose through obedience to God. When a man embraces this kind of strength, he becomes a pillar others can rely on, a protector in uncertain times, and a builder of things that last beyond his lifetime. This is the strength God created in man - not to dominate, but to serve with power, to stand with integrity, and to leave a legacy that reflects Him.

There is a divine authority placed within a man that cannot be explained by the world's standards. It is a quiet strength, rooted deeply in identity, formed through surrender, and sustained by truth. This authority carries a weight that steadies a man's steps and anchors his soul when everything around him begins to shake. He knows who he is, whose he is, and what he stands for and that clarity produces an unshakable presence. This kind of authority is cultivated in the hidden places where a man learns to trust God fully. It is forged in moments where obedience is chosen over comfort, and integrity is held when compromise would be easier. A man who walks in this divine authority brings order where there is chaos, stability where there is fear, and direction where there is confusion. He does not need to force his influence because his life speaks for him. And when he stands, he does so not in his own strength, but in the authority given to him by God, firm, grounded, and immovable.

True authority is entrusted to a man by God. When he understands this, it reshapes how he carries himself. He no longer strives to prove his strength or demand recognition, because he knows his authority has already been established by God. This realization produces a steady confidence and a quiet strength that does not need to announce itself. He recognizes that what has been given to him can also be taken if it is mishandled, so he walks carefully, aware that he is accountable to the One who entrusted him with it. A man walking in true power does not dominate, manipulate, or control for his own benefit. Instead, he serves, protects, and leads with integrity. He understands that authority is not a platform for personal elevation, but a responsibility to lift others, to bring order where there is chaos, and to reflect the character of God in how he leads. He becomes a man who consistently uses his strength to serve, his influence to guide, and his life to honor God.

The world often tries to redefine manhood. It tells men to shrink back instead of stand firm, to question their strength instead of steward it, and to apologize for the very traits God placed within them. But God does not make mistakes. The strength, courage, and responsibility placed inside a man are not flaws to be corrected - they are gifts to be cultivated. God has never called a man to diminish who he is - He calls him to rise into who he was created to be. True manhood is about disciplined strength, sacrificial leadership, and unwavering conviction. It is the courage to stand when others sit, to speak truth when others stay silent, and to lead with integrity when compromise is easier. When a man rejects the world's confusion and embraces God's design, he becomes steady, grounded, and effective. He no longer lives to please culture but lives to honor his Creator. And in doing so, he reflects a strength that does not waver, a purpose that does not fade, and a calling that cannot be redefined by the world.

Weakness, when embraced as identity, becomes a cage the soul was never meant to live in. It whispers lies that shrink a man's vision, dull his purpose, and silence the calling God has placed within him. What may begin as a moment of struggle can quietly become a mindset of limitation if it is accepted as permanent. When a man begins to see himself only through the lens of weakness, he forgets who he was created to be capable, resilient, and called to something greater. A man of faith does not deny his struggles, but he refuses to bow to them. He brings them before God, allowing them to become the very ground where strength is built. True growth begins when he stands firm and rises up, not because life is easy, but because God has placed strength within him to endure and overcome. Weakness may visit, but it does not get to stay. He was built to rise, to fight, and to press forward with courage becoming stronger, wiser, and more grounded in purpose with every step he takes.

A man must be willing to confront the quiet, persistent voices that tell him he is not enough, that he lacks what it takes, that he should shrink back instead of step forward. These lies often feel familiar because they have been rehearsed over time, but familiarity does not make them true. God did not design a man to live confined by insecurity or defined by limitation. He created him with purpose, strength, and the capacity to grow into the calling placed on his life. To replace these lies, a man must remind himself that he is not insignificant, but intentional; not incapable but developing; not unqualified, but being prepared. Transformation begins when he aligns his thoughts with what God says rather than what fear suggests. As his thinking changes, he stands with greater confidence, moves with clearer direction, and embraces responsibility instead of avoiding it. When a man learns to think rightly about who he is in God, he breaks the grip of weakness and steps into the strength he was created to carry.

God's design does not remove the weight of life - it prepares a man to carry it with purpose. He is not shaped for ease, but for endurance. The challenges he faces are not signs of abandonment, but opportunities for revelation. In the pressure, what has been placed inside him begins to surface - faith that holds, courage that stands, and strength that does not break. Comfort may feel safe, but it never builds capacity. It is in resistance that a man discovers who he truly is, and more importantly, who God created him to become. The man who understands this no longer fears the struggle - he embraces it. He does not retreat when pressure rises; he leans into it with trust in God's design. Every obstacle becomes a proving ground, every hardship a refining fire. He rises not because life is easy, but because he has been equipped to overcome. And as he stands firm, he becomes unshaken not by the absence of trials, but by the presence of strength that was forged through them.

There is power in knowing who you are because identity shapes direction. A man who understands that he was created with intention no longer drifts through life reacting to circumstances - he begins to move with purpose. Passivity loses its grip. He becomes deliberate in his actions, focused in his pursuit, and grounded in truth. He is no longer trying to become someone - he is learning to walk in who he already is. When a man's identity is secure, his decisions carry weight because they are no longer driven by insecurity, fear, or the need for approval. He stands firm in conviction, not easily shaken by opinions or pressure. He knows what he stands for, and that clarity gives him stability in uncertain moments. This kind of man does not waste his life chasing distractions - he invests it in purpose. He leads with confidence, lives with intention, and moves forward with quiet strength. Because when a man knows who he is, he also understands what he was made to do and he refuses to live beneath it.

A man created with power does not sit idle waiting for the right moment or the approval of others. Instead, he moves with purpose because he understands that growth is not optional, it is obedience. He recognizes that God did not design him to remain stagnant, but to be developed, stretched, and strengthened over time. While others delay, making excuses or waiting for ideal conditions, he leans into responsibility. He disciplines his mind, sharpens his character, and takes intentional steps forward, even when the path is uncomfortable. This kind of man refuses to let circumstances dictate his direction. He understands that growth often comes through resistance, and instead of shrinking back, he presses in with faith and determination. Because he knows that one day he will stand before God accountable for what he did with what he was given. And so he grows now, not later - steadily, faithfully, and with conviction becoming the man he was created to be.

This kind of man refuses to be trapped in the endless cycle of comparison. He is not distracted by what others have, what others achieve, or how others are perceived. His focus is higher. He looks to God as his standard, knowing that true strength is not found in outperforming others, but in faithfully becoming who he was created to be. He understands that his identity is anchored in truth. Because of this, he moves with purpose and his life reflects intention rather than imitation. His strength is revealed in his obedience and forged through discipline in the daily decisions that shape his character. He knows that real power comes from living in step with truth, not from being seen as strong by others. This kind of man grows steadily, rooted deeply, and stands firmly because his foundation is unshakable. When challenges come, he does not question his worth but leans into his calling. And in doing so, he becomes a man whose life is not defined by comparison, but by conviction.

When a man understands who he is in God, he is no longer driven by the need to be seen, praised, or affirmed by others. His identity is settled. His direction is clear. This kind of confidence is steady, grounded, and unwavering. It allows him to walk into uncertainty without fear, to make decisions without hesitation, and to stand firm when others waver. He is not moved by opinions because he is anchored in truth. This confidence produces a life of consistency and strength. A man no longer adjusts himself to fit the expectations of the world - he aligns himself with the standard of God. Whether he is seen or unseen, celebrated or overlooked, he remains the same. There is no performance, no striving to prove his worth, because he already knows it has been established by his Creator. And in that security, he moves forward with purpose, discipline, and peace. His life becomes a reflection of quiet strength unshaken by noise, unmoved by pressure, and unwavering in conviction.

When a man embraces God's design, something shifts within him that cannot be manufactured or imitated. It is not a loud transformation, but it is unmistakable. His posture reflects purpose. His mindset becomes clear and focused. He is no longer tossed around by confusion or insecurity because he understands that his identity is not something he creates but is something he receives from God. He walks with direction, speaks with clarity, and carries a quiet authority that comes from alignment with truth rather than approval from others. This kind of man no longer wastes energy trying to prove himself. He is not searching for validation because he has already been anchored in who God says he is. His actions become intentional, not reactive. He lives with discipline because he knows his life carries weight. Every decision is shaped by purpose, not impulse. He is no longer drifting through life asking, "Who am I?" Instead, he moves forward with conviction, living out the answer every single day.

Rejecting weakness does not mean pretending the struggle is not real. It means refusing to let that struggle write your identity. Every man will face moments of doubt and resistance but those moments are not meant to define him; they are meant to develop him. Weakness becomes dangerous only when it is embraced as a permanent condition rather than a temporary challenge. When a man chooses to see himself through God's design instead of his current difficulty, he stops making excuses and starts making progress. True strength is formed when a man does what is right even when it is hard, when he stays committed even when it is inconvenient, and when he keeps moving forward even when he feels stretched. Purpose begins to sharpen his focus, and discipline begins to shape his character. And though the struggle may still exist, it no longer controls him, because he has decided that who he is becoming matters more than what he is going through.

God did not design man to sit on the sidelines of his own life watching opportunities pass and purpose remain untouched. He created man to step forward, to engage with intention, to lead with conviction, and to build with vision. There is a divine urgency woven into manhood, a call that refuses to be silenced by comfort or fear. Answering this call requires more than desire; it requires strength of spirit, discipline of mind, and courage of heart. A passive man waits for life to happen, but a man aligned with God's design steps into what has been entrusted to him. He understands that his life carries weight, that his decisions shape outcomes, and that his obedience matters. Strength is not optional - it is necessary. Not strength for pride, but strength for purpose. And when a man embraces this truth, he no longer drifts through life - he advances with clarity, anchored in calling, and committed to becoming everything God created him to be.

Every man reaches a moment where the question can no longer be avoided, "Will I accept who God created me to be, or will I walk away from it?" This decision is deeply personal. God has already established the design, but it is up to the man to embrace it. To accept that design is to step into responsibility, purpose, and growth. To reject it is to drift, to live without direction, and to settle for less than what was intended. The weight of that choice is real, because it determines not just what a man does, but who he becomes. When a man chooses to accept God's design, he stops living passively and begins living intentionally. His decisions gain clarity. His actions carry purpose. But when he rejects that design, confusion replaces clarity, and comfort begins to take priority over calling. The truth is simple but powerful: the direction of a man's life is not determined by chance - it is determined by choice. And the man who chooses God's design chooses a life of meaning, strength, and eternal impact.

When a man chooses to walk in the power God has given him, everything begins to realign from the inside out. His thinking is no longer shaped by fear, insecurity, or comparison, but by truth, purpose, and conviction. He begins to see himself through the lens of God's design, and that vision reshapes how he lives. His habits start to reflect discipline instead of drift. His decisions carry intention instead of impulse. When a man knows who he is, he no longer lives scattered; he lives anchored. As he steps into that God-given power, his influence begins to expand without striving or self-promotion. There is a quiet authority in his life that others recognize not because he demands attention, but because he carries clarity, consistency, and strength. He is no longer trying to become something he is not; he is stepping fully into the man God designed him to be from the beginning. In that place, there is confidence without arrogance, authority without pride, and strength without compromise.

There is a divine imprint on your life - an intentional design that carries authority, purpose, and the capacity to lead. When you begin to see yourself through the lens of God's truth instead of your past limitations, your posture changes. You stand taller, think clearer, and move with conviction. The life you were created to live is impactful, disciplined, and anchored in purpose. The defining moment in a man's life is not when he realizes what he carries, but when he decides to walk in it. Every day presents the choice to rise or to retreat, to lead or to remain passive, to step forward in faith or shrink back into comfort. God has already placed what you need within you, but He will not force you to act. You must choose to walk in alignment with His design. And when you do, you will discover that the strength you once questioned becomes the very thing that carries you forward, enabling you to stand firm, lead with authority, and fulfill the purpose you were created for.

| 3 |

"THE IMAGE OF THE LION"

From the earliest pages of scripture, God has used imagery to awaken understanding deep within the human spirit. The lion stands among the most striking of these images. It does not strive to be noticed; it simply is. Its authority is not negotiated, and its presence shifts the atmosphere wherever it goes. In the same way, a man aligned with God does not need to force recognition or chase validation. His words carry weight, his actions carry purpose, and his presence carries influence. The call placed on every man is not to imitate the lion in pride, but to reflect what the lion represents in spirit. True boldness is having the courage to stand firm when compromise is easier, to lead when others hesitate, and to remain faithful when no one is watching. When a man walks in step with God, he does not shrink back from responsibility or retreat from challenge. He rises up and carries a presence that speaks before he ever says a word. Not because he demands it but because heaven has placed it within him.

The lion does not pace in anxiety or roar to convince others of its strength. It carries authority simply by being what it was created to be. In the same way, a man who is grounded in God does not need to chase approval or perform for acceptance. When a man understands that he is designed with purpose, called with intention, and formed by the hand of God, the need to prove himself begins to fade. He no longer lives for the opinions of others, because he is anchored in the truth of who God says he is. This kind of identity produces a quiet confidence that cannot be shaken by comparison or pressure. It is not loud, but it is undeniable. It does not demand attention, but it commands respect. A man walking in this understanding moves with clarity, stands with conviction, and leads with peace. He is no longer striving to become something - he is simply living out what has already been placed within him. His life reflects the authority that flows naturally from the design God established from the very beginning.

A lion leads by presence, not pressure. It does not scramble to assert control, nor does it manipulate to maintain authority. Instead, it stands firm, watches closely, and acts decisively when needed. In the same way, a man walking in God's authority understands that leadership is not about being served, but about serving. It is about protecting what has been entrusted to him, bringing stability where there is chaos, and reflecting the character of God in how he leads. True authority is steady, not forceful; it is purposeful, not self-seeking. The lion does not demand trust - it earns it through consistency, courage, and quiet strength. This is the kind of leadership God calls men into. When a man embraces this, he becomes someone others can rely on because his life demonstrates integrity. His leadership brings peace, direction, and security. And in doing so, he reflects the King of kings, whose authority is perfect, whose rule is just, and whose leadership is rooted in love.

When scripture says the righteous are bold as a lion, it reveals a courage that flows from alignment with God's will. This kind of boldness does not need to prove itself or draw attention - it simply stands. It remains firm when others shift, holds to truth when compromise is convenient, and refuses to bow to pressure when the cost of obedience rises. Like the lion, it carries a presence that does not come from noise, but from authority rooted deep within. This boldness also moves when others hesitate. It speaks when silence would protect comfort but betray conviction. It steps forward even when fear is present, because fear no longer has the final say. A man walking in this kind of courage is not fearless - he is faithful. He has learned that obedience to God outweighs the opinions of people, and that truth is worth standing for no matter the outcome. This is the boldness of the lion - not wild aggression, but controlled strength; not pride, but purpose; not self-reliance, but confidence in the One who called him to stand.

Too many men have been taught to retreat instead of rise. Culture rewards comfort, silence, and blending in, but the Spirit of God calls men to something higher. The image of the lion confronts that passivity. It awakens something deeper - a reminder that a man was not created to shrink back when things become difficult, but to stand firm, to engage, and to carry what has been entrusted to him. A lion does not question its role or apologize for its presence. It walks in quiet authority because it knows what it was created to be. In the same way, a man must stop hiding from his calling and start embracing it with courage. This means leading when leadership is needed, speaking when truth must be spoken, and standing when others step back. When a man refuses to retreat from responsibility, he becomes a reflection of God's strength on the earth. And in that place, he not only transforms his own life - he becomes a source of stability, protection, and direction for others.

At the center of this powerful symbolism stands Jesus Christ, the Lion of Judah - a title that reveals far more than His role as Savior. It declares Him as King. Not a distant or passive ruler, but one who carries undeniable authority, unshakable dominion, and complete victory. The Lion of Judah is bold, decisive, and triumphant. He faced sin, death, and darkness head-on and conquered them fully. This means that everything that once held power over humanity has been broken under His rule. His kingship is active, reigning, and eternal. For the man who follows Him, this truth changes everything. The same authority, courage, and victory that define Christ now shape the identity of those who belong to Him. You are not called to live timid, uncertain, or overcome by fear. You are called to stand firm, to walk boldly, and to reflect the strength of the Lion. When you understand who He is, you begin to understand who you are in Him. You stop living like you are fighting for victory - you begin living from it.

The Lion of Judah reveals a kind of strength that the world often misunderstands. His fierceness is not driven by impulse or ego, but by righteousness and divine purpose. It was never excessive, never misdirected, never self-serving. Jesus shows us that true authority is steady, intentional, pure, and always purposeful. For a man seeking to walk in that same strength, this truth becomes a foundation. It calls him to move beyond emotional reactions and into disciplined response. It challenges him to bring his desires, decisions, and actions under the authority of God. A lion does not need to prove its power - it demonstrates it through presence and precision. In the same way, a man who submits his strength to God becomes both firm and trustworthy. He does not misuse power; he channels it for protection, leadership, and truth. This is the strength of the Lion of Judah reflected in a man - fierce when necessary, but always righteous, always submitted, and always aligned with a greater purpose.

When men look at Jesus as the Lion of Judah, they are encountering a standard for their own lives. The Lion represents disciplined strength anchored in righteousness. To reflect Him is to become grounded in who God says you are, not swayed by pressure, fear, or the opinions of others. It is a call to courage - the kind that stands firm when compromise is easy. A man shaped by this truth does not waver with circumstances; he remains anchored because his identity is rooted in Christ. The strength of the Lion is never separated from His righteousness. It is power under control, authority submitted to God, and boldness guided by truth. When a man walks in this, his presence begins to change the atmosphere around him. He brings clarity where there is confusion, stability where there is chaos, and conviction where there is compromise. In reflecting the Lion of Judah, a man becomes both a protector and a pillar, carrying strength that is not only seen, but deeply felt.

To reflect the nature of the lion is to walk in a kind of authority that cannot be manufactured or assigned by man. It is formed in the quiet place of intimacy with God. When a man consistently seeks Him, listens to Him, and submits to His leading, something begins to change within. His words carry substance. His decisions carry clarity. His life carries conviction. This authority is steady, grounded, and undeniable. A man who walks closely with God begins to carry a spiritual weight that others can sense, even if they cannot explain it. His presence brings peace into chaos, clarity into confusion, and strength into weakness. Environments shift because of the presence of God resting on his life. He does not strive to control or dominate - he simply stands firm in truth, and that truth carries power. This is the nature of the lion. It is authoritative because it is anchored in something greater. And when a man lives this way, he becomes a vessel through which God's authority is revealed on the earth.

To embrace the nature of the lion is to embrace responsibility without hesitation. A lion does not neglect what has been entrusted to it - it watches, guards, and stands ready. In the same way, a man is called to be vigilant over his life and the lives connected to him. He protects his family not only through provision, but through presence. He protects his values by living them out consistently, even when no one is watching. He protects his calling by refusing to drift into distraction or complacency. A man must be willing to stand against what is wrong, even when it is uncomfortable or unpopular. He refuses to allow compromise to quietly take root in his heart, his home, or his convictions. He knows that what is tolerated will eventually grow, so he chooses to confront it early with truth and courage. This is not about control - it is about recognizing that what God has placed in his care is valuable, and it is worth defending with unwavering faith, wisdom, and resolve.

Reflecting the lion's nature requires a courage that is anchored in conviction. The lion does not shift with the crowd or retreat when challenged - it stands firm in its identity. In the same way, a man grounded in God does not measure his steps by public approval, but by divine alignment. He understands that truth is not negotiable, and obedience is not optional. Even when his voice shakes or the path grows difficult, he remains steady, because his foundation is not built on comfort, but on calling. This kind of courage is the willingness to be misunderstood, rejected, or even opposed, if that is the cost of righteousness. The lion within does not seek conflict, but it does not run from it either. It stands with clarity, conviction, and confidence in God's authority. And in doing so, it becomes unshakable. When a man chooses obedience over approval, he steps into a strength that cannot be taken from him. He becomes a man who does not just speak truth but lives it, no matter the cost.

This kind of life requires discipline. Lions are not careless - they move with purpose, with awareness, and with restraint. In the same way, a man who is called to reflect strength must first learn to govern himself. His thoughts cannot be allowed to wander without direction, his words cannot be released without consideration, and his actions cannot be driven by impulse. Discipline is the ability to bring every part of your life under control so that it serves a greater purpose. Without it, even great strength becomes dangerous, misdirected, and ultimately destructive. But when strength is anchored in discipline, it becomes something powerful and transformative. A disciplined man does not waste his energy - he invests it. He does not react emotionally - he responds with wisdom. He becomes dependable and effective in everything he puts his hand to. His life carries weight because it is ordered, intentional, and surrendered to God. Discipline refines strength into something that builds, protects, and endures.

There is a quiet strength in the lion that speaks louder than noise ever could. It does not react out of fear or move out of panic - it moves with purpose, with awareness, and with control. In the same way, a man who walks closely with God develops a steady spirit. He is not easily shaken by uncertainty or overwhelmed by pressure, because his foundation is not built on what he sees, but on who God is. While the world may rush in anxiety and react in fear, he remains grounded, knowing that God is not hurried, and neither is His plan. This calmness is the settled confidence that comes from knowing that God is in control, even when circumstances feel unstable. A man anchored in that truth does not need to force outcomes or strive in his own strength. He can move with intention, speak with clarity, and act with wisdom because he is led, not driven. His peace becomes a testimony, showing that true strength is not found in constant motion, but in unwavering trust in the One who leads every step.

There is a wisdom in the lion that does not move out of pressure or emotion, but out of purpose. In the same way, a man who walks with God learns to discern the moment. He knows that not every situation requires a reaction, and not every silence is weakness. There are times to be still and listen, allowing God to give direction, and there are times to rise with clarity and act without hesitation. This kind of discernment is developed through relationship with God, where a man learns to recognize His voice above the noise of fear, pride, and impulse. A man reflecting this nature becomes steady and trustworthy. He speaks when it matters, steps in when it is right, and stands firm when truth is on the line. He is not controlled by urgency, nor is he paralyzed by uncertainty. Instead, he moves with a quiet confidence, knowing that obedience is more important than speed. When a man learns to act at the right time, in the right way, with the right spirit, his presence begins to shape the world around him.

A lion does not look around the wilderness wondering if it should be different. It does not measure itself against other creatures or try to imitate what it was never designed to be. It simply walks in the fullness of what it is. In the same way, a man who understands his identity in God stops striving to prove himself. He stops comparing his journey, his calling, and his progress to others. Instead, he anchors himself in the truth that he was intentionally created, uniquely formed, and purposefully assigned. When identity is rooted in God, it becomes unshakable, because it is no longer dependent on opinions, achievements, or external validation. This kind of identity produces clarity and clarity produces confidence. When a man knows who he is, he knows what he stands for, what he is responsible for, and what he must refuse. He is no longer easily distracted or pulled off course by the expectations of others. His decisions become sharper, his convictions stronger, and his direction clearer.

When a man embraces the identity God has given him, everything begins to align. He is no longer pulled in every direction by culture, pressure, or impulse. The confusion that once clouded his path gives way to clarity, and that clarity produces purpose. He begins to move with intention, not reacting to life but leading within it. His steps become deliberate. His words carry weight. His presence reflects direction. He is no longer searching for who he is - he is walking in it. And when a man knows who he is in God, he stops drifting and starts building a life that actually means something. This transformation reshapes how he makes decisions. No longer driven by comfort or convenience, he is guided by conviction and calling. He understands that ease is not the goal - obedience is. Even when the right path is difficult, he chooses it because he knows it leads to purpose. His life becomes anchored in something deeper than temporary satisfaction. It becomes rooted in eternal significance.

Transformation is a process. Just as a lion does not begin its life in full strength but develops it over time, a man is formed through seasons of stretching, refining, and learning. God uses every challenge and every test to build something deeper in the man's inner self. He is not just improving behavior; He is shaping character, forging identity, and strengthening the foundation a man will stand on. This process can be painful at times, but it is never wasted. Growth requires pressure. Refinement requires fire. And maturity requires time. The man who embraces this journey, rather than resisting it, begins to see that the difficulty is not working against him - it is working for him. With each step of obedience, he becomes stronger. With each season of refinement, he becomes clearer in his calling. And over time, what once felt like struggle becomes strength and what once felt uncertain becomes conviction proving that the man who stays committed to the process will rise into the man God created him to be.

God did not create men to be timid, passive, or disconnected from purpose. He formed them with strength, intention, and the capacity to carry responsibility with courage. To embrace the image of the lion is to step into that original design - to walk in the authority that comes from alignment with God, not from striving for recognition. When a man understands who he is in Christ, he stops shrinking back and starts standing firm, not in arrogance, but in quiet, unshakable confidence. This kind of boldness reflects Christ, who carried both power and humility, authority and obedience. To live this way is to lead with conviction, to act with purpose, and to remain steadfast when pressure rises. It is a life that refuses compromise, not because of pride, but because of devotion. When a man walks in this reality, his presence begins to carry weight because he reflects the Lion of Judah. And in that reflection, he becomes exactly what God designed him to be: strong, faithful, and unwavering.

When a man truly reflects the Lion of Judah, his life begins to move into the realm of eternal impact. His presence brings stability because it is rooted in God. In moments of chaos, he does not waver and in times of uncertainty, he does not retreat. He stands firm because there is a quiet authority about him, not forced or self-made, but formed through surrender and alignment with Christ. His words carry weight because they are shaped by truth, lived through experience, and backed by conviction. This kind of man does not live for himself; he lives as a reflection of something greater. His life becomes a signpost pointing others to God. Through his actions, people see consistency. Through his character, they see integrity. Through his leadership, they experience protection and direction. He leads when it is difficult, protects what has been entrusted to him, and stands when others fall back. In doing so, his life becomes a testimony that a man fully aligned with God cannot help but influence the world around him.

| 4 |

"THE COST OF PASSITIVITY"

There is a war being waged against masculinity, and it rarely announces itself with open confrontation. Instead, it works in subtle ways - through culture, conversation, and quiet expectations that reshape how a man sees himself. What God designed to be strong is often reframed as dangerous. What was meant to lead is portrayed as oppressive. Over time, these distortions begin to wear down a man's clarity, causing him to question his role, suppress his convictions, and hesitate in moments where he was created to rise. The answer is not for men to become less, but to reclaim strength with humility, leadership with servanthood, and conviction with love. This kind of man is not shaped by culture, but by calling. He does not shrink to fit the expectations of a confused world; he stands anchored in the design of his Creator. And when he does, he becomes a force for good - walking with quiet confidence, knowing that the strength he carries is not something to hide, but something to steward well.

This cultural pressure has quietly eroded the very traits men were designed to carry. Scripture never portrays strength, courage, or conviction as flaws to be suppressed, but as qualities to be refined and surrendered to God. The enemy understands that a hesitant man is far less dangerous than a decisive one, so the attack is subtle, shaping men to shrink back instead of rising up. But God has not called men to live in confusion. He has called them to clarity, to conviction, and to a boldness rooted not in pride, but in purpose. A man who rejects this pressure embraces responsibility instead of avoiding it, knowing that leadership is not about control, but about service and accountability before God. When a man stands firm in truth he becomes a stabilizing force in a shifting world. His life gains direction and his presence brings security to those around him. This is restored masculinity, shaped by God, anchored in truth, and strong enough to stand when everything else gives way.

Passivity begins when a man chooses not to speak when truth is needed, when he delays obedience, when he trades discipline for comfort. Each compromise dulls conviction. Each act of avoidance weakens resolve. What once required courage begins to feel optional, and what once stirred conviction becomes easy to ignore. A man who was designed to lead, build, and stand firm slowly finds himself retreating because he stopped resisting the drift. What starts as occasional hesitation becomes a way of life, where silence replaces strength and comfort replaces purpose. Yet this drift can be reversed. The same small decisions that led a man into passivity can lead him out. When he chooses truth over silence, action over delay, and obedience over comfort, strength begins to return. God did not create men to withdraw, but to engage, to stand, and to carry responsibility with courage. And the moment a man recognizes the drift and decides to fight it, he steps back into the life he was created to live.

The cost of passivity is never contained to one man. When a man withdraws from his responsibility to lead, protect, and stand firm, the ripple effects reach far beyond his own life. His family feels it first. Where there should be clarity, there is confusion. Where there should be strength, there is instability. Where there should be guidance, there is silence. Passivity creates a vacuum, and that vacuum will always be filled either by disorder, by weaker influences, or by voices that were never meant to lead. A man may believe his inaction only affects him, but in reality, it quietly shapes the atmosphere of his home, the direction of his relationships, and the security of those who depend on him. But it does not stop there. Communities begin to erode when men refuse to stand for what is right. When conviction is replaced with comfort, and courage is traded for convenience, the standard begins to fall. What one generation tolerates, the next will normalize. And what is normalized will eventually define the future.

A passive man may believe he is preserving peace by avoiding conflict, but what he is truly preserving is comfort. Real peace is not the absence of tension; it is the presence of order, truth, and alignment with what is right. When a man refuses to step into responsibility, he leaves a vacuum and that vacuum will always be filled by disorder. Problems do not disappear because they are ignored; they multiply. What feels like calm on the surface often hides deeper fractures beneath. By choosing silence, he quietly permits what should be confronted, corrected, and led. There are moments when silence becomes a form of surrender and surrender to what is wrong always carries a cost. Families drift, standards erode, and truth becomes blurred when no one rises to uphold it. A man of faith does not seek conflict but neither does he run from it when truth is at stake. He chooses action over avoidance, and in doing so, he becomes a force that restores order where chaos once had room to grow.

There is a quiet deception in comfort that makes it seem harmless, even deserved. It whispers that ease is the reward, that resistance is unnecessary, that a man can drift without consequence. But comfort, when it takes the place of purpose, softens his edge, silences his convictions, and numbs the fire that once drove him to stand, build, and fight. A man who lives only for comfort may avoid struggle, but he also forfeits growth, strength, and the calling that requires him to rise. A man was not designed to be ruled by ease, but to be refined by challenge and anchored in purpose. When a man chooses purpose over comfort, he awakens something within him a resolve to live intentionally, to stand when it is hard, and to pursue what truly matters.

Comfort may offer temporary relief, but purpose produces lasting impact. And the man who refuses to be trapped by ease will discover that real life is not found in avoiding the fight, but in stepping fully into it.

Men were not designed for a life of passive existence. From the beginning, they were formed to build what is broken, to protect what is vulnerable, to lead with courage, and to stand firm when pressure rises. This design is woven into the very identity God placed within a man. But when that calling is ignored, silenced, or traded for comfort, his strength becomes unused, his voice grows quiet, and his conviction weakens. A man cannot thrive in passivity because passivity contradicts who he was created to be. When he avoids responsibility, resists leadership, or shrinks back from challenge, he slowly disconnects from his calling. But when he steps into his God-given role - when he chooses courage over comfort, action over hesitation, and conviction over compromise - something comes alive again within him. Strength returns. Clarity sharpens. Purpose ignites. This is where a man begins to truly live - not merely existing but fully engaged in the mission he was created for.

When a man steps back from his responsibility to lead, protect, and confront what is wrong, he unknowingly creates an opening. And that opening will always be filled by something. If truth is not spoken, deception will speak louder. If righteousness is not upheld, compromise will take its place. This is why silence in the face of wrong is never harmless. A man may believe he is avoiding conflict, but in reality, he is allowing something far more destructive to take root. What a man refuses to confront will grow and eventually dominate. Whether it is in his home, his relationships, or his own heart, neglected issues gain strength over time. But God did not call men to shrink back; He called them to stand firm, to bring order where there is chaos, and to carry the courage to face what others avoid. When a man rises and takes his place, he does more than push back darkness

- he restores alignment, establishes peace, and becomes a stabilizing force in a world that desperately needs strong, faithful men.

Many men cloak their hesitation in spiritual language. They call it wisdom, patience, or "waiting on God," when in reality it is often fear dressed in acceptable terms. True wisdom does not shrink back when responsibility calls - it steps forward with clarity and conviction. There is a difference between being still before God and being silent in the face of what must be confronted. One posture builds strength and alignment; the other slowly erodes courage and purpose. A man of discernment learns to recognize that difference. He understands that delay can be obedience, but it can also be disobedience in disguise. There are moments when waiting is right, and there are moments when action is required. Avoidance will always feel safer in the moment, but it leads to greater consequences over time. When a man chooses courage over comfort, he stops hiding behind hesitation and begins moving with purpose, knowing that obedience to God often requires bold, decisive action.

The danger of silence is far greater than most men realize. When truth is left unspoken, deception does not hesitate to fill the void. Lies grow louder, bolder, and more convincing when they are not challenged. What begins as a moment of hesitation can quickly become a pattern of compromise, and over time, that silence reshapes the environment around him. Truth was never meant to whisper in the shadows; it was meant to stand firm in the light. A man who refuses to speak when it matters most sends a message, whether he intends to or not. He teaches those watching him that truth is negotiable and that courage is optional. But leadership demands a voice anchored in conviction. Speaking truth does not require arrogance or aggression, but it does require boldness and clarity. When a man chooses to stand and speak with integrity, he sets a standard that others can follow. He becomes a barrier against compromise and a voice that restores direction, proving that courage is a responsibility.

Comfort and silence often form a quiet alliance that weakens a man from within. The more he settles into ease, the less urgency he feels to rise, to speak, or to confront what is wrong. What once stirred conviction begins to feel inconvenient, and what once demanded action is slowly ignored. Comfort shifts his focus toward preserving peace, avoiding tension, and protecting his own convenience. Over time, this pattern reshapes his influence. Where there should be strength, there is hesitation. Where there should be clarity, there is silence. His presence, once capable of bringing direction and stability, becomes passive and easily overlooked. But a man was not created to blend into comfort - he was created to stand firm in truth. Growth requires friction. Impact requires courage. When a man chooses to step out of comfort and reclaim his voice, his influence returns with strength. He begins to lead again with quiet conviction, steady courage, and a life that speaks louder than his words.

What a man consistently models through his actions, his words, and his discipline becomes the silent blueprint that others will follow. Whether he realizes it or not, the next generation is watching, learning, and building their lives from the example he leaves behind. Influence does not pause simply because a man is silent - it continues, shaping minds and expectations in the background. But this truth is not only a warning; it is also an opportunity. A man who chooses to live with courage, conviction, and integrity can alter the course of those who follow him. When boys see strength expressed through responsibility, truth spoken with boldness, and leadership carried with humility, they begin to understand what manhood truly looks like. One man's decision to rise can break cycles that have existed for generations. His life becomes more than his own - it becomes a standard, a guide, and a living example that calls others higher. This is what being a man is all about.

But there is always a turning point available - a moment where a man can wake up, take ownership, and choose a different direction. He is not trapped by his past patterns, nor defined by seasons of passivity. The drift can be recognized, and what is recognized can be confronted. But this kind of change does not happen casually. It requires a man to stand face to face with the truth about himself. No excuses. Just honesty. He must be willing to acknowledge where he has been silent when he should have spoken, where he has stepped back when he should have stood firm, and where comfort has taken priority over calling. When a man chooses truth over self-protection, he positions himself for transformation. From that place, real change begins. The same areas where he once avoided can become the very places where he now leads. The turning point is found in making the right decision. And when a man chooses courage over comfort, he steps into the man he was always meant to become.

Breaking free from passivity is a matter of action. It requires a man to do what is uncomfortable, to speak when silence would be easier, and to step forward when others retreat. Courage is not proven in theory; it is revealed in moments of decision. When truth needs a voice, he becomes that voice. When responsibility calls, he answers, even when the weight feels heavy. Every act of engagement strengthens his character and sharpens his resolve. As he chooses to engage rather than withdraw, something within him comes alive again. His confidence is no longer based on ease, but on obedience. His strength is no longer passive, but purposeful. Responsibility, once avoided, becomes the very thing that builds him. With each step forward, he reclaims ground that was once lost to hesitation. Over time, his life becomes one marked by courage, consistency, and conviction. And in that transformation, he not only changes himself - he influences everyone around him to rise as well.

There is a cost to courage, and it is not light. A man who chooses to stand firm will often face resistance, misunderstanding, and even criticism from those who prefer comfort over conviction. He may feel the weight of standing alone, the tension of going against the current, and the discomfort of doing what is right when it is not popular. But this cost is not destructive - it is refining. It strips away fear, exposes weakness, and forges strength that cannot be easily shaken. What feels like pressure in the moment becomes power over time, shaping a man who is steady, clear, and unmovable in his purpose. And in that refinement, his influence begins to carry real weight. People may not always agree with him, but they will recognize the consistency of his life and the depth of his conviction. This kind of man does not need to demand respect; he earns it through the way he lives. Though courage may cost him comfort, it produces something far greater: clarity, strength, and a life that leaves a lasting impact.

True masculinity is measured by how faithfully he can carry what has been entrusted to him. It is responsibility embraced, not power demanded. It is strength that is governed, not strength that runs wild. A man of true character is dependable when others are uncertain, steady when circumstances shift, and anchored when pressure rises. His life reflects discipline, restraint, and purpose - qualities that do not seek applause but produce lasting impact. He is not loud for recognition, nor does he need to prove himself through force. Instead, he is unwavering when it matters most. When others compromise, he remains firm. When others retreat, he stands his ground. His strength is seen in his consistency, his integrity, and his willingness to protect what is valuable whether that is his family, his faith, or his calling. This kind of masculinity is not built on image, but on substance. And because of that, it does not fade with time - it endures, influences, and leaves a legacy worth following.

The death of passive men is not a tragedy - it is a transformation. What is being put to rest is not the man himself, but a lesser version of who he was never meant to be. Passivity, avoidance, and a life built around comfort were distortions that kept him from his true calling. For something greater to emerge, something weaker must first be surrendered. This kind of death is necessary. It clears away the habits, mindsets, and fears that have kept a man small, making room for strength, clarity, and purpose to take root. In its place, a different man begins to rise - one who accepts responsibility, speaks with conviction, and stands firm when it matters most. He is no longer driven by ease, but by calling. No longer controlled by fear but guided by truth. This new strength is steady, disciplined, and intentional. It is the kind of strength that builds, protects, and leads. As this man rises into his calling, his life becomes a powerful influence that strengthens, inspires, and reshapes the lives of everyone around him.

The world needs men who are willing to stand, to speak, and to act when it matters most. Men who refuse to be governed by fear or lulled into silence by comfort, but who are anchored in purpose and guided by conviction. These are men who do not wait for perfect conditions; they respond to what is right. They understand that truth requires a voice, that responsibility demands action, and that courage is essential. Their lives are not passive, but intentional. And when men rise into who they were created to be, the impact reaches far beyond themselves. Homes become stronger, communities become steadier, and future generations gain a clearer example of what it means to live with integrity. One man's decision to stand can shift the atmosphere around him, breaking cycles of passivity and setting a new standard of courage. Change begins not through words alone, but through men who embody truth in both word and action. When that kind of man rises, everything around him begins to change.

So let passivity end here. Draw a line, make a decision, and refuse to drift any longer. Let silence be replaced with truth that is spoken with clarity and conviction. Let comfort be exchanged for calling, even when that calling demands more than what feels easy. This is the moment where excuses lose their power and responsibility is embraced. A man does not become who he was created to be by waiting - he becomes that man by choosing. Choosing to speak. Choosing to act. Choosing to stand when it would be easier to sit back. And let every man rise - not gradually, not reluctantly, but with boldness and purpose. Let him rise with a clear mind, a steady heart, and a strength that is rooted in truth. The life he was created to lead is not passive - it is intentional, impactful, and anchored in responsibility. When he steps into that life, everything begins to align - his actions, his influence, and his legacy. This is not just a call to change; it is a call to become. And the time to answer that call is now.

| 5 |

"STRENGTH UNDER CONTROL"

Power is often misunderstood because it is so often measured by outward force instead of inward control. The world applauds the man who is loud, aggressive, and dominant, but heaven recognizes the man who is steady, restrained, and wise. True strength is not found in the ability to overpower others - it is revealed in the ability to govern oneself. A man who cannot control his temper, his words, or his impulses is not powerful; he is unstable. But the man who can feel the surge of emotion and still choose patience is a man who possesses real power. Strength under control is disciplined authority. It is the quiet confidence of a man who does not need to prove himself because he is already anchored. There is power in restraint, and there is authority in composure. When a man chooses wisdom over reaction, he demonstrates mastery not over others, but over himself. And that is the highest form of strength - a strength that builds, protects, and honors God in every response.

There is a clear distinction between power and aggression, though many confuse the two. Aggression is often fueled by insecurity, fear, or the need to prove worth. It reacts quickly, speaks loudly, and pushes forward without restraint, hoping that force will create respect. Power, on the other hand, is rooted much deeper. It is calm, measured, and grounded in identity. A powerful man does not strive to prove himself because he already knows who he is and whose he is. This kind of power is steady and unshaken. It listens before it speaks, considers before it acts, and remains composed even when pressure rises. Where aggression seeks control over others, true power exercises control within. It stands firm with quiet authority, choosing wisdom over reaction and purpose over pride. A man who walks in this kind of power reflects strength that is refined, not reckless - a strength that builds rather than breaks, that leads rather than forces, and that ultimately honors God through its restraint.

A man who is aggressive may appear strong in the moment, but time will reveal what he truly is. Without control, his reactions become weapons that wound the very people he is called to lead and protect. Words spoken in anger cannot be taken back, and actions driven by impulse leave lasting damage. Trust begins to erode, relationships grow strained, and unnecessary conflict follows wherever he goes. What once looked like strength is exposed as instability. Aggression may command attention for a moment, but it cannot sustain respect. It burns fast and bright, creating the illusion of power, yet leaving behind a trail of broken connection and regret. True strength is proven in the ability to remain steady when emotions rise. A man who learns restraint builds trust, stability, and influence that lasts. Where aggression destroys, disciplined strength restores. And over time, it becomes clear that the man who masters himself will always stand stronger than the man who is mastered by his reactions.

True power is anchored deep within a man who has learned to stand firm regardless of what surrounds him. When challenged, he does not lose control; he gains clarity. His thoughts sharpen, his spirit steadies, and his response becomes intentional rather than reactive. This kind of strength is composed, grounded, and unwavering. It is the result of a man who has built his life on truth, discipline, and trust in God, rather than fleeting feelings. A powerful man does not feel the need to engage every conflict or respond to every offense. He discerns wisely, knowing that not every battle is worth fighting and not every voice deserves his attention. This restraint is not passivity - it is authority under control. It reveals a man who is not ruled by the moment but guided by conviction. And in that steadiness, he becomes a source of strength for others - someone who brings peace into chaos, direction into confusion, and honor to God through the way he carries himself.

The world often celebrates aggression because it is loud, visible, and dramatic. It draws attention and creates the illusion of strength, rewarding those who react quickly and forcefully. But the man who can hold his tongue when provoked, who refuses to be pulled into unnecessary conflict, and who walks away from offense with dignity is displaying a strength that cannot be faked. It is a strength rooted in discipline, humility, and trust in God rather than the need to prove himself to others. This kind of restraint is power under control. It takes far more strength to remain composed than to react in anger. It requires a man to govern his spirit, to filter his words, and to choose peace when his flesh demands retaliation. In those moments, his character is revealed, and his maturity is proven. He becomes a reflection of godly strength - a man who demonstrates a deeper authority that is not driven by emotion but guided by wisdom and anchored in the approval of God rather than the applause of the world.

This kind of strength is forged through discipline. Discipline is what teaches a man to restrain himself when anger rises, to stay committed when motivation fades, and to choose what is right when what is easy is within reach. Without discipline, strength is unstable. It reacts instead of responds. It seeks control instead of stewardship. But when a man submits himself to discipline, his strength becomes steady, reliable, and anchored in purpose rather than driven by impulse. Discipline guards a man from misusing what he has been given. Power without discipline becomes reckless. Influence without discipline becomes harmful. But when discipline is present, strength is refined into something that builds rather than destroys. A disciplined man becomes a man who can be trusted with responsibility, with influence, and with the lives of others. In this way, discipline is not just the pathway to strength - it is what makes that strength safe, effective, and honoring to God.

Discipline trains a man to govern himself long before he is ever called to lead others. It reaches into his thoughts and actions and brings them under control. Where emotion would rise and take over, discipline steps in and steadies the mind. Where impulse would lead him astray, discipline redirects his path. He is no longer tossed back and forth by moods or circumstances but stands firm because he has learned to rule himself. Over time, discipline builds a life of consistency where chaos once had room to grow. It forms daily habits that quietly shape character, reinforcing strength even when motivation fades and feelings grow weak. A disciplined man shows up when it is hard, stays steady when it is inconvenient, and presses forward when others would quit. This kind of life produces quiet power. It is unshakable and, in that steadiness, a man becomes dependable, trustworthy, and strong because he has learned that true strength is not found in bursts of effort, but in the daily decision to remain faithful.

A disciplined man builds his life on truth, not impulse; on conviction, not convenience. When anger rises within him, he pauses, examines it, and brings it into submission. He asks, "Is this righteous or reckless? Will this build or destroy?" In doing so, he transforms what could have been a moment of damage into an opportunity for growth. This is the quiet, unshakable strength of a man who refuses to be ruled by what is temporary. When pressure intensifies, he does not unravel - he becomes more anchored. While others react, he responds. While others panic, he steadies his soul and leans into God. He knows that true strength is controlled, intentional, and grounded in discipline. This kind of man does not need to prove his strength by overpowering others; he proves it by governing himself. His restraint becomes his power. His discipline becomes his defense. And in a world driven by reaction, he stands apart - a man whose strength is not just seen in what he does, but in what he chooses not to do.

God did not create you without feelings; He created you with the ability to govern them. Anger, fear, excitement, and desire all have their place, but none of them were meant to sit on the throne of your life. When emotions take the lead, decisions become reactive, unstable, and often regrettable. But when a man brings his emotions into alignment with truth, wisdom, and the Spirit of God, he begins to live with clarity and strength. He filters every emotion through conviction, purpose, and obedience, refusing to let temporary feelings dictate permanent decisions. When pressure rises, he steadies himself. When anger stirs, he channels it. When fear whispers, he stands firm in faith. This is the difference between instability and maturity. Self-control produces consistency, and consistency builds trust both with others and with God. In the storm, while others are tossed by every wave of feeling, he remains anchored. Not because he feels nothing, but because he is ruled by something greater than what he feels.

The Bible reveals meekness as strength under control. It is the picture of power that has been disciplined, refined, and brought into alignment with God's will. A meek man chooses restraint because he understands timing, purpose, and obedience. His strength is not wild or reckless; it is governed. Like a sword in steady hands, his power is controlled, intentional, and effective. Meekness is knowing you have the ability to respond with force yet choosing the response that honors God and serves the greater purpose. A meek man does not need to prove his power but demonstrates it through restraint, wisdom, and steady control. When provoked, he responds with clarity. When challenged, he stands firm with quiet authority. This is strength that can be trusted. It is strength that builds, protects, and leads. And in a world that often confuses noise with power, meekness stands as a higher form of strength - one that is anchored in purpose and aligned with God.

A meek man is aware of his strength, grounded in his identity, and ready to act when the moment requires it. He understands that unrestrained strength becomes destructive, but disciplined strength becomes effective. Because of this, he does not move impulsively. He waits, he discerns, and he acts with intention. He knows that timing, direction, and purpose matter just as much as power itself. There is a quiet authority in a man who does not need to prove himself. While others strive to display their strength, he demonstrates it through control. He does not raise his voice to command attention, nor does he force his way to establish dominance. Instead, his consistency, composure, and clarity speak for him. When he acts, it carries weight because it is measured and purposeful. His restraint reveals his maturity, and his discipline reveals his strength. In a world that often rewards impulsive displays, the meek man stands steady, intentional, and anchored in a power that is both controlled and undeniable.

Jesus demonstrated the truest form of strength. He possessed the authority to call down angels, to silence every false accusation, and to step away from the suffering that awaited Him. Yet He chose restraint. He chose obedience. In the face of injustice, He remained steady. In the presence of mockery, He remained composed. Every step He took was governed by purpose, not emotion. His strength was not proven by what He did in power, but by what He refused to do in submission to the Father's will. That is the highest form of strength - a power so secure that it does not need to assert itself. Jesus showed that true authority is revealed in obedience. While others would have fought to escape the cross, He endured it to fulfill a greater mission. His restraint was the clearest evidence of His strength. And for the man who follows Him, the lesson is not in reacting to every offense, but in remaining faithful to your purpose. This is the kind of strength that redeems, transforms, and leaves an eternal impact.

Meekness steadies a man when everything around him is unstable. While others are driven by panic, anger, or confusion, he remains composed because his strength is under control. His calm is not indifference; it is discipline. In tense moments, he becomes a point of clarity, able to think, to speak, and to act without being pulled into the emotional storm around him. This is what allows him to lead effectively. There is a quiet authority in a man who does not need to raise his voice to be heard. His strength is felt, not forced. He can stand firm without becoming hostile, correct without condemning, and lead without dominating. People are drawn to that kind of stability because it creates safety and direction in moments of uncertainty. Meekness gives him the ability to bring peace where there is chaos, not by overpowering others, but by anchoring himself. And in doing so, he reflects a higher strength - one that is rooted in control, guided by purpose, and capable of transforming the atmosphere around him.

When strength is not under control, it becomes a liability instead of an asset. Power without discipline turns into impulsiveness, and impulsiveness leaves damage in its wake. A man may have the ability to lead, to build, or to influence but if he is ruled by unchecked anger, pride, or emotion, that same strength can harm people, close doors, and tear down what should have been established. Undirected strength is unpredictable, and what is unpredictable cannot be trusted. What could have been a tool for impact becomes a source of destruction when it is not submitted to wisdom and restraint. But when strength is disciplined and guided, it becomes a force that brings life instead of damage. A man who has learned to govern his strength becomes dependable - someone others can follow, trust, and lean on. His power creates stability, fosters growth, and leaves things better than it found them. This is the kind of strength that reflects maturity - the kind that serves a purpose greater than itself.

A man who develops strength under control becomes a man others can trust. His reliability is not rooted merely in his ability, but in his character. People know that when pressure rises, he will not react recklessly or allow his emotions to dictate his actions. Instead, he responds with wisdom, restraint, and clarity. His strength is consistent, not unpredictable. Because of this, others feel safe placing responsibility in his hands, knowing he will carry it with integrity. Trust is built on how a man handles both opportunity and pressure. When others see that he acts with intention rather than impulse, they gain confidence in him. They know he will not compromise under stress or abandon his principles when challenged. His strength becomes a steady foundation others can lean on, not a force they must brace against. In every situation, he demonstrates that he is dependable. And that kind of man stands out because in a world full of unpredictability, controlled strength is rare, and it is deeply needed.

This kind of man does not crumble when pressure rises, nor does he erupt when tested. He has trained his inner world, so his outer responses remain steady. In moments that shake others, he becomes anchored. He pauses, discerns, and responds with clarity instead of reacting with emotion. His strength is controlled and purposeful. Because of this, he is able to navigate difficulty without losing direction. He does not allow circumstances to dictate his behavior; he allows conviction and wisdom to lead him through them. His strength is deeply felt by those around him. There is a stability in his presence that brings order to confusion and calm to tension. People recognize that he can be relied on, not just to act, but to act rightly. He carries himself with a quiet confidence that consistently delivers under pressure. In every situation, he becomes a steady force - one who strengthens others simply by standing firm himself. This is the kind of strength that leaves an impact, because it stabilizes everything it touches.

So do not confuse noise with strength, or aggression with true power. The loudest voice in the room is not always the strongest - often it is the least controlled. Real strength does not need to announce itself or force its presence. It is steady, composed, and intentional. A man who is truly strong does not react to every provocation or rise to every challenge thrown at him. He chooses his responses carefully, understanding that power is revealed not in how quickly he acts, but in how wisely he responds. Where there is discipline, there is clarity. Where there is control, there is authority. True strength is measured and guided by purpose, not driven by impulse or ego. It is rooted in character, shaped over time through obedience, restraint, and integrity. A man who walks in this strength does not need to prove himself because his life speaks for him. And in a world that often celebrates intensity without direction, he stands apart as a man whose power is not just present, but properly governed.

Become a man whose strength is not only powerful, but trustworthy. Train your mind, your emotions, and your actions to come under control, so that your strength serves a purpose greater than yourself. Do not chase power without character, because power without discipline will eventually betray you. Instead, pursue consistency, restraint, and integrity. As you do, your strength will become steady, reliable, and aligned with what is right. Embrace meekness until it shapes how you respond in every situation. Let it teach you when to act, when to wait, and how to lead with both strength and wisdom. The man who has strength under control is trusted with responsibility. Others will see that he does not react recklessly, that he does not misuse his power, and that he remains grounded under pressure. And because of that, greater opportunities will come his way because he proved he could carry them. This is the kind of man who is built for more because he has first mastered himself.

| 6 |

"THE BATTLE WITHIN"

Every man carries a battlefield within him. It is not marked by noise or visible conflict, but by quiet tensions of the heart - thoughts that wrestle for control, desires that pull in opposite directions, and convictions that are tested in silence. It is in these unseen places that integrity is either strengthened or compromised, where discipline is either developed or neglected, and where faith is either anchored or abandoned. What a man consistently chooses in private will shape who he becomes in public. These internal battles are not signs of weakness - they are evidence that something worth fighting for is alive within him. The struggle between flesh and spirit is real, but it is also necessary. A man who learns to win within himself gains a strength that cannot be shaken by external pressures. He becomes steady, grounded, and led by purpose rather than impulse. When a man wins the war inside, he steps into a life of clarity, authority, and quiet confidence that no outward circumstance can take away.

The struggle within is not a sign of weakness - it is evidence that something greater is at stake. There is a war being waged inside every man, a conflict between who he is and who he is called to become. This tension is not accidental; it is part of the process of growth and transformation. The pull of the flesh will always resist the direction of the Spirit, and the easier path will often compete with the right one. But this internal battle reveals that a man is not asleep, not passive, not surrendered to complacency. It shows that he is aware of the call, aware of the cost, and aware that his life carries purpose. The discomfort he feels is not something to escape, but something to engage, because within that tension is the shaping of his character and the strengthening of his spirit. Victory in this battle does not come from ignoring the struggle, but from confronting it with discipline, truth, and dependence on God. A man does not become stronger by avoiding resistance - he becomes stronger by overcoming it.

Each decision to choose what is right over what is easy, each moment of obedience when compromise would be simpler, is a step toward becoming the man he was created to be. The war within must be won before any external victories can be sustained. When a man learns to govern his thoughts, master his desires, and align his life with God's direction, he becomes unshakable. The struggle is not there to defeat him - it is there to refine him, to prepare him, and to prove that what is being built within him is stronger than anything that comes against him. At the center of every man's internal battle is a relentless conflict - the flesh pulling him toward comfort, ease, and immediate satisfaction, while the spirit calls him higher into discipline, obedience, and purpose that reaches beyond this moment. The flesh whispers, "Take the easy road. Do what feels good now." It craves indulgence, avoids resistance, and resists anything that requires sacrifice.

But the spirit speaks with a different voice. It urges a man to stand firm, to deny what is temporary for the sake of what is eternal, and to choose what is right even when it is difficult. These two forces do not negotiate - they collide. One leads to weakness and regret, the other leads to strength and life. A man who wins in life is first a man who learns to win within. Victory does not begin on the outside - it is forged in the unseen decisions of the heart. Every moment presents a choice: to feed the flesh or to strengthen the spirit. And what a man feeds will grow. When he disciplines his thoughts, guards his desires, and aligns himself with God's truth, the spirit gains ground. But when he gives in to comfort and compromise, the flesh tightens its grip. This war is constant, but it is not unwinnable. Through surrender to God, daily discipline, and a commitment to walk in the spirit, a man can rise above his impulses and live with purpose, strength, and unshakable conviction.

The flesh is subtle, but it is not harmless. It does not shout - it whispers. It appeals to comfort, convenience, and self-justification, telling a man he has earned the right to relax his standards, to compromise in private, to take what costs him nothing but weakens him over time. The flesh thrives in darkness because it depends on secrecy to survive. It avoids accountability, resists discipline, and quietly pulls a man away from the strength he was called to walk in. But the man who recognizes this battle does not negotiate with it - he confronts it. He understands that strength is not built in moments of comfort, but in moments of resistance. When the flesh whispers, he answers with truth. When it tempts him to take shortcuts, he chooses the harder path that leads to growth. This is where real victory begins not in public displays of strength, but in private decisions of integrity. A man who learns to rule himself in secret will stand unshaken in the open, because he has already won the battle within.

The spirit speaks with clarity and conviction. It calls a man to rise above comfort and live with intention, reminding him that his life carries accountability before God. It urges a man to stand firm when compromise would be easier, to choose what is right when no one is watching, and to honor God even when obedience comes at a cost. The voice of the spirit does not always promise comfort, but it always leads to purpose, shaping a man into someone who can be trusted with greater responsibility. A man who listens to the spirit walks with discipline, not because it is easy, but because it is necessary. He understands that integrity is built one choice at a time, and that strength is forged in moments when he chooses obedience over desire. The spirit calls him higher - not to burden him, but to build him. And when he answers that call, he becomes steady and unshakable. His life begins to reflect something greater than himself, because he is no longer led by what he feels, but by what he knows is right.

Every decision a man makes is a vote cast in an ongoing battle. There is no moment that does not shape him in some way. What he entertains in his mind, what he tolerates in his habits, and what he pursues with his time and energy are all feeding something within him. If he continually gives space to compromise, distraction, and indulgence, the voice of the flesh will grow louder and more persuasive. But if he chooses discipline, truth, and obedience - even in small, unseen moments - the voice of the spirit will become stronger, clearer, and more dominant in his life. The direction of a man's life is not determined in a single defining moment, but in the accumulation of daily decisions. A wise man understands this and becomes intentional about what he allows to take root in his life. He does not casually entertain what could quietly weaken him, nor does he ignore what needs to be confronted. Instead, he feeds what strengthens him - time with God, obedience to His Word, and choices that align with truth.

The real danger is not the presence of the flesh, but the quiet surrender to it. Many men do not fall in a single moment of weakness - they drift through a pattern of small compromises that go unchallenged. What once stirred conviction begins to feel acceptable. The battle that should have been fought is avoided, and over time, the line between right and wrong becomes blurred. But a man who refuses to normalize what God has called him to resist begins to reclaim his ground. He confronts what he once excused and draws a clear line where compromise used to live. He understands that conviction is not his enemy - it is his guide. Instead of silencing it, he listens and responds with action. He chooses to fight, not perfectly, but persistently. And in that fight, something begins to change. What once had power over him begins to lose its grip. The flesh no longer sets the standard - truth does. And as he stands firm, he becomes a man marked not by what he surrendered to, but by what he overcame.

The man who is serious about growth draws a line and refuses to make peace with anything that is working against him. He understands that every unchecked desire, every undisciplined habit, and every quiet compromise carries a cost that over time will demand his strength, his clarity, his purpose, and even his calling. Because of this, he becomes intentional, disciplined, and aware, knowing that growth requires resistance and that strength is built through consistent, deliberate choices. This kind of man takes responsibility for his actions and ownership of his direction. He replaces passivity with purpose and excuses with accountability. When something threatens his character, he addresses it - not later, but now. And through that commitment, he begins to transform. His habits align with his values, his decisions reflect his faith, and his life gains momentum in the right direction. He becomes a man who is not easily shaken, because he has refused to build his life on anything that could quietly tear it down.

Winning the battle within begins with honest awareness. A man cannot overcome what he refuses to acknowledge. The areas he hides, minimizes, or excuses are often the very places where he is most vulnerable. Pretending something is harmless does not make it so - it only gives it room to grow unchecked. Real strength is found in truth, in the willingness to look within and say, "This is where I struggle, and this is where I need to change." Awareness is the starting point of transformation. What is brought into the light can be addressed, but what is ignored will continue to quietly shape a man's life. A man who is serious about growth invites accountability, seeks wisdom, and replaces denial with action. As he becomes more aware, he also becomes more equipped. The struggle may still be real, but it no longer controls him. Step by step, decision by decision, he begins to take ground. Because the man who refuses to ignore his weaknesses is the man who eventually overcomes them.

It also requires discipline. Victory is not built on what a man intends to do - it is built on what he consistently does. Good intentions may inspire him, but they will never transform him without action. Discipline is the bridge between desire and change. It is choosing to say no to what weakens him and yes to what strengthens him, even when it feels difficult. This kind of training does not happen overnight; it is forged through repetition, through daily decisions that align with purpose rather than impulse. Over time, what was once hard becomes natural, and what once controlled him begins to lose its power. A disciplined man understands that growth requires effort and consistency. He does not wait until he feels motivated - he acts because he is committed. He builds habits that reinforce strength, guards his time and attention, and refuses to give space to what undermines his progress. Even when he stumbles, he does not quit - he corrects course and continues forward.

This kind of discipline is not built in a moment of inspiration - it is forged over time, in the quiet consistency of daily choices. It is developed in the unseen places, where there is no applause, no recognition, and no external pressure. In those moments, character is shaped. When he chooses what is right instead of what is easy, he is building something far stronger than temporary success - he is building integrity. These small, repeated decisions may seem insignificant in isolation, but together they form the foundation of a life that is steady, trustworthy, and resilient. Over time, this consistency begins to transform him. What once required effort becomes a pattern, and what once felt difficult becomes a standard. He no longer depends on emotion or convenience to guide him. His strength is the result of countless moments where he chose discipline over ease. This is the man who cannot be easily shaken, because his life is built on decisions he made when only God was watching.

It is possible for a man to appear disciplined, confident, and strong in public, while privately fighting battles he has not yet confronted. But outward appearance is not the true measure of strength - private integrity is. What a man does when he is alone, when there is no accountability and no audience, reveals the condition of his character. It is in those quiet moments that real decisions are made, and those decisions shape the direction of his life far more than any public display ever could. A man who understands this brings his private life into alignment with his public image, refusing to live divided or compromised. He knows that what is hidden will eventually be revealed, so he chooses to deal with it now rather than later. In the solitude of those hidden places, he makes choices that honor God, even when it costs him. And over time, that consistency produces a strength that is real, not performative - a strength that holds under pressure because it was built in the places where no one was watching.

God is not searching for a man who has it all together - He is searching for a man who is willing to lay it all down. Perfection is not the requirement; surrender is. When a man stops hiding his weaknesses, stops pretending he is stronger than he is, and brings his struggles honestly before God, something begins to shift. Pride loses its grip, and grace takes its place. It is in that moment of humility that real transformation begins, because God can work with what is surrendered. A man who is honest before God is being strengthened from within. The moment a man chooses humility over self-reliance, he opens the door for God's power to meet him in his weakness. He learns to depend, to trust, and to walk in a strength that is greater than his own. This is not a one-time decision, but a continual surrender that says, "God, I need You." And in that place, the man who once felt weak becomes steady, not because he has no struggles, but because he has learned where his true strength comes from.

The spirit grows by what a man consistently feeds it. Time in God's Word sharpens his thinking, prayer strengthens his connection, and obedience aligns his life with truth. These are not empty routines to check off a list; they are lifelines that sustain and empower him.

When a man neglects them, his spiritual strength begins to fade, but when he commits to them, something within him comes alive. His discernment becomes clearer, his convictions become stronger, and his ability to stand firm increases. What he feeds will grow and when he feeds his spirit, he equips himself for the battles he faces. These practices are not passive - they are powerful. They are weapons in the fight for his soul, his focus, and his direction. Through them, he gains the strength to resist what would pull him down and the clarity to pursue what will build him up. A man who is rooted in God's Word, consistent in prayer, and committed to obedience is not easily shaken, because he is being fortified from the inside out.

At the same time, the flesh loses its power when it is consistently denied. Every time a man says no to what pulls him away from truth, he is breaking its influence little by little. Starving the flesh is not about deprivation for its own sake - it is about creating space for strength to grow. A man who learns to deny what weakens him is not losing something valuable; he is gaining control, clarity, and freedom. What a man consistently refuses will eventually lose its hold on him. The cravings that once felt overwhelming begin to quiet. The habits that once seemed impossible to break begin to weaken. This does not happen instantly, but it happens steadily as he remains committed. Each act of discipline reinforces his authority over his desires, reminding him that he is not controlled by what he feels. And over time, the balance shifts - the flesh grows weaker, the spirit grows stronger, and the man himself becomes more grounded, more focused, and more aligned with the life he was meant to live.

There will be moments when a man falls short of the standard he is striving to live by. The danger is not in falling; it is in staying down, in allowing shame or discouragement to convince him that the fight is over. Every man who grows will face moments where he stumbles, but those moments do not define him unless he allows them to. What matters is what he does next. Will he retreat, or will he rise again with greater awareness, stronger resolve, and a deeper dependence on God? The battle is not won by those who never fail - it is won by those who refuse to quit. A man who gets back up, who learns from his mistakes, and who continues to move forward is a man who cannot be defeated. Each time he rises, he becomes wiser, more disciplined, and more resilient. He begins to understand that setbacks are not signs to stop, but opportunities to grow stronger. And over time, that perseverance builds a quiet confidence within him. He knows that no matter how many times he falls, he will rise again.

Over time, the man who consistently chooses the spirit over the flesh begins to experience real transformation from the inside out. His desires start to shift because something deeper is being reshaped within him. His thinking becomes clearer, no longer clouded by impulse or distraction, but guided by truth and purpose. This is the quiet work of growth. It is steady, consistent, and unmistakable. It is not always dramatic, but it is powerful, and it changes the direction of his life. As this transformation takes root, he is no longer easily pulled in different directions, because he has learned to govern himself. The things that once controlled him no longer hold the same authority. He walks with greater clarity, greater discipline, and greater confidence, not in himself alone, but in what God is doing within him. This is what happens when a man chooses the spirit again and again. He becomes anchored, refined, and free - no longer driven by what once mastered him but led by a strength that has been built over time.

This is why the battle within must be won first. A man cannot effectively lead others, carry weight, or step into his purpose if he is being overruled by what is happening inside him. No amount of outward effort can compensate for inward defeat. Before a man can stand strong for others, he must learn to stand firm within himself. The private victories, the disciplined choices, and the alignment of his heart and mind are what prepare him to handle greater responsibility without collapsing under it. Internal victory is the foundation for external impact. When a man governs his thoughts, controls his desires, and walks in integrity, his influence becomes steady and trustworthy. He is no longer easily shaken, because his strength is rooted deep within. He can now lead with clarity and serve with humility. His life begins to carry weight because of what has been established inwardly. And when the battle within is won, he is no longer divided - he is focused, grounded, and ready to make a lasting impact.

So fight the battle. Do not ignore it or push it aside, hoping it will resolve on its own. What is left unchallenged will only grow stronger. Face it with honesty and with discipline, choosing what is right even when it costs you. Do not run when it becomes uncomfortable or difficult. Lean into the fight with a steady resolve, knowing that every step forward matters. And above all, do not try to win it in your own strength. Depend on God, because true victory is not found in self-reliance, but in surrender to the One who strengthens you. The man who conquers himself becomes a man who cannot be easily defeated. He is not perfect, but he is anchored. His strength runs deeper than circumstances, and his stability is not shaken by pressure. He has faced the hardest opponent - the one within - and learned to stand firm. And from that place, he moves forward with clarity, confidence, and purpose. A man like that is dangerous to defeat, because he has already won where it matters most.

| 7 |

"AWAKENING COURAGE"

Courage is not handed to a man at birth - it is forged through the fires he chooses to walk through. It is built when he steps forward even while his heart pounds and his mind questions. It is in the moments where the path is unclear, where the outcome is uncertain, and where fear whispers loudest that courage begins to take shape. Every act of obedience in those moments becomes a hammer strike, shaping his spirit into something stronger, steadier, and more resilient. God does not call a man to a life free of fear - He calls him to trust Him in the middle of it. Courage grows when a man refuses to retreat, when he stands firm despite resistance, and when he moves forward knowing he is not alone. Fear may still be present, but it no longer has authority. With every step taken in faith, courage deepens, and the man who once hesitated becomes the man who stands. Not because the fear disappeared but because his trust in God became greater than the fear before him.

Many men delay their obedience, waiting for a sense of readiness that never fully arrives. They convince themselves that once they feel confident, then they will move but confidence is rarely the starting point. It is the result. Courage is what comes first. It is the decision to act while uncertainty still lingers, to step forward while fear is still present. The man who waits for perfect conditions will remain stuck, but the man who moves anyway begins to discover that strength is not something he needed beforehand - it is something that is built as he goes. When a man chooses to act in faith, something begins to shift within him. Confidence starts to rise, not because the situation becomes easier, but because he is becoming stronger. Each step of obedience reinforces his trust in God, and what once felt overwhelming begins to feel manageable. In time, the man who once hesitated becomes steady and bold - not because he waited until he was ready, but because he chose to move when he wasn't.

Every challenge a man faces carries within it the opportunity to become stronger, braver, and more grounded in faith. In the moment of pressure, when hesitation creeps in and doubt begins to whisper, he stands at a crossroads. One path leads to retreat, comfort, and missed growth. The other leads to rising, trusting God, and stepping into the man he is called to become. Courage is built in these exact moments, when the decision truly matters. God uses these crossroads to shape a man's character. Each time he chooses to rise instead of retreat, something within him is strengthened. His faith becomes more resilient, his spirit more steadfast, and his identity more aligned with God's purpose. What may feel like a small decision in the moment is actually forming the foundation of who he is becoming. Over time, these choices compound, and the man who consistently rises becomes unshakable not because he has avoided challenges, but because he has allowed them to build courage within him.

Courage is not the absence of fear - it is the refusal to be ruled by it. Fear will always show up when a man stands at the edge of something meaningful, something that requires faith, risk, and surrender. It is often confirmation that he is standing in a place where growth is about to happen. The presence of fear reveals the weight of what is before him. And in that moment, courage is the choice to step forward anyway, trusting that God is greater than whatever stands ahead. God never promised a life without fear, but He did promise His presence in the midst of it. When a man chooses to move forward despite the tension in his heart, he begins to experience a deeper strength that is not rooted in his own ability, but in his reliance on God. Fear may still walk beside him, but it no longer leads him. With every step of faith, his confidence in God grows, and what once intimidated him begins to lose its power. Courage rises not because fear disappears, but because trust becomes stronger than fear.

The man who spends his life avoiding fear will also avoid the very things that could shape him into something greater. Safety may feel secure, but it slowly shrinks his world, limits his potential, and keeps him from stepping into the fullness of his calling. God did not design a man to live confined by caution, but to walk by faith even when that path stretches him beyond what feels familiar. Avoiding fear may preserve ease, but it will always cost growth. But the man who chooses to confront fear begins to expand in ways he never imagined. Each step into the unknown strengthens his spirit, sharpens his trust in God, and awakens the capacity within him that comfort could never reveal. What once intimidated him becomes the ground where his faith takes root and grows deeper. He discovers that courage is about refusing to let fear define his limits. And as he continues to move forward, he becomes the man he was created to be - steadfast, bold, and fully alive in his God-given purpose.

Facing fear head-on begins with truth. A man cannot overcome what he refuses to acknowledge. God does not call a man to deny his fears - He calls him to bring them into the light. It takes humility to admit what intimidates you, what unsettles you, what causes you to hesitate. But that honesty is not weakness; it is the first act of courage. What is hidden remains powerful, but what is exposed begins to lose its grip. When a man confronts his fear with honesty, he creates space for God to work within him. No longer controlled by avoidance, he can begin to move forward with clarity and purpose. What once felt overwhelming becomes something he can face, step by step, with God at his side. Fear does not vanish instantly, but it no longer dominates him. Instead, it becomes something he walks through, not something he runs from. And in that process, he discovers that what is confronted in faith can be overcome, and what once intimidated him can no longer define him.

There is undeniable power in stepping directly into the very thing that once caused you to hesitate. The first step often feels the heaviest, as if fear is trying one last time to hold you in place. But that single act of movement breaks its grip. What once felt immovable begins to shift the moment you choose to act. Fear thrives in stillness and hesitation, but it weakens the instant a man decides to move forward. That first step is a declaration that fear will no longer dictate his direction. When a man moves forward despite resistance, he invites God's strength into his weakness. Each step that follows becomes a little lighter, not because the challenge disappears, but because his confidence begins to grow. Avoidance may feel easier in the moment, but it quietly strengthens fear over time. Movement, however, dismantles it piece by piece. And as a man continues to press forward, he discovers that what once held him back has lost its power, and he is walking in a freedom that only courage can produce.

Fear has a way of distorting reality, turning obstacles into giants and challenges into impossibilities. It whispers worst-case scenarios and magnifies the unknown until a man feels paralyzed before he even begins. But much of what fear presents is illusion, not truth. When a man stands still, those exaggerations grow stronger, but when he stands firm and chooses to act, clarity begins to replace confusion. The moment he steps forward, he starts to see that what once looked overwhelming is not as powerful as it appeared. God brings clarity to the man who moves in faith. As he takes action, his perspective shifts and his confidence grows. What once felt impossible becomes something he can face, handle, and overcome one step at a time. The challenge may still be real, but it is no longer inflated by fear. Instead, it is met with truth, strength, and trust in God's presence. And in that clarity, the man realizes he was never as outmatched as fear led him to believe - he simply needed the courage to see it rightly.

Courage is not built in a single moment - it is strengthened through repetition. Every time a man chooses to step forward instead of withdrawing, he is reinforcing something deeper within himself. Each act of obedience, each decision to face what once intimidated him, adds another layer of strength to his character. What once felt overwhelming begins to feel familiar, not because the challenge has changed, but because he has. Courage grows through consistent action, through repeated choices to trust God rather than retreat. Over time, the very things that once held power over him begin to lose their grip. Fear does not disappear overnight, but it weakens with every step of faith he takes. What once caused hesitation becomes something he can face with steadiness and clarity. God uses this process to transform him from within, shaping him into a man who is no longer easily shaken. And through that repetition, courage becomes a natural part of who he is.

God never promised a path without fear - He promised His presence within it. The life He calls a man to is not one of comfort, but of overcoming. Fear, difficulty, and uncertainty are often the very places where faith is meant to rise, the places where God most often reveals Himself. It is there, when the weight feels real and the outcome uncertain, that a man learns God is near, steady, and unshakable. His faithfulness is not measured by how easy the road becomes, but by how present He remains through every step of it. When a man chooses to trust God in the midst of fear, he begins to experience a strength that is not his own. He finds peace in pressure, clarity in confusion, and endurance in the face of opposition. The challenge may not disappear, but his confidence in God grows stronger than the challenge itself. And through that process, he becomes a man who does not run from fear but walks through it, knowing God is with him every step of the way.

Trusting God in moments of intimidation changes everything. When a man is faced with something that feels bigger than him, his natural instinct is to focus on the size of the challenge, the uncertainty of the outcome, and the weight of what could go wrong. But the moment he shifts his focus - lifting his eyes from the problem to the power of God - something begins to break. The challenge may remain the same, but his perspective transforms, and with it, his response. As he anchors his trust in God's strength rather than his own limitations, fear begins to lose its authority over him. It no longer dictates his decisions or controls his direction. Instead, faith rises and takes its place. He begins to move with confidence, not because he feels capable, but because he knows God is faithful. In those moments, intimidation gives way to clarity, and hesitation is replaced with boldness. The man who trusts God discovers that what once tried to stop him becomes the very place where his faith grows strongest.

Trust is the foundation upon which courage is built. Without it, a man will be governed by what he sees, what he feels, and what he fears. But when a man places his trust in God, something shifts at the core of who he is. He is no longer relying on his own strength or understanding - he is anchored in something greater. That trust steadies him when circumstances shake, and it gives him the confidence to move forward even when the path is unclear. With trust in God, intimidating situations are no longer barriers - they become invitations. What once caused hesitation becomes an opportunity to obey, to grow, and to deepen his faith. The challenge may still be real, but it is no longer overwhelming because it is no longer faced alone. Trust transforms the way a man sees everything. Instead of asking, "Can I handle this?" he begins to ask, "Can God lead me through this?" And the answer to that question changes everything because where trust is present, courage will always follow.

A man who truly trusts God does not lean on his own strength as his foundation. He understands that his ability is limited, his perspective is incomplete, and his strength alone is not enough for what he is called to face. He recognizes that the calling itself carries the provision, and that God never leads a man into something without also supplying the strength to walk through it. This kind of trust frees him from the pressure of having to be enough on his own. Courage, then, is something he receives and sustains through his relationship with God. In moments of weakness, he does not collapse; he leans in. In moments of fear, he does not retreat; he remembers who goes before him. The source of his courage is not found within himself, but in the faithfulness of God. And because God does not change, his courage can remain steady. The man who understands this walks with a quiet confidence not because he believes in himself, but because he trusts fully in the One who never fails.

In moments of pressure, when everything feels intense and uncertain, trust becomes the anchor that steadies a man's heart. It quiets the noise of fear and reminds him that he is not alone, not abandoned, and not left to figure things out on his own. Trust shifts his focus from what is happening around him to who is with him. God's presence becomes more real than the pressure, and in that awareness, his heart begins to settle. Trust also reminds him that he is not unequipped for what lies ahead. God does not call a man into battle without first preparing him for it. Every lesson, every trial, every season of growth has been building something within him for this very moment. What he needs has already been placed within reach through God's provision. And as he leans into that truth, he finds strength rising where there was once uncertainty, and confidence growing where there was once doubt because he knows that with God, he has everything required to stand and move forward.

Courage is awakened the moment trust begins to outweigh fear. As long as fear holds the greater voice, a man will hesitate, second-guess, and hold back. But when he truly believes that God is with him, for him, and actively working through him - something shifts within.

Fear loses its grip, not because it disappears, but because it is no longer the loudest voice. In that place, courage rises naturally from a heart that is anchored in faith. When a man walks in that kind of trust, boldness begins to define his steps. He no longer waits for perfect conditions or complete certainty - he moves because he knows who goes before him. His confidence is not rooted in his own ability, but in God's faithfulness. And that changes everything. What once intimidated him becomes something he can face, and what once held him back becomes the very ground where his faith grows stronger. Courage comes alive when trust takes its rightful place, and the man who walks in it begins to live with a strength that cannot be shaken.

This kind of courage is not loud, impulsive, or driven by the need to prove something. It is steady, grounded, and unshakable. It does not rise and fall with circumstances, nor does it depend on everything going right. While the world often equates courage with bold displays and outward strength, this deeper courage is quiet and consistent. It stands firm in the face of pressure, not because the situation is easy, but because the man has learned where to anchor himself. His confidence is not in outcomes, but in the One who holds them. When a man's foundation is rooted in God, his courage becomes immovable. Storms may come, opposition may rise, and uncertainty may surround him, but he does not waver. This kind of courage does not need recognition or validation; it simply endures. And in that endurance, it becomes a powerful testimony - a life that stands firm, not because it avoided hardship, but because it was built on a foundation that cannot be shaken.

With every new season comes new challenges, new fears, and new opportunities to trust God in deeper ways. A man never outgrows the need for courage; he simply grows in his capacity to walk in it. What once tested him may no longer shake him, but new levels will always require new faith. This is how God continues to shape him - leading him from one step of trust to the next, each one stretching him, strengthening him, and refining his character. Each moment he chooses faith over fear adds strength for what lies ahead. The battles he faces today are preparing him for the responsibilities of tomorrow. Over time, he begins to walk with a quiet confidence, not because challenges have disappeared, but because he has seen God prove Himself again and again. And through that ongoing journey, he becomes a man who is not intimidated by what's next but is ready for it, knowing that the same God who brought him this far will carry him through whatever comes.

So do not wait for fear to disappear before you move. If you wait until everything feels comfortable, you will remain where you are. But when you choose to move forward in faith, even with uncertainty in your heart, you begin to build courage in real time. Each step you take weakens fear's hold and strengthens your resolve. Facing what intimidates you is not easy, but it is necessary, because growth will always be found on the other side of obedience. Trust God completely as you step forward, knowing you are never walking into the unknown alone. He is already ahead of you, preparing the way, strengthening your spirit, and guiding your steps. What feels uncertain to you is already known to Him. And as you move, you will discover that He meets you in the action - in the step of faith, not before it. Courage will rise, not because fear vanished, but because your trust in God became greater. And in that trust, you will find the strength to keep going, no matter what stands before you.

| 8 |

"THE VOICE OF AUTHORITY"

A man does not step into authority the moment he raises his voice - he steps into authority the moment he aligns his voice with truth. Authority is formed in the quiet places where a man submits himself to what is right, even when it costs him. When his words are rooted in truth, they no longer need to be loud to be powerful. There is a steadiness, a clarity, and a weight behind what he says that cannot be ignored. True authority is not about being heard - it is about standing on something unshakable. When a man knows what is right, believes what is true, and stands firmly on it, his words begin to carry weight far beyond his natural ability. He is no longer speaking to impress - he is speaking to represent. And when a man represents truth, he carries a kind of authority that does not come from himself, but from the One who established that truth. He does not need to demand respect - he commands it through consistency, courage, and unwavering alignment with what is right.

There is a powerful distinction between a man who speaks to fill silence and a man who speaks from substance. One is striving for validation, hoping his words will earn him attention. The other is grounded in truth, speaking because something within him has been formed, tested, and made clear. When a man has not cultivated his inner life, his words often come out rushed, scattered, and uncertain - driven by the need to be noticed rather than the responsibility to be accurate. But when a man has spent time in quiet refinement with God, his voice carries weight. He is not trying to impress - he is trying to be faithful. And that difference changes everything. The man who walks closely with God does not need to chase attention. His words become steady because his heart is settled. His speech becomes focused because his mind is anchored in truth. And when he speaks, people listen - not because he is the loudest in the room, but because there is clarity behind his voice and integrity behind his life.

Speaking with conviction is not something a man manufactures in the moment - it is something he has forged over time in the hidden places. In those quiet moments, God shapes his heart, aligns his thoughts, and strengthens his spirit. The man who has spent time with God does not need to search for courage when it is time to speak. What flows from his mouth is the natural overflow of a life that has already been anchored in truth. Because of this, he does not shrink back or second-guess what he knows to be right. His confidence is not rooted in his own ability, but in the truth he has already settled within his soul. He has faced the internal battles and surrendered his fears before God. So when he speaks, there is clarity. There is authority. There is peace. His words carry weight not because they are loud, but because they are backed by a life that has been lived in alignment with God. And when a man lives that way, his voice does more than speak - it leads, it strengthens, and it calls others higher.

Truth is what gives a man his backbone. Without it, he becomes unstable - shifting with opinions, swayed by pressure, and shaped by whatever voice is loudest in the moment. But when truth is deeply rooted within him, something changes. He is no longer easily moved or manipulated. He stands firm, not out of stubbornness, but out of conviction. His life is anchored, his decisions are steady, and his direction is clear. Truth becomes the foundation beneath his feet, and because that foundation does not shift, neither does he. From that place of stability, his voice begins to carry weight. His words are not driven by emotion or insecurity, but by clarity and purpose. There is a steadiness in how he communicates, a strength that others can feel. In a world full of confusion and compromise, his voice brings direction. It cuts through the noise, not with arrogance, but with authority rooted in truth. And when a man speaks from that place, he doesn't just contribute to conversations - he shapes them.

Many men silence themselves, not because they lack truth, but because they fear people. The fear of man is a subtle but powerful enemy. It tells him to hold back, to remain unnoticed rather than risk rejection. And if he listens long enough, that voice begins to shape him. What was once bold becomes hesitant. What was once clear becomes compromised. Over time, the strength of his voice is slowly surrendered. But a man was never created to be governed by the opinions of others; he was created to be anchored in the truth of God. When he fears people more than he reveres God, his voice will always shrink. But when he chooses to honor God above all else - his courage begins to return. He realizes that silence in the face of truth is hesitation rooted in fear. And as he breaks free from that fear, his voice is restored. Not loud for the sake of attention, but strong for the sake of purpose. Because a man who fears God more than man will stand, he will speak, and he will lead with authority.

A man who fears people will measure his words by approval instead of truth, adjusting his convictions to match the comfort of those around him. In that process, he begins to trade what is solid for what is accepted, what is eternal for what is temporary. He softens truth to avoid rejection, trims conviction to avoid conflict, and slowly reshapes himself until he is no longer speaking from who he is but from what others want him to be. And in doing so, he forfeits the very authority his voice was meant to carry. A compromised voice repeats what is already being said, reinforces what is already accepted, and blends into the noise instead of rising above it. Leadership requires clarity, courage, and conviction, and those cannot coexist with the fear of man. But when a man chooses truth over acceptance, his voice regains its strength. It may not always be popular, but it will always be purposeful. And in a world full of echoes, the man who speaks with uncompromised truth becomes a voice that others can follow.

Overcoming the fear of man requires a decisive shift in allegiance. A man must settle, once and for all, whose approval truly matters. As long as he lives for the affirmation of people, he will be constantly adjusting, constantly second-guessing, constantly striving to be accepted. But when he chooses to live for the approval of God, the need to perform fades. He is no longer driven by how he is perceived, but by what he knows is right. His identity is no longer shaped by the crowd - it is anchored in truth. From that place, freedom emerges. He can speak clearly without fear, stand firmly without apology, and act boldly without hesitation. The opinions of others no longer have the power to control him because they no longer define him. There is a quiet strength in him, a steady confidence that comes from knowing he is aligned with God. And when a man lives that way, his voice carries authority, his actions carry integrity, and his life becomes a reflection of something far greater than human approval.

This does not mean a man becomes harsh or careless with his words. Authority is not arrogance, and boldness is not brutality. A man who truly walks in authority does not speak just to prove a point or to win a moment. He speaks with purpose. His words are shaped by wisdom and guided by truth. He knows when to speak and when to remain silent, when to confront and when to counsel. Strength is present, but it is controlled. Because of that, his voice carries not just power, but precision. True authority does not tear people down - it builds them up while still refusing to compromise what is right. When correction is needed, it is given with clarity, not cruelty. When leadership is required, it is exercised with humility, not domination. A man like this does not lead by force; he leads by example. His life reflects the very truth he speaks, and that consistency earns trust. People are not driven away by his strength - they are drawn to it, because they recognize that his authority is rooted not in pride, but in purpose.

A man who is no longer intimidated by people is finally free to speak as he truly believes. He no longer hides behind vague language, softened statements, or uncertain tones designed to keep everyone comfortable. Instead, his words become direct, steady, and understandable. What he says reflects what he believes, and what he believes is anchored in truth. That clarity brings strength - not only to his voice, but to every area of his life. Clarity is a mark of confidence rooted in conviction. It does not mean he speaks harshly, but it does mean he speaks plainly. People know where he stands because he is not shifting with the moment. His words provide direction, his voice brings order, and his presence removes uncertainty. In a world filled with blurred lines and mixed messages, a man who speaks with clarity becomes a steady guide. And when he lives this way, his voice does more than communicate - it establishes truth, sets boundaries, and leads others with confidence.

Clarity is a mark of true leadership. When a man speaks with clarity, he removes the fog that causes hesitation and doubt. He brings definition where there was confusion, and purpose where there was wandering. His words do not leave people guessing; they give them something solid to stand on. His voice becomes a steady line that points the way forward. That kind of clarity comes from conviction rooted in truth. Because of this, his voice becomes a source of stability to those around him. He provides vision that others can follow and direction that others can trust. His leadership is not built on noise or constant talking, but on intentional, clear communication that carries weight. People feel strengthened in his presence because they know where he stands and what he stands for. And when a man leads with that kind of clarity, he does more than guide others - he creates an environment where strength can grow, confidence can rise, and purpose can be pursued without confusion.

Boldness is courage expressed through words. It is the quiet but unshakable resolve to say what must be said, even when it is uncomfortable, even when it costs something. A bold man does not measure his words by how they will be received, but by whether they are true and necessary. He refuses to remain silent when truth is needed. His courage is not found in volume, but in conviction. And because of that, even his calmest words can carry great weight. True boldness understands that words have power, and with that power comes accountability. A bold man does not speak carelessly or impulsively; he speaks with purpose, guided by wisdom and grounded in truth. He knows that silence in the wrong moment can cause harm, just as much as careless speech can. So he chooses his words carefully, but he does not withhold them when they are needed. And when a man walks in that kind of boldness, his voice becomes a force for clarity, direction, and transformation in the lives of those around him.

A man who leads with boldness does not wait for perfect conditions, because he understands that those conditions rarely come. If he waits until everything feels comfortable, aligned, and risk-free, he will remain silent when his voice is needed most. He recognizes that silence in critical moments can cause more damage than imperfect speech. Truth delayed can become truth denied, so he speaks not because he is fearless, but because he is faithful to what is right. He does not enjoy confrontation, nor does he seek conflict for its own sake. But he values truth more than comfort, and that priority shapes his actions. His boldness is driven by responsibility. He understands that leadership often requires stepping into difficult moments and saying what others are unwilling to say. And when he does, his courage creates clarity, his voice establishes direction, and his example gives others permission to rise. A man who values truth above comfort leads with conviction that transforms the environment around him.

The voice of authority is shaped in the moments that demand something from a man, when speaking truth comes with a cost and standing firm comes with resistance. There will be times when his words are not welcomed, when his convictions set him apart, and when doing what is right feels isolating. But these moments are the very forge where strength is built. Every time he chooses truth over comfort, courage over compromise, his voice is being refined and strengthened. In those difficult seasons, he learns that authority is not dependent on applause, but on alignment with what is right. He becomes less concerned with being accepted and more committed to being faithful. And as he endures those tests, his voice gains weight because it has been proven. When he speaks, it carries the steadiness of conviction, and the strength of a man who has stood when it was not easy. That is what gives his voice authority - the fact that it has been forged in the fire and has not been shaken.

Every time a man chooses truth over comfort, something within him is strengthened. Each decision to stand firm builds a deeper confidence, a steadier voice, and a stronger sense of purpose. These moments may seem small in isolation, but over time they form a life marked by courage rather than compromise. When he resists the urge to stay silent, when he speaks even in the face of resistance, his authority begins to grow. Authority is never handed to the passive - it is developed through the consistent practice of courage. It is built in the daily choice to do what is right regardless of how it feels or how it is received. A man who lives this way does not wait for a moment of greatness to suddenly become bold - he has been training for it all along. And when the defining moments come, he is ready. His voice carries weight because it has been exercised. His leadership carries influence because it has been proven. Authority is formed not in comfort, but in courage lived out over time.

A man must also learn when to speak and when to remain silent. Not every moment requires his voice, and not every situation benefits from more words. There is power in restraint, in the discipline to hold back until the right moment arrives. A man who understands this is not driven by impulse or the need to be heard - he is guided by wisdom. He speaks when it matters, and because of that, his words carry greater impact. His silence is not weakness; it is control. There is strength in timing, and a wise man respects it. He does not waste words on empty conversations or speak just to fill space. He knows that weight is built through intentional use, and that careless speech diminishes authority. So when he does speak, people listen. His words are measured, purposeful, and aligned with truth. In a world full of noise, his voice stands out not because it is constant, but because it is meaningful. And that is the mark of true authority - a voice that is not overused but rightly used.

When he does speak, people listen. Not because he demands attention, but because his words have earned it. There is a pattern of truth, integrity, and consistency that people have come to recognize. He does not speak carelessly, and he does not speak often without purpose. Others listen to him because they trust what comes from him. His authority is not forced - it is established through a life that aligns with what he says. Over time, consistency builds credibility, and credibility gives authority its staying power. A single bold moment may gain attention, but a consistent life earns trust. Day by day, decision by decision, he proves that his words are reliable. He follows through, stands firm, and remains anchored in truth even when it is inconvenient. That steady consistency forms a foundation that cannot easily be shaken. And from that foundation, his authority endures not as something temporary or situational, but as something lasting, rooted in a life that has been proven over time.

The voice of authority ultimately reflects the condition of the heart. What is happening within a man will always surface in how he speaks. A divided man cannot speak with clarity, because he is pulled in different directions. His words carry hesitation because his heart is unsettled. A compromised man cannot speak with consistency, because he is not firmly anchored in truth. His voice shifts depending on the situation, revealing the instability within him. But a man who is aligned with God speaks differently. His confidence does not come from self-reliance, but from surrender. He is not trying to manufacture authority - he is walking in it because his heart is settled, his direction is clear, and his words reflect that alignment. There is a steadiness in his voice, a quiet confidence that does not waver with circumstance. And when a man lives from that place, his voice carries more than sound - it carries conviction, clarity, and the authority that comes from being aligned with something greater than himself.

He understands that true authority is not self-generated but is God-given. Because of this, he faithfully stewards what has been entrusted to him. He recognizes that every opportunity to speak, lead, and impact others is a responsibility, not a platform for self-promotion. This perspective keeps him grounded. It reminds him that the power behind his voice is not his own, and that his role is not to elevate himself, but to honor the One who gave him the assignment. This understanding produces humility and purity in how he leads. He does not speak to impress or control - he speaks to serve and to guide. His voice is not driven by ego, but by obedience. And because of that, there is a sincerity in his words that people can feel. That commitment keeps his voice clear, free from manipulation and pride. And when a man walks in that kind of humility, his authority becomes something others trust - not because it is loud or forceful, but because it is rooted in God and carried with integrity.

So speak with conviction. Not because it elevates you, but because it aligns you with what is right. Faithfulness is not found in staying silent when truth is needed - it is found in the willingness to speak when God calls you to. Your words are not meant to be shaped by fear or filtered through the opinions of others. They are meant to flow from a heart that has been grounded in truth and surrendered to God. When you speak from that place, your voice carries purpose, not pressure, and conviction, not insecurity. Let your words be rooted in truth, steady and unshaken, regardless of the response they receive. Let your voice be guided by purpose, not controlled by the shifting opinions around you. You are not called to echo the room - you are called to bring clarity into it. And when you live and speak this way, your faithfulness becomes evident. Your voice becomes more than sound - it becomes a vessel through which truth is established, direction is given, and others are strengthened to stand.

And when the moment comes to speak - do not shrink back. Do not hesitate when truth is needed most. Stand firm in what you know is right, even if your voice trembles at first. Speak clearly, without hiding behind uncertainty or softening what must be said. Lead boldly, not with arrogance, but with conviction rooted in truth. These moments are opportunities to step into the responsibility you've been prepared for. And every time you choose courage over fear, you strengthen the voice God has placed within you. Because a man who has found his voice in truth becomes a man others can follow. His words carry direction because they are anchored in something unchanging. His presence brings stability because he is not easily moved. People are drawn to that kind of leadership not because it is loud, but because it is real. And when he stands and leads from that place, he becomes a guide, a steady voice in uncertain times, and a reflection of the strength that comes from living aligned with truth.

| 9 |

"THE DISCIPLINE OF A WARRIOR"

A warrior is not forged in the noise of battle, but in the silence of daily surrender. Long before the pressure rises and the moment of testing arrives, a man is being shaped in the unseen places - through early mornings, quiet prayers, disciplined choices, and obedience when no one is watching. These are the moments that define him. Strength is not something he reaches for in crisis; it is something he has already built through consistency. While others wait for motivation, he has trained himself to move by conviction. While others rely on emotion, he stands on discipline. Because when the storm comes, a man does not rise to the level of his intentions - he falls to the level of his training. Discipline is the hidden foundation beneath visible strength. It is the steady, faithful repetition of what is right, even when it is hard, unnoticed, or inconvenient. Every small decision to stay committed, to resist compromise, and to press forward lays another brick in the structure of his character.

Daily habits are the quiet chisels in a man's life, shaping him with every unseen strike. Character is built in the ordinary rhythms of daily obedience. The man who chooses discipline in the small things is laying a foundation that will hold under the weight of greater responsibility. Each decision to pray when he doesn't feel like it, to choose integrity when compromise would be easier, to show up when comfort calls him away are the moments that carve strength into his soul. The repetition of right choices creates a momentum that shapes his identity and directs his path. While others wait for motivation, the disciplined man builds structure. While others rely on emotion, he relies on commitment. If a man guards his daily habits, he will not have to chase greatness - he will grow into it. Because in the kingdom of God, it is not the dramatic moments that define a man, but the steady, faithful ones that prepare him. Over time, those small, faithful actions compound into a life of strength, clarity, and purpose.

Strong men are not shaped in seasons of ease, but in moments when they choose what is right over what is comfortable. Convenience may feel good in the moment, but it never builds the strength required to carry purpose. Commitment, on the other hand, forges a man from the inside out. When a man chooses discipline over comfort, he is refusing to stay where he is. He embraces the process that stretches him, refines him, and calls him higher. Discipline always requires a cost, but it never leaves a man empty. What it takes in effort, it returns in strength, clarity, and endurance. It transforms potential into reality and intention into action. A disciplined man understands that growth is not accidental, it is intentional. Those daily choices of choosing discipline, choosing consistency, and choosing commitment become the foundation of a life that is unshakable. Because in the end, the man who masters himself is the man who is prepared for anything.

The body is not separate from a man's calling - it is the vessel that carries him into it. Every assignment God gives requires strength to endure, energy to sustain, and resilience to keep going when comfort would say stop. When a man neglects his body, he often limits his capacity to fulfill what he has been entrusted with. But when he trains it, he is not just building muscle, he is building endurance for the journey ahead. Physical discipline becomes a proving ground where he learns to push past resistance, to stay consistent when it is inconvenient, and to finish what he starts. The habits formed in the physical realm often reveal and reinforce the condition of the inner man. A lack of discipline in the body can spill into the mind, the spirit, and the decisions he makes daily. But when a man brings his body under control, he is also sharpening his ability to lead with strength and clarity. He becomes more resilient under pressure, more steady in adversity, and more prepared for the weight of responsibility.

A warrior's strength is not proven by muscle alone, but by mastery of his mind. While the body may endure hardship, it is the mind that determines direction, restraint, and resolve. A disciplined mind does not wander into fear, doubt, or distraction - it stands guard at the gates of thought. It filters what is allowed in and rejects what weakens its purpose. Such a man trains himself to think clearly, to focus intentionally, and to remain steady when everything around him is uncertain. He does not react impulsively to pressure; he responds with wisdom. The man who governs his mind will not be ruled by his circumstances. Storms may rise, pressure may mount, and opposition may come, but his thoughts remain anchored in truth and purpose. He refuses to let temporary situations dictate his identity or direction. Instead, he fixes his mind on what is right, what is strong, and what is eternal. This kind of discipline is not accidental but is developed daily through intentional focus, prayer, and surrender to God.

When a man learns to take authority over his thoughts he steps into a strength that cannot be shaken because his stability is no longer tied to what happens around him, but to what has been established within him. If he continually feeds on negativity, impurity, or passivity, he will find his strength drained and his convictions weakened. But when he intentionally fills his mind with truth, discipline, and things that stir courage and faith, he builds an inner foundation that cannot be easily shaken. Guarding the mind is not about restriction; it is about protection. It is the daily decision to reject what poisons and embrace what produces life. A disciplined mind is forged through consistent, intentional choices. A man must learn to filter what he listens to, be selective about what he watches, and be mindful of what he entertains. The man who trains his mind in this way will not be easily led astray because his thoughts have been conditioned to align with strength, purpose, and the voice of God.

Above all, a warrior must be disciplined in spirit. When the storms of life rise and everything around him begins to shake, it is not his emotions, his circumstances, or even his physical strength that will hold him steady - it is his connection to God. Spiritual strength becomes the unseen anchor, keeping him grounded when fear presses in and uncertainty surrounds him. Time in prayer is where he aligns his heart with heaven. Time in the Word is where truth replaces confusion and strength replaces doubt. Time in quiet reflection is where God refines his thoughts and sharpens his discernment. These are the daily disciplines that build an unshakable man. A man who neglects his spirit may appear strong for a season, but pressure has a way of exposing what is lacking beneath the surface. Without spiritual discipline, cracks will form, and under enough weight, he will eventually collapse. But the man who invests in his spirit daily builds a foundation that cannot be easily broken.

The spirit is where true transformation begins. A man may refine his appearance, sharpen his skills, and build strength in the natural, but if his spirit is neglected, everything he builds rests on unstable ground. Real change does not start outwardly - it starts in the hidden places where a man meets with God. Without time in prayer, time in the Word, and a heart that seeks God daily a man may look solid on the surface, but underneath, his foundation remains fragile and vulnerable to collapse. Only what is anchored deeply in God will endure the pressure, the uncertainty, and the weight of life's battles. Discipline in the spirit produces a stability that carries into every area of a man's life - his thoughts, his decisions, and his relationships. He is no longer easily shaken by circumstances because his strength is not dependent on them. Instead, he stands firm, grounded in truth, steady in faith, and unmovable in conviction. What is built in the spirit becomes the strength that sustains him everywhere else.

Consistency is the mark of true discipline. A disciplined man is not built on bursts of emotions; he is built on habits. Day after day, he chooses prayer over distraction, truth over impulse, and obedience over comfort. This steady faithfulness forms a strength that cannot be shaken, because it is not dependent on how he feels, but on who he has decided to become in God. The warrior understands that progress is not rushed but is forged over time. He does not chase quick results or temporary victories, because he knows that what is built fast often breaks easily. Instead, he commits to lasting growth, trusting that each small act of discipline is laying another stone in a solid foundation. Over time, those unseen choices produce clarity in his thinking, stability in his life, and endurance in the face of pressure. While others burn out or drift away, he remains. And in that consistency, he becomes a man who is not only strong for a moment, but strong for a lifetime.

Intensity may start the journey, but consistency is what sustains it. A man who relies only on inspiration will be at the mercy of his emotions - strong one day and stagnant the next. But a disciplined man is not governed by how he feels. He understands that growth is not built in moments of excitement, but in the quiet, repeated choices to stay committed. When the initial fire fades, discipline remains. It carries him forward when feelings fail, anchoring him in purpose rather than impulse. He shows up when it is hard, when it is inconvenient, and when no one is watching. In those unseen moments, his character is being formed, and his strength is being forged. He prays when he's tired, stands firm when he's pressured, and chooses obedience when compromise would be easier. This kind of consistency builds a life that is steady and unshakable. While others drift based on circumstance, he moves forward with intention, becoming a man whose faith is grounded in discipline and sustained by devotion to God.

There will be days when your body is tired, your mind is weary, and your spirit feels stretched thin. In those moments, quitting will whisper like an easy escape, offering relief from the pressure. But those are the very moments that reveal who a man truly is. Anyone can stand strong when it's easy, but real strength is proven when everything in you wants to stop and you choose to keep going anyway. It is in that tension between comfort and calling that character is forged and conviction is made unshakable. Choosing to press forward in those moments is what separates the strong from the weak. The strong man is not the one who never struggles, but the one who refuses to surrender when he does. He leans into God, drawing from a deeper source that does not fail. Step by step, choice by choice, he pushes through resistance and builds a resilience that cannot be broken. And over time, those hard moments become the very things that shape him into a man of endurance, faith, and unwavering resolve.

Discipline requires sacrifice. A man cannot cling to comfort and expect to grow stronger. What is easy will keep him where he is, but what is necessary will take him where he is called to go. Every step forward demands that something be left behind - old habits, shallow thinking, and the pull of convenience. A disciplined man understands this trade. He does not resent the cost; he embraces it, knowing that every sacrifice is shaping him into something greater than he was before. Growth always demands a price, and discipline is the currency. It is paid in early mornings, in hard decisions, in saying no to what feels good so he can say yes to what builds strength. While others choose the path of least resistance, he chooses the path of purpose. And over time, those daily deposits of discipline produce a life marked by strength, clarity, and endurance. He becomes a man who is not controlled by comfort but refined by commitment - a man who has paid the price to become who God has called him to be.

A disciplined man does not make excuses. He refuses to hide behind blame or justify his shortcomings, because he understands that growth begins with ownership. When he falls short, he does not waste time protecting his pride; he corrects his course. With humility and clarity, he studies where he went wrong, strengthens what was weak, and moves forward with greater resolve. His focus is not on appearing strong, but on becoming strong where it truly matters. When he fails, he does not quit; he refocuses. He knows that setbacks are not the end of the journey, but part of the process that refines him. Every failure carries a lesson, and every lesson, if received, becomes fuel for growth. Instead of being discouraged, he becomes sharper, wiser, and more resilient. What once caused him to stumble becomes the very ground he now stands firmly upon. This is the mindset of a disciplined man. He is the one who turns every setback and every challenge into an opportunity to rise stronger than before.

The warrior builds structure into his life because he understands that strength is formed through intentional living. He does not drift through his days hoping to grow; he designs his days to ensure that he does. He establishes routines that align his spirit with God, sharpen his mind, and discipline his body. Prayer is scheduled and time in the Word is prioritized. He removes what weakens him and reinforces what strengthens him, knowing that what he consistently practices will ultimately shape who he becomes. Every choice, every habit, and every commitment is aligned with a greater purpose. While others are ruled by impulse and distraction, he is guided by discipline and direction. This structure empowers him, giving him clarity, focus, and stability in a chaotic world. Over time, these intentional patterns build a life that is steady, fruitful, and strong. The warrior becomes a man who is not easily shaken, because his life is built on purpose, anchored in truth, and strengthened by daily discipline.

Discipline becomes part of who he is. What once required effort, focus, and constant correction begins to feel natural, almost instinctive. The man who once had to push himself to pray now seeks God without hesitation. The man who once struggled to stay in the Word now hungers for it daily. The battle that once felt intense becomes steady ground beneath his feet. This is how transformation works - not in sudden leaps, but in steady, repeated obedience that reshapes his desires, his mindset, and his identity. The habits he once had to fight for now sustain him automatically. They no longer feel like burdens; they become the very structure that carries him forward. In moments of pressure, he responds from what has been built within him. This is the power of consistent training. It produces a man who is not easily shaken because his strength has been forged over time. What was once difficult has now become the source of his endurance, stability, and lasting spiritual strength.

The man who embraces discipline begins to walk with confidence not because life has become easier, but because he has become stronger. His confidence is built in the quiet, unseen places where he has trained his spirit, guarded his mind, and strengthened his character. When challenges arise there is a steady assurance within him not rooted in pride but in the knowledge that he has been faithful in the process God has given him. He trusts the process that has shaped him. He no longer rushes outcomes or fears pressure, because he understands that every step has been preparing him for what lies ahead. Even when things feel uncertain, he remains grounded, knowing that discipline has built a foundation that will hold. This confidence is quiet but powerful. It does not need to be announced, because it is evident in how he lives, how he leads, and how he stands firm. He walks forward with clarity and conviction, a man strengthened not by ease, but by the faithful work that has formed him.

Discipline produces freedom. At first, it can feel like boundaries are limiting your life rather than improving it. But over time, those very boundaries become the structure that strengthens you. Discipline sharpens your focus and brings clarity to your decisions. It trains your spirit to seek God first, your mind to think rightly, and your actions to align with purpose. What once felt like restriction becomes protection, guiding you away from what weakens you and leading you toward what builds lasting strength. The undisciplined man is ruled by whatever is easiest, by whatever demands his attention. But the disciplined man rules himself. He is not controlled by emotions, distractions, or fleeting desires. Instead, he chooses his path with intention, anchored in truth and guided by conviction. True freedom is not the ability to do anything, but the strength to do what is right. And in that self-mastery, he becomes a man who is steady, focused, and capable of walking fully in the life God has called him to live.

And when the battle finally comes, the disciplined man does not scramble for strength because he has already built it in the quiet places. While others are overwhelmed by the weight of the moment, he stands steady, anchored by what has been developed within him over time. He does not have to rise to meet the occasion, because his life has already been prepared for it through consistent obedience, prayer, and discipline. He falls back on the level of his training. What he has practiced in private becomes his strength in public. The prayers whispered in secret become bold faith in the open. The discipline formed in unseen moments becomes confidence under pressure. Nothing is wasted for every act of faithfulness has been shaping him for this very moment. And when the battle comes, he does not hesitate or retreat. He stands firm, moves with clarity, and endures with strength, because he is not relying on sudden courage - he is walking in what has already been forged within him.

So commit to the process. Build the habits that shape your days and, in time, will shape your life. Train your body to endure, sharpen your mind to think clearly, and strengthen your spirit to stay anchored in God. These are not separate pursuits - they work together to form a man who is whole, steady, and prepared. Every disciplined choice, no matter how small it seems, is laying a brick in a foundation that will one day be tested. Because the man who disciplines himself today is the man who will stand strong tomorrow. When pressure rises and challenges come, he will not be scrambling to become something new - he will simply stand in what he has already been becoming. His strength will not be temporary or situational; it will be rooted, proven, and reliable. While others are shaken, he remains steady. While others retreat, he advances. And in that moment, it becomes clear - the quiet work of discipline was never wasted. It was preparation for a life that would stand firm when it mattered most.

| 10 |

"GUARDING YOUR TERRITORY"

A man who understands his calling recognizes that his mind is a battlefield, his home is a sanctuary, and his purpose is a divine assignment. He does not allow every thought to take root, every influence to enter, or every distraction to pull him off course. Instead, he stands guard with intention, filtering what he entertains and strengthening what God has entrusted to him. He knows that what is unguarded will eventually be overrun, so he disciplines his mind, leads his home with conviction, and protects his calling with unwavering focus. This man sees territory not as something physical, but as something spiritual. His territory is his influence, his integrity, his family, and the ground God has assigned him to stand on. And because he understands its value, he defends it. He does not surrender ground to fear, compromise, or passivity. He pushes back against anything that threatens what God has built in his life. Like a watchman on the wall, he stays alert, aware that neglect is an open door to loss.

Guarding your territory begins in the unseen battlefield of your mind. Before a man ever falls in his actions, he first compromises in his thoughts. What you repeatedly allow to take root in your thinking will eventually shape your decisions, your character, and your direction. If your mind is left unguarded, it becomes vulnerable to fear, doubt, temptation, and deception. That is why a man of God must refuse to give space to anything that weakens his faith or clouds his purpose. A strong man takes authority over his thoughts with intentionality and conviction. He does not passively accept every idea that enters his mind, but instead filters it through truth, righteousness, and alignment with God's Word. Guarding your mind is a daily act of vigilance. As you take control of your inner world, you strengthen your outer life. Victory is not first won in circumstances; it is won in your thinking. And the man who masters his mind becomes a man who cannot easily be defeated.

The thoughts you allow to linger, the voices you give access to, and the patterns you tolerate in your mind will quietly take root and grow into something stronger over time. Fear, when entertained, expands until it distorts your perspective and weakens your resolve. Compromise, when excused, becomes a habit that erodes your integrity. Negativity, when welcomed, clouds your vision until you begin to expect defeat instead of victory. A man is not only shaped by what he does, but by what he consistently allows to dwell within him. The battlefield is within you. But when a man chooses to guard his mind with truth, discipline, and faith, something powerful begins to happen. Truth anchors him when emotions try to drift. Discipline trains him to reject what is harmful and embrace what is right. Faith strengthens him to stand firm even when circumstances are uncertain. Over time, this intentional guarding builds a fortified inner life giving him a mind that is not easily shaken by pressure, temptation, or fear.

Your home is sacred ground entrusted to you, a place where your leadership is not spoken about but lived out daily. As a man, you are called to stand watch over what enters your home, what is allowed to remain, and what must be driven out. Your presence should bring stability, your words should bring life, and your example should point everyone under your roof toward God. Peace, order, and spiritual strength are the result of intentional leadership and daily obedience. You set the spiritual climate by what you prioritize, what you tolerate, and what you pursue. Prayer must be practiced, not postponed. Truth must be spoken, not softened. Love must be demonstrated, not assumed. When you lead with conviction and consistency, your home becomes a stronghold of faith, a refuge from chaos, and a place where God is honored. Do not underestimate your influence. What you build within your home will shape lives, establish legacies, and echo far beyond your walls.

A man who guards his home knows that every word spoken, every image watched, and every attitude tolerated carries weight. This is why he filters what is allowed through the doors of his home and through the atmosphere of his family. He does not entertain what weakens, corrupts, or confuses. Instead, he cultivates what is pure, what is true, and what is life-giving. His home becomes a place of clarity in a world of compromise, a refuge where truth stands firm and love is not diluted by the noise outside. His life becomes the blueprint his family can follow. He speaks with intention, corrects with wisdom, and protects with vigilance. He stands watch over his home like a faithful guard, knowing that what he permits today will shape tomorrow. And because he chooses to guard it well, his home becomes a place of strength, order, and purpose where faith is not just spoken, but lived, and where those under his care are strengthened, not scattered.

A man who leads well pays attention to the atmosphere of his home, the condition of hearts, and the subtle shifts that signal something is off. He does not ignore tension, dismiss warning signs, or hope problems resolve themselves. Instead, he leans in with discernment, seeking God for wisdom and responding with calm strength. He understands that what he allows will grow, and what he confronts with truth and grace can be healed. A passive man, however, creates silent openings. Where he is absent, something else will take his place whether it be unhealthy influences, confusion, or spiritual drift. Leadership means closing those gaps. It means speaking when it would be easier to stay quiet, guiding when it would be easier to withdraw, and standing firm when compromise tries to creep in. A godly man recognizes that his presence carries weight. His words shape direction. His example sets the tone. So he chooses to be engaged, intentional, and watchful - not out of fear, but out of responsibility.

Guarding your territory also means protecting your calling. God has entrusted you with an assignment that carries eternal weight. Every man has a field to tend, a responsibility to carry, and a purpose that demands focus. But distraction is subtle and dangerous. It often appears as something harmless, even appealing. Yet anything that pulls your attention away from obedience to God is a threat to your calling. A man who is careless with his focus will slowly drift from his purpose, not because he was overpowered, but because he was unfocused. If the enemy cannot stop you, he will try to sidetrack you. He will fill your path with noise, tempt you with comfort, and lure you into pursuits that drain your strength but produce no eternal fruit. This is why a man must stay watchful, stay anchored in prayer, and stay grounded in the Word. The man who fulfills his calling is not the one who does the most things, but the one who stays faithful to the right things. Guard your focus and refuse to be pulled off course.

A focused man knows who he is, and more importantly, he knows what he has been called to do. That clarity gives him power. His time, energy, and attention are no longer up for negotiation. He understands that purpose requires protection, and he guards it with discipline. The world may offer him applause, comfort, or quick success but discernment becomes his shield. He recognizes that not every opportunity is from God and not every invitation deserves a yes. Where others are entangled, he remains free because he filters everything through truth and purpose. He is not driven by urgency, but by obedience. This kind of man cannot be easily distracted, manipulated, or worn down, because his eyes are fixed and his spirit is anchored. And over time, that focused, disciplined obedience builds a life of impact, strength, and spiritual authority. A man like this does not just move forward - he moves with precision, with power, and with unwavering resolve.

Spiritual responsibility is not optional for a man - it is essential. Whether he realizes it or not, his words, his habits, and his convictions shape the atmosphere around him. In his family, he is not just present, he is foundational. In his workplace, he is not just an employee, he is an example. In his community, he is not just a face in the crowd, he is a voice that either strengthens or weakens what others build upon. The man who understands this stops living casually and starts living intentionally. He understands that his influence carries weight, and he refuses to misuse it or neglect it. When pressure comes, he does not fold, he anchors himself deeper in truth. When those around him drift, he becomes a steady point of direction. This kind of man recognizes that his life is not his own; it is a vessel meant to impact others for something greater. And when he embraces that responsibility, he becomes a force for stability, strength, and spiritual covering in every place God has positioned him.

Many men want authority, but they avoid responsibility. They desire influence, respect, and a voice that carries weight, but they resist the cost that comes with it. True authority is forged in the decision to step up and take the hit and to carry the burden instead of complaining about its weight. A man who embraces responsibility leads by example and becomes a stabilizing force wherever he goes. In moments of chaos, he brings clarity. In times of pressure, he remains steady. When others panic, he positions himself with purpose and resolve. His presence calms storms because it is anchored in conviction, not emotion. He becomes trustworthy because he does not run from problems - he faces them. People begin to lean on him, not because he demands it, but because he has demonstrated that he can be depended on. True authority is not about control, but about influence rooted in character. And the man who carries it well becomes strong, reliable, and unshaken no matter where he stands.

Guarding your territory requires strength, but it also requires consistency. A man builds strength through repeated, intentional choices. He watches what he allows into his mind, what he entertains in his heart, and what he tolerates in his environment. He becomes vigilant, not just in moments of pressure, but in the quiet, ordinary rhythms of life. He prays when no one is watching, chooses integrity when no one would know, and stays aligned when it would be easier to relax his standards. The small, unseen decisions are what determine long-term strength. Every disciplined thought, every resisted temptation, every quiet act of obedience is laying another brick in a foundation that will either stand or crumble under pressure. What looks like sudden strength is actually the result of steady faithfulness over time. And the man who commits to that kind of daily discipline becomes rooted, reliable, and ready, able to hold his ground and protect what has been entrusted to him.

Standing watch means showing up when no one applauds, staying alert when others relax, and holding your position when nothing seems to be happening. Endurance is forged in these moments. A man who is committed to his calling learns to draw strength from God. He presses on not because it feels exciting, but because it is necessary. And in doing so, he develops a kind of resilience that cannot be manufactured in comfort. Every unseen act of obedience, every disciplined decision, every moment he refuses to quit is strengthening his foundation. When pressure comes, he is not scrambling to stand; he is already established. His endurance has prepared him. His faithfulness has anchored him. What others see as sudden strength is actually the result of sustained commitment over time. And because he did not abandon his post in the hard seasons, he becomes a man who can be trusted with greater responsibility - a man whose life stands firm, steady, and unmovable.

Being a watchman means you pay attention. You stay alert to what is happening within you and around you. You do not ignore warning signs or excuse what should be confronted. Small compromises may seem harmless in the moment, but you understand they are seeds that are always growing. So you guard your thoughts, your habits, and your environment with intention. You do not allow negativity, temptation, or complacency to quietly take root. Instead, you confront it early, when it is still manageable. Awareness sharpens a man's discernment and strengthens his discipline. This kind of man is not easily caught off guard, because he is already paying attention. He learns to read the condition of his own heart and the direction of his life, making corrections before things drift too far. And because he refuses to ignore what needs to be addressed, he builds a life marked by clarity, strength, and control - a life that is guarded, intentional, and prepared for whatever comes.

A man who stands watch does not live with a spirit of fear, but with a posture of awareness. He keeps his mind clear, his spirit grounded, and his priorities in order. This kind of man knows that leadership is about vigilance, and vigilance requires him to stay awake to what others might overlook. Sleeping on your responsibility will cost you more than you think. Small issues become major problems, subtle compromises become strongholds, and neglected areas become points of vulnerability. A man who chooses comfort over alertness will eventually face consequences that could have been avoided. But the man who remains watchful builds a life of stability and strength. He catches things early. He corrects course quickly. He protects what has been entrusted to him with diligence and care. And because he refuses to let his guard down, he becomes a steady, reliable leader - one who is not shaken by what comes, because he has been prepared long before it arrived.

When you are spiritually strong, you become harder to move. You have spent time in the presence of God, you have disciplined your mind, and you have settled your convictions. So when challenges arise, you respond with clarity and control. The storms may hit, but they do not carry you away. You remain grounded, steady, and un-movable because your strength has been developed where it matters most. And when your foundation is firm, everything built on it becomes stronger. Your leadership gains stability and your relationships gain security. Others begin to feel the strength of your life because it creates an environment of confidence and peace. You are not immune to difficulty, but you are prepared for it. Spiritual strength builds a man who can withstand, who can endure, and who can continue to move forward with purpose no matter what comes. And because his foundation is secure, his life becomes something that not only stands tall but supports and strengthens others as well.

Guarding your territory will require you to say no. Not everything deserves access to your time, your energy, or your attention. A man who understands his calling refuses to spend himself on what does not align with his purpose. He is not harsh, but he is clear. He is not closed off, but he is disciplined. He knows that distractions will slowly drain his strength and derail his focus, so he chooses carefully. He protects his priorities. He honors what matters most by refusing what does not. A man who sets boundaries is making space for what is essential and guarding the future he is building. When he says no to what is unnecessary, he is saying yes to what is meaningful. He is not pulled in every direction, because he has drawn the lines that keep him grounded. And because he values what has been entrusted to him, he does not allow just anything to influence it. This is how a man protects his future - by choosing with intention, living with discipline, and guarding his life with wisdom.

Guarding your territory will require courage. There will be times when you must confront what others ignore, address what others avoid, and stand where others choose to sit back. A man who leads well acts when it is necessary. He understands that ignoring problems now is what brings calamity in the future. This is why he faces what needs to be faced, even when it costs him ease and temporary comfort. But a man who refuses to stand will eventually lose ground little by little, compromise by compromise, until what once was strong begins to erode. Courage protects what passivity surrenders. The man who holds his position, who speaks when it matters, and who remains anchored in truth builds a life that endures. He may feel the weight of resistance, but he also carries the strength of conviction. And over time, that courage establishes him as a man who cannot be easily moved - a man who keeps what has been entrusted to him because he refused to back down when it mattered most.

At the end of the day, guarding your territory is about stewardship. It is about recognizing that what you have been given is entrusted to you by God Himself. Your mind matters, because it shapes your direction. Your home matters, because it sets the atmosphere for everyone within it. Your calling matters, because it carries purpose beyond yourself. A man who understands this takes ownership of what has been placed in his hands and treats it with value. When a man embraces stewardship, his life begins to reflect strength, clarity, and purpose. He stays engaged, proactive, and disciplined. He guards his thoughts, leads his home, and walks in his calling with consistency. He understands that what he protects today will shape what he experiences tomorrow. And because he values what has been entrusted to him, he refuses to treat it casually. This is the heart of stewardship - it is not about control, but about care. And the man who lives this way builds a life that is prepared, positioned, and purposeful.

So stand your ground. Guard what has been entrusted to you with conviction and clarity. Do not drift into passivity or allow life to be shaped by neglect. Lead with strength, live with awareness, and stay anchored in purpose. Every day becomes an opportunity to reinforce what matters, to strengthen what has been built, and to remain aligned with what God has called him to do. A man who stands watch faithfully becomes a man who builds something that lasts. His consistency forms a foundation that can withstand pressure, his awareness keeps him from drifting, and his strength allows him to endure when others fade. Over time, his life becomes a place of stability for himself and for those around him. What he builds is not temporary or fragile, but rooted and resilient. And because he refused to look away, refused to back down, and refused to grow passive, he becomes a man whose life carries weight, purpose, and lasting impact - a man who did not just exist, but established something that endures.

| 11 |

"THE ROAR OF IDENTITY"

There is a sound that rises from a man who knows who he is. It does not strive to be heard, yet it cannot be ignored. This is the roar of identity. It is the steady confidence of a man who has settled the question of his worth at the feet of Christ. He no longer lives for approval because he has already been accepted. He no longer competes for validation because he has already been chosen. His life is not driven by insecurity but anchored in truth. And from that place, everything changes - his posture, his decisions, his endurance. This roar is not loud, but it is powerful. It is heard in the way he stands firm when others compromise, in the way he remains faithful when others drift, and in the way he carries peace in the middle of pressure. It is the sound of a man who is no longer searching for identity. His confidence is not in his strength, but in his Savior. And because of that, his life speaks with authority. This is the roar of a man who knows who he is, and because he knows who he is, he knows how to live.

Most men spend years searching for identity in things that were never designed to carry its weight. Titles can be stripped, accomplishments can be surpassed, and the opinions of people can shift overnight. When a man builds his identity on these things, he lives in a constant cycle of proving, performing, and protecting an image that was never secure to begin with. The applause of others is a moving target - it

100

cheers one moment and criticizes the next. But a man who finds his identity in Christ steps onto unshakable ground. He no longer borrows worth from the world - he receives it from God. He does not have to defend who he is, because his identity was not given by people and cannot be taken by them. In Christ, he is already accepted, already chosen, already called. When identity is rooted in truth rather than opinion, a man can stand firm, walk boldly, and live with a quiet confidence that does not need to be announced because it is already established.

The man who is in Christ no longer lives from a place of striving, but from a place of being. In Christ, he has already been made new. He is not working toward sonship; he is walking in it. He is not laboring to gain God's approval; he is living from it. On the cross, identity was secured, not suggested. And now, instead of exhausting himself trying to become enough, he stands as one who is already chosen, redeemed, and called by name. This truth changes everything. When a man understands that identity is received, not achieved, the pressure to perform begins to fall off his shoulders. His confidence is rooted in who God says he is, not in what the world demands he prove. From that place, he doesn't live passively - he lives powerfully. He obeys not to earn love, but because he is loved. He fights not for acceptance, but from acceptance. And when he truly grasps that he is already a son, already valued, already secured in Christ, he stops striving to become and starts walking boldly in who he already is.

When a man truly understands who he is in Christ, everything within him begins to realign. His identity is no longer shaped by opinions, failures, or comparisons, but by the unchanging truth of what God has spoken over him. His decisions are no longer driven by fear or the need for approval, but by purpose and conviction. He begins to walk with clarity, because he knows he is called, chosen, and positioned. The confusion that once clouded his direction starts to lift, and in its place comes a steady confidence rooted not in self, but in Christ. This shift transforms the way he lives. He no longer strives to earn what has already been given through grace. Instead of chasing validation, he walks in inheritance. Instead of proving his worth, he lives from it. His priorities change because his perspective has changed. He now values what is eternal over what is temporary, what is purposeful over what is comfortable. In Christ, he realizes he is already accepted, already equipped, and already established.

Insecurity begins to loosen its grip the moment a man anchors his identity in the truth about who God is and who God says he is. When identity is rooted in Christ, it is no longer dependent on opinions, achievements, or comparisons. It becomes steady, unshaken by the success or status of others. A man who knows who he is does not need to measure himself against another, because he understands that his worth was never meant to be weighed on someone else's scale. He stops striving to prove himself and starts walking in what has already been declared over him. He realizes that God did not design him to imitate, but to fulfill a specific assignment that no one else can carry in the same way. The gifts, experiences, and even the struggles he carries are tools to help him fulfill his assignment from on high. With sharpened focus he starts moving forward, fully engaged in the path God has set before him, confident that faithfulness and not comparison is what leads to a life that truly counts.

Every life carries a distinct assignment, a calling that cannot be fulfilled by imitation. When a man truly understands this, comparison begins to lose its grip on him. The pressure to perform like others fades, and in its place comes a deep sense of responsibility to become exactly who God designed him to be. What God has placed inside him is not accidental; it is purposeful, powerful, and necessary. And when he begins to cultivate those gifts, he steps into alignment with something far greater than human approval - he steps into divine intention. This shift changes everything. He stops competing for attention, status, or validation, and instead commits himself to growth, discipline, and obedience. His focus sharpens. His energy is no longer scattered trying to keep up with others but is invested in becoming stronger, wiser, and more faithful in his own calling. He understands that greatness is not found in outdoing another man, but in fully becoming the man God created him to be.

The roar of identity is anchored in truth. When a man truly knows who he is in Christ, insecurity loses its grip and comparison loses its appeal. He no longer measures his worth by the opinions of others or the shifting standards of the world. Instead, he stands on the unshakable foundation that he is chosen, called, and equipped by God Himself. This identity is rooted in grace that gives a man the boldness to walk with confidence, not in himself, but in the One who has defined him. When this truth takes hold, a man stops striving to prove his value and starts living from it. From that place, he walks in purpose, leads with conviction, and lives with clarity. He is not driven by fear of failure or the need for approval, but by the assurance that his position in Christ is secure. And when a man lives from that identity, his life becomes a testimony that grace is enough, and that who God says he is will always be greater than what the world tries to make him believe.

Your identity is not something the world gets to assign, and it is not something your past gets to rewrite. Your identity is anchored in Christ, and it is unchanging, unshaken, and secure. What God has spoken over you is greater than anything that has happened to you. You are who He says you are. You are redeemed, not rejected. Chosen, not overlooked. Made new, not permanently marked by old mistakes. Jesus did not die to give you a second chance at your old identity - He died to give you a completely new one. You stand firm in who you are in Christ, walk confidently in that identity, and refuse to bow to anything that contradicts it. Because when your identity is rooted in Him, no lie can overthrow it, and no past can reclaim it. The man who knows his identity stands firm when pressure rises. He may feel the weight, he may bend in the storm, but he does not collapse beneath it because his life is not anchored to emotion, approval, or circumstance - it is anchored to truth.

Feelings rise and fall but truth remains constant. When a man builds his life on what is unchanging, he becomes unshakable. The storm may test him, but it cannot define him. The pressure may shape him, but it cannot destroy him. His strength is in knowing who he is, even when everything around him feels uncertain. A man grounded in truth does not need perfect conditions to remain steady. He carries stability within him because his identity is rooted in Christ, not in the shifting opinions of others or the instability of life. When pressure comes, it reveals what he is built on and, because he is built on truth, he stands. He does not panic when things shake, because he knows his foundation cannot be moved. He does not abandon his calling when it gets hard, because truth reminds him who he is and why he stands. And in a world that bends to every wave of emotion and circumstance, he becomes a man who endures, a man who remains, a man who does not break.

Confidence is not rooted in personality, charisma, or how loudly you can make your presence known. It is rooted in your position in Christ. A man who understands this does not chase attention or strive to prove his worth to others. He is not driven by insecurity or the need to dominate the room. Instead, he is anchored. Steady. Grounded. While others are trying to be seen, he is simply standing firm. His confidence flows from identity, not image. And because that identity is secured in Christ, it cannot be shaken by opinions, rejection, or comparison. A confident man does not have to overpower others to feel powerful, because his strength is not something he has to manufacture - it is something he draws from. He knows where his strength comes from, and that changes everything. It gives him the ability to remain calm under pressure, to speak with clarity instead of noise, and to lead without arrogance. He doesn't need to elevate himself by putting others down, because his value is already established.

A man who knows who he is no longer drifts through life reacting to everything around him. Instead, he moves with intention. His steps are not random; they are directed. His choices are not impulsive; they are anchored. He no longer chases every opportunity or follows every voice, because he is no longer searching for himself - he has found his identity in Christ. And when identity is clear, direction follows. It doesn't mean the path is always easy, but it does mean it is no longer confusing. He may face resistance, but he is not lost. He may encounter obstacles, but he is not distracted. His life begins to carry weight, purpose, and precision. A man with settled identity becomes focused in a world full of noise. He knows what he is called to build, what he is called to protect, and what he is called to pursue. He stops wasting energy on things that do not align with his purpose and starts investing himself in what truly matters. He is no longer driven by pressure or comparison, but by his heavenly calling.

Purpose is something you walk in daily. It unfolds step by step as you live from the truth of who you are in Christ. When a man understands his identity, he no longer runs in circles trying to find his purpose, because purpose is no longer hidden from him - it flows through him. Identity fuels direction. It gives clarity to his decisions, alignment to his actions, and conviction to his path. Without identity, everything feels uncertain and scattered. But when identity is settled, life begins to move with meaning. He stops striving and starts walking steady, intentional, and grounded in truth. Without identity, purpose becomes confusion - constantly shifting, always out of reach. A man may be busy, but he is not effective. He may be moving, but he is not progressing. But when identity is established in Christ, purpose becomes clarity in motion. He begins to recognize what he is called to do because he knows who he is called to be. His steps gain direction, his efforts gain focus, and his life gains impact.

There is a boldness that rises from identity that is steady, rooted, and unshakable. It is the kind of boldness that does not need to prove itself, because it is already grounded in truth. When a man knows who he is in Christ, his words carry weight, his decisions carry conviction, and his life carries direction. He is no longer swayed by the fear of rejection or the pressure to conform because his identity is no longer up for negotiation. This boldness is about standing firm. It is not about being the strongest voice in the room, but about being anchored in the One who never changes. And from that place, he speaks not to impress, but to reflect truth. He leads not to control, but to serve with strength and clarity. He lives not to gain approval, but because he is no longer afraid to walk in who God created him to be. This is the boldness that transforms a man from the inside out. And when a man walks in that kind of boldness, his life becomes a testimony of what happens when identity is fully surrendered to Christ.

The need for approval begins to lose its power when identity is rooted in Christ. What once felt like pressure to conform now becomes an opportunity to stand. And even when that stand costs him comfort or acceptance, he remains steady, because he knows his worth is not determined by the crowd but secured by truth. He stops negotiating truth just to be received by others. He no longer waters down what he believes to make it more palatable or easier to accept. Identity gives him the strength to stand without compromise - to hold the line when others blur it, to speak truth when others avoid it, and to live with integrity when others bend. This is not arrogance; it is alignment. It is a man who knows who he belongs to and therefore knows what he stands for. And when a man reaches that place, he becomes immovable - not harsh, not prideful, but unwavering. Because when identity is settled in Christ, compromise is no longer an option - it is a contradiction.

The roar of identity doesn't need to be loud to be powerful. It is seen in the man who shows up when it's hard, who keeps moving forward when motivation fades, who stands his ground when compromise would be easier. This kind of strength is not built in moments of visibility, but in seasons of quiet obedience. It is forged in the discipline to stay, the courage to endure, and the conviction to remain. While others rely on bursts of passion, his life speaks not through noise, but through steady, unwavering faithfulness. And that is the true sound of a man who knows who he is. He remains faithful when no one is watching, because his identity is not dependent on an audience. He stands firm when it is costly, because truth is more valuable to him than comfort. He doesn't need recognition to stay committed, because his foundation is not built on praise but on purpose. Day by day, choice by choice, his life shows that he is unshaken, unmoved, and fully grounded in who God has called him to be.

When identity is secure, comparison loses its grip. A man no longer measures his worth against another man's progress, platform, or praise. Jealousy begins to fade because he is no longer looking sideways - he is looking forward. He understands that God did not create him to compete for purpose, but to walk in it. The need to outdo others weakens when he realizes he has a unique assignment that cannot be replaced or replicated. And from that place, he learns to genuinely celebrate others. He can honor another man's success without feeling threatened, because he knows it does not subtract from his own calling. He is not intimidated by greatness - he is inspired by it. He understands that there is room for every man to fulfill his purpose, and that God's plan is not limited or competitive. So instead of striving against others, he walks alongside them focused, secure, and steady knowing that what God has for him is his to carry, and no one else can take it away.

He becomes free from the exhausting cycle of trying to measure up, free from the pressure to perform for approval. He no longer wakes up trying to earn what has already been given or prove what has already been secured. His identity is not on trial, and his worth is not up for debate. Because of that, he can live with clarity instead of striving, with peace instead of pressure. He begins to walk in the freedom of being fully known and fully accepted by God. And from that freedom, a different kind of strength is formed. It is the kind of strength that holds steady in storms, that does not collapse under criticism, that keeps moving forward when others give up. This strength is sustained by truth. It remains when emotions fluctuate and when challenges intensify. It is quiet but powerful, steady but unbreakable. And as that strength grows, it carries him through pressure, through opposition, through seasons of difficulty because a man who is free in Christ is a man who cannot be easily shaken.

And from that place, a man begins to walk fully in his purpose. He is no longer drifting through life, reacting to whatever comes his way. He is moving with intention. He leads with conviction, not confusion. He loves with clarity, not hesitation. He serves with strength, not insecurity. And he lives with direction, not doubt. His life gains focus because his identity is settled. He is not guessing his way forward - he is walking it out, step by step, anchored in truth. Even when the road is difficult, he does not lose his footing because he knows who he is and why he is here. So let the roar of identity rise within you. Let it be the steady, unshakable confidence that comes from knowing you belong to Christ. Reject insecurity. Reject comparison. Refuse to live beneath what God has called you to be. Stand firm in your identity and walk boldly in your purpose. Because when a man truly knows who he is, everything changes - his mindset, his direction, his impact. And that man cannot be easily shaken.

| 12 |

"THE POWER OF OBEDIENCE"

Obedience is not weakness - it is strength brought under control and surrendered to the authority of God. In a culture that celebrates self-rule and personal freedom above all else, choosing obedience is a radical act of faith. It declares, "I trust God more than I trust myself." It takes a forged, steady spirit to say no to the flesh and yes to righteousness. Obedience is where faith becomes action, where belief becomes evidence, and where a man proves that God's voice carries more weight than his own feelings. True strength is revealed in restraint, in submission, and in alignment with God's will even when it costs you comfort, reputation, or immediate gratification. It is easy to live by what feels right in the moment, but it is powerful to kneel, to listen, and to follow. Every act of obedience builds spiritual muscle, shaping a man who is not ruled by emotion but anchored in truth. And in that place, he becomes unshakable not because he is in control, but because he is fully surrendered to the One who is.

Strength is revealed in moments of obedience. Anyone can move when the path is smooth, when the outcome is guaranteed, and when the applause is loud. But true spiritual strength is proven when a man chooses to obey God in the unseen places, in the quiet battles, and in the costly decisions. Obedience in those moments is not weakness or restriction; it is power under control; a will surrendered to something greater than self. That is where character is forged - in the fire of costly obedience. When doing right requires sacrifice, when standing firm means standing alone, and when trusting God demands letting go of comfort and control, a man is being built into something unshakable. Immediate rewards may not come, recognition may never arrive, but heaven takes notice. And over time, that consistent obedience forms a foundation that cannot be broken. Because the man who learns to obey God when it is hardest will be the man who stands strongest when it matters most.

Obedience is forged through discipline. A man who lives by obedience does not wait until he feels ready, motivated, or inspired. He rises anyway. He acts anyway. He aligns himself with truth even when his emotions resist it. Feelings are unstable; they rise and fall with circumstances, pressure, and perception. But God's Word stands firm, unmoved by the shifting winds of life. The disciplined man understands this, and he trains himself to respond to truth rather than react to emotion. In doing so, he strengthens his spirit, sharpens his character, and builds a life that is not easily shaken. Over time, this kind of obedience produces an unshakable man. He is steady when others are wavering. He is clear when others are confused. He is anchored when others are drifting. Why? Because his life is built on what he knows to be true. Conviction becomes the compass that guides his steps, and truth becomes the unshakable foundation upon which he builds a life that honors God.

Each time you lay down your desires and choose God's way instead, something eternal is forged within you. Your spirit becomes more discerning, your convictions more unshakable, and your inner strength more resilient. God is not merely asking for compliance; He is cultivating character. In every act of obedience, He is sharpening you into a man who can stand firm, think clearly, and walk boldly in truth. Obedience is a battlefield where weak impulses are defeated and godly strength rises. It is the training ground where God molds ordinary men into vessels of honor fit for His purpose and ready for

His use. The more you obey, the more aligned your life becomes with His power. This refining fire may be uncomfortable, but it is never wasted. It is producing a man who does not bend under pressure, who does not compromise under temptation, and who does not retreat when the cost is high. Stay in the fire because what God is building in you is far greater than anything you are leaving behind.

Delayed obedience is disobedience. When God speaks, His voice carries both authority and urgency, and every moment we postpone is a moment we subtly choose our will over His. Partial obedience is rooted in control - it is us deciding which parts of God's command we will honor and which parts we will ignore. True obedience does not edit God's instructions; it submits fully, trusting that His way is higher, wiser, and always right. Immediate obedience, however, is a safeguard for the soul. It keeps the heart tender, aligned, and responsive to the Spirit of God. When you act quickly on His voice, you cut off the opportunity for fear to take root and for distractions to pull you away. You remain anchored in trust rather than tossed by uncertainty. God is not looking for negotiation or delayed compliance - He is looking for surrender that moves without hesitation. The man who obeys swiftly walks in clarity, strength, and peace, because he has chosen to trust God not just in word, but in action.

Many men miss their moment not because they are incapable, but because they hesitate. They wait for the fear to disappear, for the path to become obvious, for the risk to be removed. But God has never required perfect conditions - He requires obedience. The tension you feel is often the very place where faith is forged. The uncertainty is not a barrier; it is an invitation to trust. While some men stand still, analyzing and delaying, the moment passes them by. But the man who responds when God speaks steps into a flow of purpose that cannot be manufactured through comfort or control. God often speaks in moments that stretch you and the man who moves anyway finds himself aligned with something far greater than his own understanding. He may not have every detail, but he has direction. He may not feel ready, but he is willing. While others wait for clarity, he walks by faith. And in that decisive obedience, he doesn't just seize a moment - he fulfills a calling.

Obedience is built on unwavering trust in the character of God. A man does not need to see the entire road to walk in the right direction; he only needs to respond when God speaks. Too often, hesitation is disguised as wisdom, when in reality it is fear waiting for certainty. The man who waits to understand everything will remain stuck, but the man who trusts God enough to move will find that revelation follows obedience. Step by step, God unfolds what He never reveals all at once. Faith is proven in motion, not in observation. It is easy to claim trust when the path is visible, but true faith rises when vision is limited and the next step feels uncertain. That is where obedience becomes powerful. Every step taken in obedience strengthens his confidence in God's guidance and sharpens his spiritual vision. What once felt unclear begins to make sense in hindsight. And in time, he realizes that God was not asking for perfection or full comprehension - He was simply asking for trust expressed through action.

There will be moments when obedience demands a real cost. It may separate you from certain relationships, pull you out of comfortable environments, close doors you once wanted open, or even cause others to misunderstand you. Obedience is often lonely, stretching, and deeply refining. But the man who walks with God understands that anything requiring disobedience to maintain is too expensive to hold onto. When God calls, obedience becomes the greater priority than comfort, approval, or personal ambition. What he gains in return cannot be matched by anything this world offers. There is a peace that comes from knowing you are in step with God, a purpose that anchors your life beyond circumstances, and a clarity that no external success can replace. While others chase temporary rewards, the obedient man sees beyond the moment and understands that alignment with God carries far greater value than fleeting gain. He stands firm knowing that what he gained in God was infinitely greater.

Trusting God when obedience comes at a cost is where faith moves from theory to power. It is easy to follow when the road is smooth, the outcome is clear, and the reward is immediate. But true obedience is forged in the moments where the path is difficult and the price feels heavy. This is where a man's heart is tested. Will he cling to what is familiar or surrender to what God is calling him into? A surrendered heart moves forward not because it feels safe, but because it knows God is faithful. Real faith is revealed in what a man does when it costs him something. Obedience in difficult seasons carries a weight of authority and depth that comfortable faith never produces. Every costly step strengthens his trust, refines his character, and deepens his dependence on God. In time, what once felt like sacrifice becomes the very place where God's power is made evident in his life. The man who obeys in hardship discovers that God meets him there not just to sustain him, but to transform him.

When a man chooses to walk in obedience, he is stepping into the very structure God established for life to flourish. It is not about earning favor; it is about living in harmony with the One who gives it. Just as a man who walks outside of shelter exposes himself to the storm, the one who ignores God's direction steps outside of His intended covering. But the man who obeys finds himself steady, anchored, and positioned where God's hand can rest upon him. When you walk in His ways, you place yourself where His favor can flow freely. There is a quiet confidence that comes from knowing you are aligned with God's will, and that alignment opens doors no man can shut. You'll have peace in the midst of chaos, clarity in the face of confusion, and strength when others are overwhelmed. The obedient man understands that God's favor is not something he chases; it is something he lives within. And as he remains faithful, he experiences a life marked by divine alignment and steady, unshakable provision.

Disobedience, on the other hand, leads a man into struggles he was never designed to carry. It introduces detours that delay purpose, burdens that weigh down the soul, and consequences that cloud clarity. What often feels like freedom in the moment becomes frustration over time. God's instructions are not meant to confine a man - they are meant to guard him. They are the boundaries that keep him on the path of life, the wisdom that prevents unnecessary pain, and the guidance that preserves his strength. The man who understands this stops resisting God's voice and starts responding to it. He no longer views obedience as a limitation, but as a lifeline. With humility, he chooses alignment over independence and trust over impulse. And in doing so, he begins to experience a life marked by clarity instead of confusion, peace instead of pressure, and direction instead of wandering. What once felt restrictive now becomes the very thing that strengthens and stabilizes his walk with God.

True authority does not come from position, titles, or recognition; it flows from alignment with God's will. The man who obeys demonstrates that he can be trusted, and trust is the foundation of promotion in the Kingdom of God. He becomes a vessel God can use because his heart is surrendered. In quiet, unseen moments of obedience, God is shaping his character, strengthening his integrity, and preparing him to carry greater weight without compromise. Obedience in the small things is the training ground for greater responsibility. The man who is faithful in what others overlook proves that he will be faithful when more is placed in his hands. As obedience becomes consistent, influence begins to grow. And when that influence comes, it is not used for self-gain, but for God's purposes. The obedient man understands that every step of submission is positioning him, not just for greater opportunity, but for greater impact under the authority of God.

The quiet acts of obedience matter more than most men realize. It is in the decisions no one applauds, the disciplines no one notices, the choices made when no one is watching that a man's true character is formed. These private victories are not small; they are foundational. While the world celebrates what is visible, God builds a man in the hidden places. Every time he chooses integrity over compromise, discipline over ease, and truth over convenience, he is becoming someone stronger than the moment requires. Long before recognition ever comes, identity is being forged in secret. What a man does in private will always surface in public. There is no shortcut around this principle. Public impact is simply the overflow of private obedience. The man who has learned to be faithful in secret will stand firm when the spotlight comes. And when that moment arrives, it will not feel like pressure to become something new, but the natural expression of a life that has been aligned with God all along.

Obedience sharpens your ability to hear God. Every time a man chooses to act on what God is prompting, his spiritual sensitivity increases. What once felt like a whisper becomes recognizable, steady, and clear. Obedience tunes the heart. It aligns the inner man with God's direction so that discernment grows stronger over time. But when that voice is repeatedly ignored, it becomes easier to overlook. The issue is not that God stops speaking, but that the heart becomes less responsive to what He is saying. Sensitivity to God is developed through consistent, faithful obedience. It is built in the daily responses to God's small promptings, quiet convictions, subtle directions. The man who honors those moments begins to walk with clarity and confidence because his connection to God is stronger. He learns to recognize God's leading in both the ordinary and the significant. Over time, he finds guidance, peace, and a growing awareness that God is actively leading him every step of the way.

There is freedom in obedience, even though the world often sees it as restriction. Obedience to God breaks the chains that sin quietly wraps around a man's life - chains of confusion, instability, and inner conflict. It frees him from being driven by impulse, emotion, or the ever-changing standards of the world. The man who walks in obedience is not confined - he is released from everything that once controlled him. When a man walks in God's will, he steps into clarity and purpose that the world cannot offer. Decisions become clearer because they are no longer rooted in uncertainty, but in alignment. His life gains direction, not because every detail is revealed, but because his path is guided. There is a deep sense of peace that comes from knowing he is where he is supposed to be, doing what he is called to do. In that place, he is no longer wandering or striving to find meaning - he is living it. Obedience does not shrink a man's life; it expands it into the fullness of what God intended him to become.

A man of obedience becomes a man of impact because his life is aligned with heaven's authority. There is a weight to his life, a substance that others can feel even if they cannot explain it. His decisions are steady, intentional, and rooted in something greater than himself. While others react, he responds. While others drift, he advances with purpose. That alignment with God gives his life a clarity and strength that naturally influences the world around him. And that kind of man becomes a force for good in a world that desperately needs it. His presence brings stability where there is chaos, truth where there is confusion, and strength where there is weakness. People are drawn to the consistency of his life and the integrity of his walk. Over time, his impact extends far beyond what he can see, touching lives, shaping environments, and leaving a lasting imprint. Because when a man walks in obedience, he is not just living for himself - he is becoming an instrument through which God moves.

So do not delay when God speaks. Do not hesitate when He calls. When you feel that inner prompting, that conviction that won't let you settle, that is your moment. Obedience requires urgency, because delayed obedience often becomes disobedience. The man who moves when God speaks steps into alignment, while the one who hesitates risks missing what was meant for him. Even when it is uncomfortable. Even when it is costly. Even when it does not make sense move anyway. God does His greatest work in the places where logic falls short and trust must rise. Comfort will try to hold you back. Fear will try to silence you. But faith pushes forward. The obedient man understands that God's direction is always greater than his understanding. And when he steps out, he finds that God meets him in the discomfort, in the uncertainty, in the cost. What begins as a step of obedience becomes a defining moment of transformation, and the man who responds becomes the man God can use.

In the end, the power of your life will not be measured by what you knew, but by what you obeyed. Knowledge can inform you, inspire you, and even impress others but obedience is what transforms you. God is not looking for men who simply understand His Word; He is looking for men who live it. It is in the doing, not just the knowing, that a man's life begins to carry weight. Every act of obedience turns belief into reality and truth into power. When a man stands before God, it will not be his awareness that defines him, but his response. What did he do with what he was given? Did he move when God spoke, or did he remain still? The legacy of his life will be written in the decisions he made to obey, especially when it was difficult. And in that obedience, his life becomes more than words - it becomes a testimony. Not of perfection, but of faith in action. Because in the end, it is not the man who knew the most who made the greatest impact - it is the man who obeyed the most.

| 13 |

"STANDING ALONE"

There will come a defining moment in every man's life when the noise dies down, the approval disappears, and the road in front of him narrows into something quiet, weighty, and alone. It is easy to stand when you are surrounded by agreement, but real strength is revealed when you must stand without it. When no one defends you and no one walks beside you, that is when your foundation is tested. And in that testing, God is showing you whether your life is anchored in shifting voices or in unshakable truth. Do not fear the lonely road, because it is there that your faith becomes your own. A man who stands firm in isolation is a man who cannot be easily moved in battle. When you choose to stand alone without applause, without reassurance, and without support, you step into a deeper level of strength that crowds can never produce. So stand anyway. Stand when it costs you relationships, recognition, or ease. Because the man who can stand alone with God will never truly stand alone at all.

Standing alone is not a sign that you have lost your way - it is often proof that you have found it. When the crowd chooses comfort over conviction and approval over obedience, the path of righteousness will naturally grow narrow. But the man of God knows that faithfulness isn't proven by applause, but by alignment with the will of God. While others turn back when the weight of obedience becomes heavy, he keeps walking forward with steady resolve, knowing that

God's presence is more valuable than man's approval. Loneliness in the will of God is far better than popularity outside of it. The man of conviction knows that standing alone does not mean he is truly alone because the One who called him walks with him. In the end, a man's legacy is not shaped by the applause of the crowd, but by his unwavering obedience to God. Many may walk away when the road gets difficult, but the man who remains will discover that God is building in him a faith that cannot be shaken.

When no one else stands with you, the illusion of borrowed strength quickly fades, and what remains is the true condition of your faith. Borrowed faith depends on the energy of others - it leans on their passion, their convictions, and their approval. But when the crowd disappears borrowed faith buckles under pressure because it was never rooted deeply enough to endure. Yet real faith is different. It has been formed in the hidden places, strengthened through testing, and anchored in a personal relationship with God. It draws its strength from a source that does not fail. Real faith that stands firm is not swayed by opinions, discouraged by isolation, or weakened by opposition. It has been proven in the fire - it has wrestled through doubt, endured seasons of silence, and chosen obedience when it would have been easier to walk away. The man who carries this kind of faith may stand alone in the natural, but he stands unshaken in the spirit, upheld by the unchanging truth of God.

There is a quiet strength that develops in isolation, far from the noise of recognition and the applause of others. It is formed in the early morning prayers whispered in stillness, the tears shed when no one is watching, the private decisions to keep moving forward when quitting would be easier. God does some of His deepest work in those hidden places, shaping character, refining motives, and building endurance that cannot be manufactured in the spotlight. This quiet strength does not crumble under pressure because it was born in it. It does not chase validation because it has already been anchored in truth. When the time comes to stand, to lead, or to endure, this strength shows itself with steady resolve. It is the kind of strength that holds the line when others falter, that remains faithful when no one is watching, and that continues forward without needing recognition. What was forged in isolation becomes unshakable in the open, a testimony that the hidden seasons were not wasted, but essential.

Conviction anchors itself in truth. It refuses to bend when everything around it demands surrender. While others adjust their beliefs to fit the moment, the man of conviction remains steady, choosing obedience over approval. He understands that truth is not determined by popularity, and righteousness is not measured by comfort. Even when the cost is high, he stands, knowing that alignment with God is worth more than acceptance by the world. Conviction gives a man the courage to speak when silence would protect him and to stand when kneeling would be easier. It is not fueled by pride, but by a deep reverence for what is right. This kind of strength does not come overnight - it is built through time, tested through pressure, and proven through action. It stands firm in the storm, unwavering and unashamed, because it knows that truth does not change to accommodate culture. In the end, it is not those who blend in who leave a mark, but those who stood firm when it mattered most.

The cost of conviction is real, and it is not to be taken lightly. It may cost you relationships with those who no longer understand your choices. It may cost you opportunities that require compromise to obtain. It may even cost you your reputation in the eyes of people who once applauded you but now question your stand. But the man of conviction does not measure his life by what he keeps - he measures it by what he honors. And when honoring God requires letting go, he trusts that what he is releasing was never greater than what he is gaining. What conviction produces in you is far greater than anything it takes away. It builds a strength that cannot be shaken by opinions, a clarity that is not clouded by pressure, and a character that stands the test of time. It refines your faith, deepens your trust in God, and anchors your identity in something eternal. In the end, the loss is temporary but what is built within you is lasting, unbreakable, and worth every cost.

A man who stands alone with God is never truly alone, no matter how empty the landscape around him may seem. Truth becomes his companion, and the presence of God becomes more real than the approval of any crowd. In those moments, he realizes that what he stands on is not fragile or temporary, but eternal and unshakable. He may stand without visible support, but he is upheld by something far greater than human agreement - he is sustained by the very strength of God. From that place, a different kind of strength begins to rise within him. It is forged in communion with God, built in trust, and strengthened through obedience. This strength cannot be manufactured by encouragement or applause - it comes from knowing who stands with you, even when no one else does. And when the moment comes to endure, to lead, or to remain faithful, that man does not waver. Because though he stands alone in the natural, he stands fully supported in the spiritual - anchored, empowered, and unshaken.

Isolation has a way of stripping life down to what truly matters. When the noise fades and the crowd disappears, everything superficial begins to fall away leaving behind the raw truth of who you are. It reveals what you genuinely believe when no one is affirming you, what you truly value when nothing is gained from appearances, and who you really serve when there is no audience to impress. Isolation does not create weakness; it uncovers reality. And in that silence, a defining choice emerges: remain faithful or drift away. There is no spotlight to perform under, no pressure to impress - only the steady call to obedience. It is there that true devotion is formed, where a man learns to walk with God for God, not for recognition. What is built in that hidden place becomes the foundation for everything that follows. Because when a man chooses faithfulness in isolation, he develops a strength and integrity that cannot be shaken by circumstance or opinion. What is proven in the quiet will stand firm in the open.

Many men fear isolation because it removes the distractions that keep their weaknesses hidden. Without the noise and the constant validation of others, they are faced with unfiltered thoughts, unresolved struggles, and areas of immaturity they can no longer ignore. That exposure can feel uncomfortable, even unsettling. But the man who chooses to embrace isolation instead of avoiding it begins to see it differently. He understands that what is being revealed is not meant to shame him, but to shape him. In the quiet, God gently uncovers what needs to change, not to condemn, but to transform. Instead of running from the silence, he leans into it. He allows God to take what is weak and begin strengthening it from the inside out. What once felt like loneliness becomes a place of growth, where roots go deeper and faith becomes more resilient. And when he steps back into the world, he does not return the same. He carries a strength that cannot be shaken because it was built with God in the quiet places.

Strength forged in isolation is different from any other kind. It is not shaped by applause, nor sustained by encouragement. It is built in the quiet places where no one is watching, where there is no reward for perseverance except the growth it produces. This kind of strength is steady, deeply rooted, and tested over time. It does not need the approval of others to exist, because it was never built on it. This is why it does not rise and fall with opinions or circumstances. It remains anchored when storms come, unshaken when pressure increases, and unmoved when others waver. This strength has already faced silence, already endured struggle, and already proven its foundation. When the winds blow and the waves rise, it holds firm not because the storm is weak, but because its roots run deep. The man who carries this strength becomes a stabilizing force in uncertain times, a quiet but powerful presence who does not collapse under pressure. What was forged in isolation becomes his anchor in every storm.

When you stand alone, the safety net of agreement is removed, and you are brought face to face with your own convictions. There is no crowd to lean on and no reassurance that others will validate your choices. In that place, your decisions are no longer shaped by approval but by truth. Standing alone exposes the depth of your integrity, revealing whether your faith is anchored in God or influenced by the opinions of others. But it is in those very moments that true character is formed. When a man consistently chooses righteousness without recognition, he builds a foundation that cannot be shaken. He learns to trust God's voice above every other voice and to follow it without hesitation. Over time, those unseen decisions shape him into someone steady, trustworthy, and strong. And while the world may not notice those quiet acts of obedience, heaven does. Because a man who chooses what is right when no one is watching is a man who can be trusted when everything is on the line.

Character is built not in the comfort of crowds but in the quiet weight of solitude. It is not formed in ease where everything flows smoothly but in pressure where every decision carries consequence. The hidden places reveal what is real, and the pressure exposes what is true. And it is there, in that refining tension, that God shapes a man's character into something genuine and unshakeable. The man who learns to stand alone develops a backbone that cannot be easily broken. He is not swayed by shifting opinions or intimidated by resistance, because his strength was not built in comfort - it was forged in adversity. He has learned to endure, to hold his ground, and to remain faithful when it would have been easier to bend. This kind of man does not collapse under pressure; he stands firm through it. What was built in solitude becomes his strength in every setting, and the character formed in those hidden seasons becomes the foundation that carries him through every challenge he will face.

There will be moments when the silence feels heavier than you expected and the road stretches farther than you can see. In those seasons, it may seem like nothing is happening, like your efforts are unnoticed and your endurance is unseen. But those are the very moments where something deeper is taking place. Beneath the surface, your roots are growing. Your faith is learning to stand on truth. What feels like stillness is God doing a quiet work within you, building depth that cannot be developed in easier seasons. What feels like emptiness is the space where God removes what is unnecessary and makes room for what is essential. It is where dependence on Him becomes real, not theoretical. Though it may not feel productive, it is purposeful. So do not rush through these moments or try to escape them. Stay faithful in the silence, because what is being formed in you now will sustain you later. What feels like a long road is actually leading you into a strength that will not fail.

God often does His greatest work far from the spotlight and untouched by human recognition. When no one is watching, He is shaping your character with careful precision, forming integrity that does not depend on an audience. When no one is affirming you, He is strengthening your faith so it no longer relies on encouragement to endure. These are the moments where your walk with Him becomes personal, steady, and real. What feels unseen is sacred ground where God is building something that cannot be easily shaken. And when no one is standing beside you, you begin to realize that He is within you. His presence becomes your confidence, His voice becomes your direction, and His strength becomes your foundation. In that place, you are not sustained by people, but by God Himself. The hidden season stops feeling like isolation and starts revealing itself as preparation. Because what He is forming in you there will carry you when the pressure increases and the stakes grow higher.

Do not mistake loneliness for abandonment. God has not left you - He has set you apart for a purpose that cannot be fulfilled in the noise of the crowd. Loneliness, when misunderstood, can weaken a man, causing him to question his worth or his direction. But when seen through the lens of faith, it becomes a sacred space where distractions are removed, where clarity is restored, and where your identity is no longer shaped by others, but anchored in God alone. There is a difference between being left behind and being set apart. One drains you, the other prepares you. In this season, God is doing a work that requires your focus, your attention, and your willingness to be still. He is strengthening what was weak, refining what was unfocused, and aligning what was out of place. What you are experiencing is preparation for something greater. And when the time comes to step forward, you will not be stepping out empty, but equipped, strengthened, and ready for what lies ahead.

The men who change the world are rarely the ones who followed the crowd. They are the ones who refused to be shaped by it. When it was easier to sit down and blend in, they stood firm. When silence would have protected them, they spoke truth. And when the road grew difficult and many turned back, they pressed forward with unwavering resolve. That kind of life requires strength that demands a willingness to be misunderstood, to walk paths others avoid, and to carry convictions that not everyone will support. But it is in that courage that history is shaped and lives are changed. The man who stands when others fall, who speaks when others stay silent, and who moves forward when others retreat becomes a force that cannot be ignored. Not because he seeks recognition, but because he is anchored in something greater than himself. And in the end, it is not the crowd-followers who leave a legacy - it is the men who had the courage to stand alone when it mattered most.

Standing alone will teach you to hear God more clearly in a way that crowded seasons never could. When the noise of opinions fades and the pressure to please others is removed, His voice begins to stand out with clarity. What once felt confusing becomes focused, and what once felt uncertain begins to settle into steady direction. The distractions that once competed for your attention lose their power, and your sensitivity to His voice grows stronger. In that place, guidance becomes less about seeking approval and more about walking in obedience. You begin to trust what God is saying, even when it does not align with what others expect. His voice becomes your anchor, steadying you when everything else feels uncertain. What once required reassurance from people now rests confidently in your relationship with Him. And as that clarity develops, so does your confidence - not in yourself, but in the One who is leading you. Standing alone positions you to be guided more precisely than ever before.

One day you will look back and realize that your season of standing alone was never wasted. In those quiet, unseen moments, God was building something within you that could not be rushed or replicated in easier seasons. Every decision to remain faithful, every moment you chose truth over comfort, every step you took without support—none of it was in vain. It was forming a foundation that would hold you when everything else around you begins to shake. What was built in that season is now unshakable. A strength that does not collapse under pressure. A conviction that does not bend with culture. A faith that does not move when circumstances shift. You are no longer the same man who entered that season for you have been refined, strengthened, and established. And when the storms come, as they always do, you will stand not because the storm is weak, but because what God built in you is strong. What once felt like standing alone has now become the very reason you can stand at all.

So stand even if you have to stand by yourself. Stand when the pressure rises and everything in you wants relief. Stand when obedience costs more than you expected and the easy path calls your name. Stand when no one else will, when the crowd thins and the voices grow quiet. Because your strength is not determined by how many stand with you, but by what you stand on. A man anchored in God does not need majority approval - he needs alignment with the will of God. And in that place, standing is unshakable power because the man who can stand alone with God is a man who cannot be defeated. He may be opposed, misunderstood, or even rejected but he cannot be moved from what is true. His foundation is not built on people, but on the presence and power of God. And that foundation does not crumble. When storms come, he remains. When pressure increases, he holds his ground. When others fall back, he stands firm because he is standing with the One who never fails.

| 14 |

"BROTHERHOOD OF LIONS"

There is a strength a man can build in solitude but there is a greater strength that cannot be developed alone. It is the strength that comes from brotherhood, from when men stand shoulder to shoulder, sharpening one another, correcting one another, and refusing to let each other fall. From the very beginning, God declared that it is not good for man to be alone, because isolation slowly erodes what connection was meant to reinforce. A man by himself may learn to endure, but without godly relationships, his blind spots go unchecked, his burdens grow heavier, and his fire can begin to fade. In true brotherhood, iron sharpens iron. A band of brothers fight not only for themselves, but for each other. They speak truth when it is hard, they lift one another when strength is low, and they remind each other of who they are when the world tries to pull them off course. This is how God designed it - men growing stronger together, standing firm together, and advancing forward together.

The brotherhood of lions does not gather for comfort, but for sharpening. They speak truth when it would be easier to stay silent, they correct when it would be easier to ignore. It is men locking arms with a shared conviction that none of them will drift back into passivity, compromise, or isolation. This kind of brotherhood makes a declaration that we rise together, or not at all. This covenant brotherhood is proven in the fire of trials, where character is exposed and commitment is tested. When one stumbles, the others do not stand back - they step in. When one grows weary, they remind him of who he is and what he is called to become. This is the brotherhood of lions - men who sharpen one another, protect one another, and push one another toward God's purpose. They do not settle for being average, and they do not allow their brothers to settle either. Bound by covenant, driven by purpose, and strengthened through adversity, they become the kind of men who do not just endure life but conquer it together.

Every man needs strong, godly relationships because life is a battlefield. The pressures of temptation, distraction, and compromise come daily, wearing down even the strongest resolve. A man who stands alone may feel strong for a moment, but isolation slowly erodes his clarity, his discipline, and his courage. Without brothers to remind him of who he is in God, he becomes vulnerable to the very things he once believed he could conquer. But a man surrounded by strong, godly brothers is sharpened, strengthened, and steadied. In the presence of true brotherhood, excuses lose their power, accountability rises, and purpose becomes clear again. These relationships are not optional - they are essential for survival and victory. When one grows weary, another lifts him. When one loses focus, another redirects him. This is how men endure. This is how men overcome. Because strength is not just built in solitude - it is sustained in brotherhood, where faith is reinforced, character is refined, and no man fights alone.

There is a lie that has quietly taken root in the hearts of many men that says real men carry their burdens in silence and never reach for help. But that is not strength; that is pride dressed up as toughness. Pride whispers, "Handle it yourself. Don't let anyone see your struggle." Yet scripture reveals isolation weakens a man, but humility strengthens him. A man who refuses help cuts himself off from wisdom, accountability, and growth. He may appear strong on the outside, but inwardly he is vulnerable, fighting battles he was never meant to fight alone. The strongest men are not lone warriors - they are brothers in arms. They understand that iron sharpens iron, and that sharpening requires contact, friction, and honesty. A humble man seeks out other strong, godly men who will challenge him, correct him, and strengthen him. He knows that accountability builds discipline, and brotherhood builds endurance. When one man grows weary, another lifts him. When one loses focus, another brings clarity.

Iron sharpens iron and iron does not become sharp without pressure. It requires contact, resistance, and friction. In the same way, godly brotherhood is not always comfortable, but it is always necessary. There will be sparks when truth collides with pride, and moments where correction cuts deep. A man who surrounds himself with those who only affirm him will remain dull, but the man who invites honest, godly voices into his life will be sharpened into strength, clarity, and purpose. A true brother refuses to let you stay weak. He will speak truth when it would be easier to stay silent. He will challenge your excuses, confront your compromises, and push you toward the man God is calling you to become. This kind of love is strong, steady, and committed to your growth. It sees beyond who you are and fights for who you could be. And if you are wise, you will not resist that sharpening - you will embrace it, knowing that every spark is evidence that God is forging something stronger within you.

Godly brotherhood is not built on the need to be liked, but on a shared pursuit of becoming the men God has called them to be. These men are not concerned with impressing one another; they are committed to sharpening one another. They speak truth even when it is uncomfortable, because they understand that silence in the face of compromise is not love - it is neglect. Each man stands guard not only over his own life, but over the lives of his brothers, refusing to let one another drift into passivity, sin, or spiritual weakness. They remind each other of who they. They lift each other when one grows weary, and they refuse to celebrate anything less than obedience to God. This is not a brotherhood of convenience - it is a brotherhood of conviction. And in a world that rewards compromise and applauds weakness, these men choose a different path. They understand that iron only sharpens iron when there is friction, and they are willing to endure that friction for the sake of becoming stronger together.

True brotherhood refuses to let a man live behind masks or excuses. It calls him higher and exposes the places where pride, fear, or compromise try to take root. What a man might justify in isolation becomes undeniable in the presence of godly men who speak truth with courage and love. This kind of accountability is iron sharpening iron, a process that may spark and sting, but ultimately produces strength, clarity, and conviction. Because what is hidden grows in darkness, but what is exposed can be healed. Sin thrives in secrecy, but it loses its power when brought into the light. Brotherhood shines that light into the corners a man would rather avoid in order to restore him. In that honest space, chains begin to break, burdens are lifted, and freedom takes root. A man surrounded by the right brothers is not weakened by being known - he is strengthened by it. And as he walks in that light, he becomes a man who is no longer controlled by what he hides but transformed by the truth he embraces.

Accountability is a shield that keeps a man standing. Left to himself, even a strong man can slowly drift through small compromises, unchecked thoughts, and quiet justifications. Emotions rise and fatigue weakens resolve but accountability steps in as a guardrail, keeping him aligned with truth when his footing becomes uncertain. It reminds him of who he is, what he stands for, and where he is going. A brother who asks hard questions is not trying to control your life - he is fighting for it. He sees what you may be tempted to ignore. He speaks when silence would be easier. He challenges when compromise would be more comfortable. That kind of brotherhood is rare, but it is powerful. It sharpens a man, strengthens his discipline, and calls him higher when he feels like settling lower. In a world that celebrates independence without accountability, the wise man chooses men who will stand close enough to correct him, bold enough to confront him, and loyal enough to never let him fall without a fight.

Weak accountability produces weak men because it leaves too much room for excuses, compromise, and quiet failure. When no one is close enough to challenge you, it becomes easy to justify drifting, to follow impulse instead of conviction, and to settle for less than who you were called to be. But strong accountability builds a man from the inside out. It sharpens his discipline, anchors his consistency, and trains him to live with purpose instead of reacting to every feeling or temptation. Strong accountability tells a man that his life matters, that his actions are not insignificant, and that someone cares enough to watch, to ask, to challenge, and to stand with him. This kind of accountability calls out the best in a man, even when he feels at his worst. It pushes him to rise when he wants to retreat, to stay disciplined when he feels weak, and to keep going when quitting would be easier. And over time, that pressure doesn't break him - it builds him into a man who is steady, intentional, and strong.

There is power in being known - not the polished version you present to the world, but the real man beneath it all. The man who wrestles with doubt, who fights private battles, who sometimes questions his own strength. When those parts remain hidden, they often grow stronger in the dark. But when they are brought into the light among trusted brothers, they begin to lose their grip. Being known strips away the illusion and replaces it with truth. It reminds a man that he is not alone in his struggles and that his weaknesses reveal where he needs to grow. And when a man is fully known it produces a confidence that cannot be shaken. Not a pride rooted in perfection, but a strength grounded in authenticity. He no longer has to prove himself because he is already seen and still stands. That kind of brotherhood frees a man to fight harder, walk straighter, and live bolder, because he knows he is not carrying the weight alone. And in that place of being fully known, he becomes not only stronger but unbreakable.

The brotherhood of lions does not sit in circles rehearsing weakness or magnifying problems; they speak life, truth, and challenge into one another. Every word is meant to refine. Every moment together is intentional. They understand that iron only sharpens iron through friction, through honesty, through pressure. So they lean into it. They embrace the discomfort of growth because they know it produces strength. This is not a passive gathering - it is an active forging of men who refuse to stay dull, distracted, or stagnant. They do not come together to stay the same - they come together to grow. They build each other up, correct each other when needed, and push one another toward discipline, consistency, and calling. In that environment, mediocrity cannot survive. Excuses lose their voice. And over time, what is produced is not just camaraderie but transformation. Men leave stronger than they came, sharper than they were, and more aligned with the life God has called them to live.

These men celebrate victories, but they do not disappear when the battle begins. They understand that true brotherhood is proven in pressure, not just in moments of success. When one man is strong, he lifts others higher, but when one man is weak, the others step in and carry the weight with him. They refuse to let a brother fight alone. If a man begins to drift, they do not stand at a distance - they pursue him, speak truth to him, and pull him back before he falls too far. Their loyalty is not seasonal; it is steadfast. They do not abandon each other in struggle - they press in closer. When the fire intensifies, so does their commitment. They remind each other of truth when lies grow loud. They strengthen what is shaky and steady what is slipping. In that kind of brotherhood, weakness is not ignored but neither is it allowed to win. It is met with strength, with truth, and with presence. And over time, this kind of unity builds men who are not easily broken, because they know they are never standing alone.

A true brother will remind you of who you are when you begin to forget. When your vision gets clouded and your resolve starts to weaken, he speaks truth back into your life. He doesn't let you shrink back into comfort or settle for less than your calling. Instead, he calls you back to the standard God has placed on your life. He refuses to let a temporary weakness redefine your identity. His words are anchored in a deep commitment to see you become the man you were created to be. He will not stand by while you compromise what God has called you to become. He steps in, not to control you, but to protect your future. That kind of brotherhood is rare in a world that often chooses comfort over confrontation, but it is incredibly powerful. It produces men who are steady, grounded, and unwilling to drift. It builds a strength that goes beyond emotion and into conviction. And when a man is surrounded by brothers like that, he grows and walks boldly in the life God has called him to live.

There is also a responsibility that comes with being part of this brotherhood. You are not there to be carried without ever carrying someone else. You are called to sharpen others just as they sharpen you, to invest strength where there is weakness, and to bring clarity where there is confusion. This kind of brotherhood calls you to engage, to listen, and to speak when it matters. Because every man in the circle is both a recipient and a contributor, and the strength of the whole depends on each man doing his part. You are called to speak truth, to stand firm, and to show up when it matters most. A true brother does not stay silent when something needs to be said, and he does not disappear when someone needs him most. He steps in, he stands up, and he holds the line. And when every man embraces that responsibility, the brotherhood becomes more than a gathering - it becomes a force. A place where men are built, strengthened, and prepared to live out their calling with conviction and consistency.

A godly man refuses to stand by while a brother drifts toward compromise or collapse. He understands that unchecked weakness grows stronger in silence. So he steps in. He speaks truth with clarity, not harshness. He confronts with purpose, not pride. He strengthens with intention, not judgment. Because love does not ignore what could destroy - it addresses it before it does. A godly man does not watch his brother fall without stepping in. He sees responsibility where others see inconvenience. He values a man's future more than a moment of comfort. And while correction may be uncomfortable, it is always rooted in care. He is not trying to tear down - he is trying to build up, to restore, and to protect. This kind of love is active, courageous, and unwavering. It says, "I will not let you walk this path alone, and I will not let you become less than who God has called you to be." And in that kind of brotherhood, men are not only challenged - they are covered, strengthened, and preserved.

This kind of brotherhood does not happen by accident. It is formed through time invested, truth spoken, and battles endured together. It is built in the moments where men open up instead of shutting down, and where they stay committed even when it would be easier to withdraw. Shared trials forge deeper bonds, and unwavering commitment holds those bonds together. This kind of brotherhood requires men who are willing to be real, to be humble, and to be accountable. Men who are not afraid to admit where they are struggling, and not too proud to receive correction. Humility becomes the foundation, and accountability becomes the structure that strengthens it. In that environment, masks fall off, truth rises up, and real growth begins. Transformation happens in honest, intentional brotherhood. And when men commit to one another, they create something powerful, something lasting, and something that shapes not just who they are but who they are becoming.

The enemy fears this kind of unity because it carries real power. A single man may be targeted, isolated, and shaken, but a group of grounded, godly men becomes a force that is difficult to move. Where one may grow weary, another stands strong. Where one may be attacked, others step in to defend. They do not scatter under pressure - they lock arms and stand firm together. And that unity becomes a barrier the enemy struggles to break. They fight together, they stand together, and they grow together. Every battle faced side by side deepens their strength and sharpens their faith. They refuse to let one another fall, and they refuse to retreat when resistance rises. In that kind of brotherhood, fear loses its grip, and courage becomes contagious. Each man draws strength from the others, and together they become steady, unshakable, and prepared for whatever comes. Because when men are united in truth, purpose, and faith, they are not easily defeated - they are built to endure and to overcome.

So build your brotherhood wisely. Surround yourself with men who make you better, men who challenge your thinking, sharpen your discipline, and refuse to let you stay where you are. Men who speak truth even when it is uncomfortable, who push you toward growth when you feel like settling, and who remind you of your calling when you begin to drift. These are the men who will strengthen your life, not just share space in it. Because the quality of your brotherhood will shape the strength of your walk. And be that man for others. Do not just look for sharpening - be willing to sharpen. Stand firm, speak truth, and show up with consistency and courage. When every man commits to that standard, something powerful is formed. Because when lions walk together, they do not just survive - they take ground. They move with purpose, with unity, and with strength that cannot easily be broken. And in that kind of brotherhood, men do not live passively - they rise, they lead, and they dominate the ground they stand on.

| 15 |

"YOUR PROVING GROUND"

There is a fire that every man must pass through. It is not sent to destroy him, but to reveal what truly lives within him. When the heat rises and the pressure builds, the masks fall away, the excuses burn off, and what remains is the real man. The fire of testing does not create weakness; it uncovers it. It brings hidden fears to the surface, exposes compromised convictions, and reveals where faith has been spoken but not yet lived. In the fire, God does His deepest work. He reshapes and rebuilds the man who is willing to endure. What feels like breaking is often the beginning of true formation. Strength is forged where comfort once ruled. Faith is anchored where doubt once whispered. And character is established where shortcuts once tempted. So do not run from the fire - stand in it. Let it strip away everything false, everything weak, everything temporary. For on the other side of the flames stands a man who is transformed - proven, purified, and prepared for the purpose God has called him to fulfill.

Trials have a way of stripping away illusion. They tear down the image we try to maintain and expose the truth beneath it. When the fire comes, excuses lose their voice, masks fall to the ground, and the comfortable lies we once believed can no longer stand. What remains is not what we claimed to be, but what we have truly become. God uses these moments to uncover the foundation of a man's life, showing whether it is built on sand or anchored in truth. When life gets hard, what is truly inside a man rises to the surface. Strength cannot be faked in the fire - it is either there, or it is not. But even in that revealing, there is grace. The fire is not only meant to expose weakness, but to refine it. God allows the heat so that impurities can be burned away and something stronger can emerge. A man who endures with faith, who leans into God instead of running from Him, comes out forged, not broken. What the fire reveals, God can redeem and what is tested by trial can be transformed into unshakable strength.

It is easy to appear strong when life is smooth. It is easy to speak boldly when nothing is at stake. But real strength is not revealed in comfort - it is forged in the fire. When the storm rises and the winds push against you, when the weight of responsibility grows heavier than you expected, when your knees feel weak and your voice wants to fall silent - that is where true strength is uncovered. God does not measure a man by how he stands in ease, but by how he endures in adversity. Pressure does not destroy a faithful man - it exposes what is within him and refines it. The storm is not your enemy; it is your proving ground. So stand when it would be easier to sit down, speak truth when silence would be safer, and hold the line when quitting whispers your name. It is in those moments that character is being built, and faith is being made unshakable. When you come through the storm, you will not be the same man who entered it. You will be deeper, stronger, and more anchored in God than ever before.

Every hardship you face, every delay that tests your patience, and every moment of pressure that feels unbearable is being used with divine purpose. What looks like a setback is often a setup, and what feels like resistance is actually refinement. In the fire of difficulty, He is shaping your character, strengthening your faith, and building a resilience that comfort could never produce. The weight you carry today is not meant to break you - it is meant to build you. What feels like opposition is often preparation. God sees what lies ahead, and He uses today's struggles to equip you for tomorrow's calling. The closed doors, the long waits, and the battles you didn't choose are all part of a greater design. You are being trained, not trapped. You are being positioned, not punished. So stand firm in the process, trust Him in the pressure, and refuse to quit in the middle of your becoming. Because when God is finished, you will see that every trial had a purpose and every moment was working for your good.

Fire does not ask permission - it simply arrives and reveals what is real. It does not negotiate with weakness or adjust itself to your comfort; it exposes, refines, and separates. In the same way, trials enter your life without invitation, confronting not your preferences but your character. They bring to the surface what could never be seen in ease. What feels like destruction is often divine inspection. God allows the heat not to harm you, but to show you what is strong, what is shallow, and what must change. And what cannot endure is burned away. The pride that collapses under pressure, the faith that only lives in convenience, and the strength that disappears when tested is consumed so that something greater can remain. What survives the fire is not weaker, but purified - faith that stands, character that holds, and a man who cannot be easily shaken. Do not fear the fire; embrace what it produces. Because when the flames settle, what remains is not who you were, but who God is forming you to be.

Many resist the fire because they misread its purpose. When the heat rises, they assume God has turned against them, that the pressure is proof of punishment. But the fire was never meant to destroy you - it was meant to reveal you. Just as gold is refined by intense heat, so your faith, your character, and your strength are being purified in the very place you want to escape. The impurities cannot survive the fire, but what is real, what is rooted in God, will come forth stronger, purer, and unshakable. God is not trying to harm you - He is strengthening you. He is building endurance where you were weak, courage where you were hesitant, and depth where you were shallow. The fire is not evidence of His absence, but of His intentional work in your life. If you run from it, you run from the very process designed to prepare you for greater purpose. But if you stand in it, trust Him through it, and surrender to what He is shaping in you, you will come out refined - not burned, but built.

A man who avoids hardship may feel safe for a moment. Comfort whispers ease, but it never builds character. The life that chases convenience will eventually collapse under pressure because it has never been tested. God did not design you to live wrapped in ease, but to be forged through resistance. Just as iron is shaped in fire, a man is shaped in adversity. The trials you face are invitations to grow, to deepen your faith, and to become the man you were created to be. Pressure is not your enemy; it is your training ground. When you endure hardship with faith, something unshakable begins to form within you. Endurance is born in the moments you refuse to quit, and from endurance comes a strength that cannot be broken by circumstance. This is the kind of strength that stands firm when everything else is falling apart. So don't run from the trial - embrace it. Let it refine you because on the other side of pressure is a man who is steady, grounded, and ready for anything God calls him to face.

Faith is proven in endurance. When life is smooth and doors open effortlessly, belief often feels natural, almost automatic. But true faith is not revealed in comfort; it is uncovered in resistance. It is in the long nights, the unanswered prayers, and the moments when heaven seems silent that faith is truly tested. Anyone can trust God when the path is clear, but it takes a forged man to keep walking when the road disappears. Endurance is the fire that separates surface belief from unshakable conviction. A forged man learns to trust not by what he sees, but by who God is. When circumstances contradict the promise, he stands anyway. When logic fails and emotions waver, he anchors himself in truth. This kind of faith is battle-tested, refined through pressure, and strengthened by perseverance. It declares, "Even here, even now, I will trust You." And in that unwavering endurance, faith becomes more than words - it becomes a living force that cannot be shaken, because it has been proven in the fire.

In the fire, God is shaping your strength. He is watching for the man who refuses to bow, the man who keeps his footing when everything around him shakes. He is looking for perseverance that doesn't quit when it's uncomfortable, and faith that doesn't waver when answers are delayed. In the middle of the flames, your character is being revealed and refined. What you choose in the fire determines who you become when the smoke clears. God is looking for trust that stands firm without needing constant reassurance. He is looking for a man who will hold his ground, even when he feels alone, even when the outcome is uncertain. This is where warriors are made. When others fall away, when excuses rise, when the pressure intensifies - that is your moment to stand in truth, stand in conviction, and stand in faith. Because the fire is not your end - it is your proving ground. And the man who stands in it with unwavering trust will walk out stronger, sharper, and ready for the purpose God has prepared.

There is something powerful about a man who refuses to break. He knows who he belongs to, and that truth steadies him when everything else feels uncertain. His strength is not built on fleeting emotions or temporary confidence; it is anchored deep in faith. When feelings rise and fall, his foundation remains. He may feel the weight but he does not collapse under it because he is held, guided, and sustained by something greater than himself. This kind of man stands different. When storms come, he doesn't panic - he plants his feet. When others give in, he leans in. His strength is quiet but unshakable, forged in surrender and sustained by trust. He understands that real power is not found in never feeling weak, but in refusing to let weakness define him. Anchored in faith, he rises again and again, not by his own might, but by the One who never fails. And that is what makes him unbreakable - not the absence of pressure, but the presence of God within him.

Pressure reveals priorities. What once seemed important suddenly fades, and what truly matters rises to the surface with clarity. In those moments, a man can no longer hide behind comfort or routine. What he loves, what he trusts, and what he lives for all becomes visible. Pressure has a way of stripping away illusion and exposing reality, and in that exposure, the mission becomes undeniable. This is where decisions are made that define a man. Not in ease, but in intensity. Not when everything is convenient, but when everything costs something. Under pressure, he must choose - will he stand firm in purpose, or fold under the weight? Will he cling to what is eternal, or reach for what is temporary? Pressure forces the question: Who are you, really? And the man who answers that question with conviction, who aligns his life with truth when it's hardest, becomes a man of clarity, strength, and purpose. Because when the pressure passes - and it will - what remains is the man he chose to be.

Gold is not purified in a moment - it is shaped through sustained heat, through cycles of fire that remove what does not belong. In the same way, God does not build strong men in seconds, but through seasons. There are stretches of waiting, moments of pressure, and times when progress feels slow or unseen. But every season has purpose. Every trial, every delay, every challenge is part of a greater process that is carefully forming strength, endurance, and depth within you. God is not in a hurry because He is building something that will last. He develops men layer by layer, teaching trust in one season, endurance in another, and faithfulness through it all. You may want instant growth, immediate answers, or quick breakthroughs but real transformation takes time. With each season you endure, something stronger is being established within you. Stay in the process because when the refining is complete, what remains will be proven and ready for the purpose only a developed man can carry.

You may feel like the fire is lasting too long, like the weight should have lifted by now. Questions rise, strength feels stretched, and you wonder why the pressure continues. But God knows exactly how much heat is required to shape you without breaking you. He sees what you cannot see: the impurities being removed, the endurance being built, the depth being formed. Every second in the fire is intentional, every ounce of pressure is purposeful. Even when you don't understand it, you can trust His process. If the fire has not lifted, it is because the work is not finished. And when the work is finished, He will bring you through at the right time - not early, not late, but exactly when you are ready. So don't retreat. Don't give up in the middle of refinement. Stay steady. Stay faithful. Because the same God who allowed the fire is the One who is watching over you in it, ensuring that what emerges is stronger, purer, and ready for the purpose He designed from the beginning.

In the moment when pressure rises and uncertainty closes in, you are standing at a crossroads - will you trust or retreat, stand or surrender? The test is not just about what you're facing; it's about who you're becoming. Each decision you make under pressure is shaping your future, carving your character, defining your direction. When you choose trust over fear, when you stand instead of stepping back, you are aligning yourself with strength, purpose, and faith. The fire reveals what is inside you, but it also gives you the opportunity to decide what will remain. The fire is not just testing you - it is training you. It is building endurance where there was weakness, conviction where there was hesitation, and courage where there was doubt. What feels like resistance is actually preparation. God is using every moment to develop a man who does not fold under pressure but grows through it. So, when the test comes, don't just try to survive it - learn from it, lean into it, and rise through it.

Men of impact are not formed in comfort - they are forged in conflict. It is in the tension, the resistance, and the battles no one else sees that true strength is built. In those hard seasons, a man must fight to hold his ground when everything pushes against him, fight to keep his faith when doubt whispers, and fight to move forward when quitting feels easier. These are the moments that separate passive men from purposeful ones. It is in conflict that identity is strengthened and purpose is clarified. Every struggle becomes a proving ground, every obstacle an opportunity to grow. God uses these seasons to build men who do not drift with circumstances but stand firm in truth. The fight is not meaningless - it is making you. It is shaping your endurance, sharpening your focus, and anchoring your faith. So don't resent the battle - embrace it. Because the man who learns to fight through adversity becomes a man who carries weight, influences others, and walks in the kind of impact that only conflict can produce.

Endurance is active, intentional, and costly. It is not simply surviving the day; it is standing when you feel weak and choosing to keep going when every emotion tells you to stop. Real endurance is a decision made over and over again - a refusal to bow to pressure or surrender to fatigue. It is strength in motion, faith in action, and discipline that does not wait for motivation. The man who endures is not the one who never struggles, but the one who refuses to let struggle have the final word. It is in these moments that true character is revealed. Endurance says, "I will not walk away from what God has called me to." Even when the path is unclear, even when progress feels slow, endurance keeps moving forward. This kind of persistence builds within you a strength that cannot be easily broken. Because every time you choose to stand instead of quit, you are becoming stronger, steadier, and more prepared for the purpose ahead. Endurance is not just how you survive the battle - it is how you win it.

The fire may be intense, but it is not permanent. Every trial has a boundary, every hardship has an end, and every moment of pressure is working toward a greater purpose. The heat is stripping away what cannot remain and strengthening what must endure. Even when you can't see the finish line, God already knows where it is and He is guiding you toward it. And when the fire has done its work, you will not come out weaker - you will come out refined. Stronger in faith, clearer in purpose, steadier in character. What once shook you will no longer move you. What once tested you will now testify through you. The same fire that tried to break you will have built you into something unshakable. So hold on in the heat. Stay faithful in the process. Because on the other side of the fire is transformation, and a man who has been refined for something greater than he ever imagined. So do not fear the fire - step into it with faith. What looks like danger is often the doorway to development.

The heat you feel is not there to consume you, but to transform you. When you trust God in the fire instead of resisting it, you allow His work to go deeper. You stop fighting the process and start growing through it. Faith doesn't wait for comfort - it walks forward in confidence, knowing that God is present even in the flames. Let the fire do what it was sent to do. Let it refine your character, strengthen your resolve, and deepen your dependence on Him. Because the man who endures the fire of testing will not come out the same - he will come out stronger, sharper, and ready. Ready for greater responsibility, ready for deeper purpose, ready to stand where others cannot. What once intimidated him will no longer control him. What once tested him will now testify of what God can do in a man who refuses to quit. So step forward, not backward. Stand firm, not fearful. Because on the other side of the fire is a version of you that is forged, focused, and fully prepared for everything God has already set in motion.

| 16 |

"THE LION IN THE STORM"

There is a kind of man who does not run when the storm rolls in. While others scramble for shelter, he plants his feet and lifts his eyes, not in defiance of the storm, but in confidence in the God who commands it. What lives in him will surface when the winds howl and the rain falls. He does not deny the danger - he simply refuses to bow to it. The storm may shake everything around him, but it cannot shake the foundation beneath him. Storms do not come to destroy the man of God - they come to reveal him. They uncover whether his roots are shallow or deep, whether his trust is in comfort or in Christ. And when the storm passes, it leaves behind a man still standing, still trusting, still unbroken not because he was untouched, but because he was anchored. This is the kind of man heaven recognizes - not the one who avoids the storm, but the one who endures it with unshakable faith. So when the thunder roars, he does not run - he rises knowing that what is revealed in the storm will echo into eternity.

The lion does not fear the storm because he knows who he is. Thunder may roar and lightning may split the sky, but it does not change his nature - it only reveals it. And so it is with you. Storms do not come to destroy a man of God - they come to prove him. When chaos rises and everything around you shakes, that is your moment to stand. Root yourself in truth. Anchor yourself in faith. Let the winds come and the rain fall but refuse to move from what God has called you to be. Steadiness is strength. Remaining is power. You do not bow to fear, you do not surrender to panic, and you do not abandon your post when the pressure builds. You stand unmoved, unshaken, and unwavering because your foundation is not built on circumstances, but on the unchanging Word of God. The storm may rage, but it cannot uproot what God has firmly planted. So lift your head. Square your shoulders. And stand like the lion you were created to be - steady in the storm, bold in the battle, and faithful until the end.

Remaining steady in chaos is a spiritual discipline forged in the quiet places long before the storm arrives. God calls all men to a place of resolve anchored not in circumstance, but in truth. When everything around you begins to shake, faith remembers that God has not changed, even when everything else has. A man of faith is not ruled by what he sees, but by what he knows. He has already settled in his heart that no storm is greater than the One who holds him. Anyone can be calm when the skies are clear, but calm in the storm is where spiritual strength is revealed. When pressure rises, what is inside you is exposed. The man who stands firm in chaos is not without emotion, but he is unmoved in conviction. He does not collapse under pressure because his foundation was built before the winds came. So when life begins to tremble, do not reach for panic - reach for God. Stand your ground. Hold your peace. And let the storm discover that you are not easily shaken.

The storm does not come to destroy you - it comes to reveal you. When the winds rise and the rain beats against your life, everything shallow begins to shake. What you built without God being at the center of it will be exposed. Comfort cannot carry you in chaos, and circumstances cannot sustain you when everything around you is shifting. The storm has a way of stripping away illusions and bringing you face to face with the truth: what are you really standing on? But the man who is anchored in God does not fear the storm - he is refined by it. When your foundation is rooted in Him, pressure doesn't destroy you, it develops you. The winds may howl and the waves may rise, but you remain unshaken because your strength is built on eternal truth. What was meant to break you becomes what builds you. The storm becomes your proving ground, and when it passes, you are not weaker - you are stronger, steadier, and more certain than ever that a life founded on God cannot be moved.

Too many men are tossed back and forth by every gust of adversity. They're steady one moment and shaken the next. Their strength is tied to circumstances, their peace dependent on conditions. But a man of God is not meant to live at the mercy of the storm. He is called to be anchored. When trials rise and pressure builds, it reveals what he is rooted in. If his foundation is shallow, the winds will expose it. But if his life is built on truth, on faith, on the unchanging character of God, then even the fiercest storm cannot uproot him. Strength is not proven when life is easy - it is revealed when everything around him is unstable, yet he remains. The lion-hearted man is different. He has trained his soul to be still when everything within him wants to panic. He has learned that peace is not the absence of noise, but the presence of God. There is a quiet authority in him because he knows that God is with him in the fire and that is enough. So he steadies his heart, fixes his eyes upward, and refuses to be moved.

You were not created to be tossed back and forth by chaos, but to stand firm in the middle of it with authority. God did not design you to be ruled by fear, emotions, or circumstances - He designed you to rule them. You rise higher. You anchor yourself in truth. You remind your soul who God is and who you are in Him. Chaos may be loud, but truth is stronger. When uncertainty whispers lies of doubt and instability, you answer with the steady voice of faith. You don't wait for everything around you to settle - you become the one who is settled. You become the calm in the storm, the steady hand when others are shaken, the grounded presence when everything else feels like it's falling apart. That kind of strength doesn't come from circumstances

- it comes from surrender, discipline, and trust in God. So stand your ground. Command your thoughts. Guard your heart. And refuse to be moved. Because when everything feels unstable, you were created to become the most stable thing in the room.

Trusting God in uncertainty is where true faith is forged. Anyone can trust when the path is visible and the answers are clear, but real faith is born in the moments when nothing makes sense. It is in the silence, in the waiting, in the unknown places where you cannot trace His hand that you must choose to trust His heart. When the path is unclear, when the outcome is unknown, and when the future feels uncertain, that is where trust must take root and grow strong. God does not ask you to understand everything - He asks you to believe that He is faithful in everything. The unseen road is not a sign of His absence, but an invitation to rely on His presence. In those moments, your faith is being refined, strengthened, and made unshakable. So stand firm, even when you cannot see the way ahead. Walk forward, even when the ground feels uncertain. Because the same God who leads you into the unknown is the One who has already prepared the way through it.

God does not always silence the wind the moment you pray but He will steady your soul in the middle of it. While the storm roars, God is building a strength that circumstances cannot shake. He teaches your heart to trust when there is no immediate change, to stand when everything around you is unstable, and to believe when you cannot yet see. The peace He gives is not dependent on calm surroundings - it rises from a settled confidence that He is still in control, even when everything feels out of control. Sometimes the greater miracle is not the storm stopping, but the man standing. When God calms the storm within you, fear loses its grip, anxiety loses its voice, and chaos loses its authority. You begin to walk with a quiet strength, unmoved by what once overwhelmed you. The waves may still crash, and the winds may still howl but they no longer define you. You are anchored, unshaken, and grounded in something greater. The storm may still rage but it no longer rules.

There is a confidence that rises in a man who knows who holds his life - not a fragile hope, not a passing feeling, but a settled certainty rooted in God Himself. When you truly trust God, you are no longer shaken by every unknown or rattled by every possibility. The questions of "what if" begin to lose their power, because your faith is anchored in the One who never changes. Even when the path is unclear, your heart is steady, because you know who is leading you. That kind of trust transforms how you live. You stop negotiating with fear and start declaring truth. You move from "what if everything falls apart?" to "even if it does, God is still faithful." Even if the door closes, even if the storm comes, even if the answer is delayed you remain unshaken. This is not denial; it is conviction. It is a bold, unyielding confidence that says your life is not in the hands of chance, but in the hands of a sovereign God. And when that truth takes hold, uncertainty no longer controls you - faith does.

Even if the storm doesn't pass quickly, and the winds seem to press harder against you with each passing moment, your foundation does not move. Even if the answers don't come when you want them and heaven feels silent and the timeline stretches longer than you planned - your trust remains unshaken. Why? Because your faith was never meant to rest on timing, comfort, or visible results. It is rooted in something far deeper - the unchanging character of God. When your faith is anchored in the One who controls all things, outcomes lose their power to define you. You are no longer tossed between hope and disappointment, because your confidence is not in what happens, but in who is over it. Whether He calms the storm or carries you through it, He is faithful. Whether the breakthrough comes now or later, He is still good. That kind of faith stands firm in every season. It does not bend with circumstances or break under pressure. It declares with quiet strength: even here, even now, I trust Him.

Strength that does not collapse is forged in resistance. It is built slowly, deliberately, through moments that test you, stretch you, and refuse to let you remain the same. Every storm you endure is teaching you how to stand under pressure instead of folding beneath it. Every challenge you face is reinforcing your foundation, driving your roots deeper so that when the winds come again, you are not easily shaken. What feels like opposition is often God strengthening what must hold in the days ahead. What you call pressure is often preparation in disguise. It is God shaping endurance into your spirit, stability into your character, and resilience into your walk. The very thing that feels like it might break you is actually building you layer by layer, trial by trial. You are becoming the kind of man who does not collapse when life presses hard, because you have been trained in the tension. So do not despise the resistance. It is producing something solid, something lasting, something unshakable within you.

Weak men spend their lives trying to escape storms, searching for comfort and control, but strong men are forged in the very battles others run from. The storm you wish would disappear is not your enemy - it is your training ground. It exposes what is shallow, strengthens what is weak, and calls out a deeper level of faith and endurance. God does not waste pressure; He uses it to shape men who can stand when others fall. What feels like disruption is actually development, chiseling away what cannot last and building something that will not break. Do not waste the storm by wishing it away. Step into it with purpose. Let it teach you, refine you, and harden your resolve. The resistance you feel is producing strength; the struggle is forming character; the fire is forging endurance. This is where you become who you were called to be - not in ease, but in adversity. So stand your ground. Embrace the process. What you are walking through is not destroying you - it is defining you.

The lion's strength is not loud - it is steady. It does not thrash in panic or waste energy trying to prove its power. It moves with purpose, grounded and controlled, fully aware of who it is. There is a quiet authority in that kind of strength - a confidence that does not need validation. In the same way, a man rooted in God does not live in constant reaction to chaos around him. He is not frantic - he is focused. His peace is not weakness; it is power under control, anchored in something unshakable. When others are losing control, the lion remains in control. While fear spreads and pressure rises, he stands firm, steady in spirit and clear in mind. This is the kind of strength God builds within you. It is not loud, not reckless, but disciplined and composed. It is the ability to hold your ground when everything around you is shifting. Your power is not proven in panic, but in the calm, unwavering confidence that says you are not ruled by the storm but grounded above it.

You do not need to match the noise of the storm - you need to master your response to it. Chaos will always be loud, demanding your attention and trying to pull you into reaction. But true strength is not measured by how quickly you respond - it is revealed in how well you remain anchored. When you are grounded in God, you are not easily provoked or shaken. You learn to pause, to steady your spirit, and to respond with wisdom instead of impulse. The storm may be wild, but your soul does not have to be. Power is not found in reacting - it is found in discipline, in an unwavering composure when everything around you is trying to pull you apart. It is the strength to hold your tongue when emotions rise, to stand firm when pressure builds, and to remain clear when confusion surrounds you. This is the kind of control God develops within you - a quiet authority that does not bend to chaos. When you master your response, you take back control. And in that place of composure, you become unshakable.

There will be moments when the weight of everything seems to press in at once - when the storm feels too strong, the path too unclear, and your strength too small for what stands before you. In those moments, it is easy to feel overwhelmed, to question, to hesitate. But this is not where your faith weakens - this is where it rises. When the pressure is greatest, your foundation is revealed. And if your trust is in God, then even in uncertainty, you are standing on something that cannot be shaken. These are the moments where your faith must stand tallest; not because the storm has less power, but because your trust has greater strength. You may not have all the answers, and you may not see the way forward clearly, but you know who is leading you. Faith is not the absence of struggle - it is the decision to stand firm in the middle of it. So when everything presses in, do not collapse but stand firm and tall. Because the same God who allowed the storm is the One who will carry you through it.

You are not alone in the storm, even when it feels like silence surrounds you. God is present, closer than you realize, steady in the midst of your uncertainty. While you may not see immediate change, He is working beneath the surface, strengthening parts of you that comfort could never reach. He is building endurance in your spirit, clarity in your thinking, and resilience in your faith. What feels like absence is often His quiet, intentional work that is shaping you for something greater than the moment you're in. In the stillness, God is removing distractions, refining your focus, and teaching you to depend on Him alone. It is in these hidden places that your roots grow deepest, where your trust becomes unshakable, and where your identity is secured not in circumstances, but in Him. You may feel set apart, but you are not forgotten. You are being prepared, strengthened, and positioned. And when the time comes, you will step forward not as someone who barely survived the storm, but as someone who was built by it.

So stand firm. Plant your feet. Lift your head. Do not yield to fear or bend under the weight of pressure. The storm may rise, the winds may push, and the noise may try to overwhelm you, but you do not have to be moved by it. There is a strength available to you that is greater than your circumstances, a stability that does not come from within yourself but from the God who holds you steady. When everything around you is shifting, you can remain grounded, fixed, and unshaken. Let the storm come and let it find you standing - not in your own strength but firmly rooted in the unshakable power and presence of God. You are not defiant in your own power, but confident in His. This is not about proving your strength; it is about trusting His. When your foundation is built on God, you do not collapse when pressure increases - you become more resolute. So hold your ground. Stay anchored. Because the strength that sustains you is not your own - it is His, and it does not fail.

Be the lion in the storm - steady when everything around you is chaotic, anchored when others are drifting, and unshaken when uncertainty tries to take hold. Strength is not proven in calm conditions; it is revealed when pressure rises and the winds push hardest. You are not called to panic - you are called to stand. To hold your ground with a quiet, unwavering confidence that comes from God. When fear whispers, you remain focused. When chaos erupts, you stay composed. This is the strength that does not break - it endures. Let the winds rise and the thunder roar, because the storm does not have the final say. What will define you is not what came against you, but how you stood in the middle of it. Did you hold the line? Did you trust when it was hard? Did you remain anchored when everything tried to move you? When the storm passes what remains is the man you became in it. Stronger. Steadier. Unbreakable. Not because the storm was weak, but because your faith was stronger.

| 17 |

"CONQUERING FEAR"

Fear has always been one of the enemy's most effective weapons against men. It convinces a man to hesitate when he should advance, to retreat when he should stand, and to stay silent when he should speak. Fear is not always loud; often it comes disguised as caution, logic, or even wisdom. But underneath it all, its purpose is the same: to stop a man from becoming who God created him to be. It clouds vision, weakens resolve, and keeps potential locked behind the prison of "what if." But God has called you to walk by faith, to move with courage, and to trust Him beyond what you can see or control. You were not designed to be mastered by fear, but to overcome it through faith. Courage is not the absence of fear; it is the decision to move forward in spite of it. When fear says "wait," faith says "go." Stand your ground. Speak when it's hard. Step forward when it's uncomfortable. Because on the other side of fear is obedience, and on the other side of obedience is the life God intended for you to live.

From the beginning, fear has been a weapon aimed at the heart of a man's calling. It takes what God has placed inside of him and tries to bury it beneath doubt. Fear magnifies the mountain while shrinking the man. It turns steps of faith into stumbling blocks and paints obedience as danger. Where God declares victory, fear predicts defeat. But fear has never spoken truth   it only echoes insecurity, hoping a man will mistake it for wisdom. Yet God's voice cuts through the noise with authority and clarity. He does not call the qualified - He qualifies the called. What He declares possible is not limited by human strength but empowered by divine strength. A man who listens to God will rise, even when fear shouts for him to stay down. Courage is not the absence of fear - it is the decision to move forward in spite of it. So step forward anyway. Obey anyway. Trust anyway. Because every time a man chooses faith over fear, he steps into the life God designed for him.

Fear isolates. It pulls a man inward until it convinces him to withdraw when he should advance, to question when he should trust, and to second-guess the very voice of God that once burned clearly in his spirit. Fear whispers that he is alone and abandoned but that is its greatest lie. Even when a man feels most isolated, God has not stepped back. The same power that called him forward is still standing behind him. But fear makes a man passive, and passivity is where defeat takes root. A man who stops moving, stops speaking, and stops standing will slowly surrender ground that was meant to be taken. Faith was never meant to make a man comfortable; it was meant to make him courageous. So he must rise, even while afraid. He must move, even when uncertain. Because courage is not the absence of fear - it is the decision to obey God in spite of it. When a man rejects passivity and steps forward in faith, he breaks the isolation, silences the lie, and proves that he was never alone to begin with.

The tragedy is not that fear exists - it's that many men surrender to it. God never designed fear to be your compass, yet so many men let it dictate their decisions, silence their convictions, and shrink their calling. Instead of advancing with boldness, they retreat into comfort, constructing lives built on avoidance rather than obedience. But a life governed by fear will always be smaller than the purpose God placed inside you. You cannot fulfill a divine calling while bowing to a human emotion. The presence of fear is an opportunity, not a defeat; it is the very place where faith must rise and take command. When a man chooses to confront what intimidates him, he steps into the authority God gave him from the beginning. Break the agreement with fear. Refuse to build your life around what makes you comfortable. Step forward, even when your voice shakes, even when the outcome is uncertain. Because on the other side of fear is growth, freedom, and the life you were created to live.

Fear whispers lies that distort what God has already declared to be true. A man who was once confident in his calling suddenly questions his purpose. Fear strips away clarity and replaces it with confusion, causing him to forget that he was chosen, not by accident, but by design. When identity is shaken, everything begins to shift. He no longer stands with conviction - he hesitates, second-guesses, and withdraws. The battle is no longer just around him; it is within him. But the truth remains unchanged, no matter how loud fear becomes. You are still called. You are still chosen. You are still equipped. Fear may try to rewrite your identity, but it has no authority to do so unless you agree with it. A man who remembers who he is will rise even while afraid. He will move forward not because fear is gone, but because truth is stronger. When identity is restored, action follows. Strength returns. Courage awakens. And the man who once hesitated begins to walk boldly again because he knows exactly who he is.

Fear has a way of bending your vision until shadows look like giants, whispering lies that feel louder than truth. It magnifies danger, minimizes faith, and convinces you that defeat is already decided before the battle even begins. But fear is not rooted in truth, but in illusion. What it declares as inevitable is often nothing more than imagined destruction dressed up as certainty. God has not handed your future over to fear, and He has not written failure into your story. So when fear begins to speak in absolutes, you must answer with truth. Where fear says, "You will fail," God says, "My grace is sufficient. I will uphold you with My righteous right hand." Where fear says you will not recover, God declares restoration, strength, and victory. Fear may be loud, but it is not final. It may feel convincing, but it is not faithful. Stand firm, reject its lies, and move forward anyway because the voice of God is greater than the voice of fear, and His promises, not your fears, will define your outcome.

Fear is an intruder that seeks to occupy ground God never gave it permission to take. It whispers lies, magnifies threats, and shrinks your calling until you forget who you are and whose you are. This is why fear must be confronted at its root. You cannot negotiate with it, because it does not come to reason - it comes to rule. You cannot wait for it to leave, because fear does not retreat on its own - it must be driven out. God has not given you a spirit of fear, but of power, love, and a sound mind. The moment you turn and face fear, its illusion of control begins to break, and the truth of God's presence rises stronger than the threat before you. Every step you take in obedience weakens fear's hold and strengthens your trust in God. The longer fear is tolerated, the deeper it roots itself but when confronted with faith, it withers. So stand your ground. Speak truth over your life. Move forward anyway. Because fear loses its power the moment you refuse to bow to it.

Fear imagines loss, defeat, and uncertainty until the heart begins to tremble. But God has not left men defenseless. He has given an antidote - faith. Faith does not deny reality; it redefines it through the lens of who God is. Where fear fixates on what cannot be seen or predicted, faith anchors itself in the unchanging character of a faithful God. He has never failed, never abandoned, never lost control. Faith reaches back into that truth and pulls it into the present moment. When a man walks by faith, he is no longer led by the shifting shadows of uncertainty but by the steady light of God's promises. Fear may still knock, but it no longer has authority to enter. Faith steadies the mind, strengthens the heart, and aligns the soul with heaven's perspective. It reminds you that God is ruling and guiding your life. And when you trust Him, even in what you cannot see, you step into a confidence that fear cannot shake. So choose faith. Speak it. Stand in it. Because when faith takes its rightful place, fear loses its voice.

Fear may rise, emotions may shake, and uncertainty may press in but faith steps in and takes its stand. It declares that God's voice is louder than fear's whisper, and His promises are stronger than any threat. Faith refuses to let fear have the final word. It looks beyond the moment and fixes its eyes on the One who holds all things together. A man of faith does not wait until he feels fearless - he chooses to trust even while fear is present. A man of faith may feel fear, but he does not bow to it. He does not surrender his calling, his obedience, or his purpose to what he feels. Instead, he moves forward anyway, step by step, trusting that God goes before him. Every act of obedience in the face of fear is a declaration of victory. Every step forward weakens fear's grip and strengthens his confidence in God. This is how faith is forged - not in comfort, but in confrontation. So rise up, stand firm, and move forward. Fear may speak, but it does not get the final say. God does.

Faith shifts perspective. It lifts a man's eyes off the chaos of the storm and fixes them on the Savior who stands above it. Storms will rage, winds will howl, and waves will rise but faith refuses to be mesmerized by the noise. Instead, it remembers who is in control. When your focus changes, your fear begins to fade. What once looked overwhelming begins to shrink in the presence of God's greatness. Faith reminds a man that he is not walking alone, not fighting alone, and not standing alone. God is with him, and that changes everything. His presence brings strength where there was weakness, peace where there was turmoil, and courage where there was hesitation. You are not abandoned in the battle - you are accompanied by the Almighty. And when a man truly grasps that truth, he stands differently, walks differently, and fights differently. Because when God is with you, the storm may still rage but it no longer has the power to define you.

When faith rises, fear loses its grip not because the storm suddenly calms, but because the man standing in it is no longer the same. His foundation deepens, his vision clears, and his heart steadies. He stops reacting to what he sees and starts responding to what he knows about God. Faith transforms the battlefield from a place of intimidation into a place of trust. The circumstances may remain, but their power over him does not. Fear thrives on a man's uncertainty, but faith roots him in unshakable truth. He no longer measures his ability - he measures God's power. He stops asking, "Am I strong enough?" and starts declaring, "God is more than enough." And when God becomes the standard, everything else is brought into proper perspective. Giants shrink. Storms lose their voice. Obstacles no longer dictate his steps. This is the strength of a man who walks by faith - he is not limited by his own capacity but empowered by God's sufficiency. And when that truth takes hold, fear has no place to stand.

Faith also fuels courage. Courage is the fire that faith ignites in a man's soul, compelling him to move when everything inside him says to stay still. Faith reminds him that God is greater than the threat, stronger than the opposition, and faithful to sustain him through whatever lies ahead. It tells him that obedience matters more than comfort, and that stepping out with God is always safer than staying back without Him. Courage is the decision to step forward when every part of you wants to step back. It is obedience when comfort is calling you to retreat. It is choosing purpose over ease, conviction over convenience, and calling over fear. A man fueled by faith moves when God speaks. And in that movement, courage is strengthened and fear is weakened. Each step of obedience builds momentum, and what once felt impossible becomes a testimony of God's power at work in him. Because when faith leads, courage follows - and together, they push a man into the life he was created to live.

Every great man of God had to face fear. They stood at the edge of moments where the risk was real, the danger was present, and the outcome was uncertain. Their minds felt the weight of what could go wrong, and the cost before them was undeniable. Yet what marked their lives was their refusal to let fear take control. They chose obedience over hesitation, trust over doubt, and action over retreat. In those defining moments, what separated them was not that they felt no fear - it was that they refused to let fear stop them. They moved forward because they believed God was greater than what stood before them. They understood that destiny is not fulfilled in comfort, but in courage. Every step they took in faith became a testimony that fear does not have the authority to dictate a man's path. And the same is true for you. The moments that scare you the most may be the very places God is calling you to trust Him the deepest. So stand up, step forward, and refuse to let fear write your story.

Moving forward despite fear is where transformation happens. When you choose to step forward anyway, you are not just overcoming fear - you are becoming someone new. God uses those very moments of tension and uncertainty to shape strength, sharpen conviction, and build a faith that cannot be shaken. What feels like risk is often the very place where purpose is forged. Growth does not happen in safety; it happens in obedience. Comfort may feel secure, but it never produces the depth or resilience that calling requires. A man becomes who he was meant to be when he answers God in the middle of discomfort, not after it passes. Each act of obedience stretches him, strengthens him, and prepares him for greater responsibility. This is where true manhood is forged - not in ease, but in endurance; not in retreat, but in resolve. So step forward, even when it's hard. Because on the other side of that step is the man God is calling you to become.

There will be moments when doubt crowds your mind, when hesitation grips your heart, and when everything in you wants to wait for a better time. But God has never required perfect feelings - He asks for faithful steps. Readiness is often a myth that keeps men standing still, while faith calls them to move. Strength is not proven in moments of comfort, but in moments when you choose to obey even when you feel weak. God does not wait for you to feel capable - He moves when you choose to trust Him. You don't have to feel any of those things to move forward. You only need to trust God enough to take the next step. One step of obedience opens the door for His power to meet you in motion. One step of faith invites His strength into your weakness. You don't need the whole path - you just need enough trust to take the next step in front of you. And as you move, confidence will grow, strength will follow, and clarity will come. But it all begins with the decision to trust God more than you trust your feelings.

Fear will always try to delay you. It will whisper, "Wait until you're certain. Wait until everything makes sense. Wait until you feel secure." But faith speaks a different language. It says, "Move. Not because you have all the answers, but because God does." Fear tells you to play it safe, to protect what you have, to avoid the risk. But faith calls you out of the comfortable and into the calling. It reminds you that safety is not found in staying still - it is found in walking with God. Fear measures the unknown and hesitates. Faith measures God and moves. When you understand that God is certain, unchanging, and faithful, it changes how you respond to uncertainty. You no longer need guarantees from the future because you are anchored in the character of the One who holds it. So when fear says, "Stay where you are," faith rises and says, "Step out." Not recklessly but obediently. Not blindly but trustingly. Because when God is leading, every step forward is secure even when the path is not fully seen.

The battle against fear is won one decision at a time. Every choice matters. Every time you choose to act instead of retreat, to speak instead of stay silent, to trust instead of doubt, you take ground that fear once occupied. It may feel small in the moment, but those decisions are building something powerful within you. Fear loses strength each time it is challenged, and faith grows stronger each time it is exercised. Victory is forged in consistent obedience. And over time, what once controlled you will no longer have power over you. The things that used to intimidate you will no longer define your response. Why? Because you have trained your spirit to trust God more than your feelings. You have proven, step by step, that fear does not get the final say. What once held you back becomes the very ground you now stand on in confidence. Freedom is built decision by decision and step by step; by putting faith over fear until the man you once were is replaced by the man God is calling you to be.

God did not create you to live controlled by fear. He formed you with intention, called you with purpose, and equipped you with authority to stand firm in truth. Fear was never meant to govern your decisions or define your identity. You were designed to walk in confidence rooted in God, not in the shifting emotions of the moment. When you understand who you are in Him, fear loses its position of influence. You are not a man built to shrink back - you are a man called to rise, to stand, and to move forward with purpose. Fear may knock at the door, but it does not have the right to live in your house. You have the authority to decide what stays and what goes. When fear comes, you don't have to entertain it, agree with it, or give it space. You confront it with truth, you answer it with faith, and you shut the door on its lies. God has given you everything you need to stand your ground. So stand firm. Guard your heart. And refuse to give fear a place in a life that was meant to be led by faith.

So confront it. Challenge it. Refuse to bow to it. Fear may try to rise up and make itself look larger than it is, but it only has the power you give it. You were not created to live intimidated - you were created to stand firm. When fear speaks, answer it with truth. When it pushes, push back with faith. Let something rise up inside you that refuses to surrender ground God has already given you. This is not the moment to retreat - it is the moment to take a stand and move forward with boldness. Let faith rise up inside you, and step forward into everything God has called you to be. The path may feel uncertain, but God is not. The step may feel difficult, but it is necessary. Because on the other side of fear is the man you were meant to become - stronger, sharper, more grounded in truth than ever before. What stands in front of you is not there to stop you, but to shape you. So step forward. Trust deeper. And become the man fear tried to keep you from becoming.

| 18 |

"LEADING WITH STRENGTH"

Leadership is the quiet resolve to step forward when others step back, to speak truth when it would be easier to stay silent, and to stand firm when pressure demands compromise. Real leaders understand that going first often means going alone, and that responsibility is not something to be avoided, but something to be embraced. A man becomes a leader the moment he stops blaming and starts owning his choices, his failures, his calling, and his influence. He no longer looks outward for excuses but inward for strength. This is the turning point where boys make excuses, but men make impact. Leadership is not about control; it is about accountability. It is the willingness to carry the burden so others don't have to, to set the standard even when it costs something, and to walk the path of responsibility with unwavering resolve. That is the kind of leadership that shapes lives, builds legacies, and reflects the strength of a man who chooses to stand.

Before a man can guide others, he must first learn to govern himself. His thoughts must be brought into alignment with truth, his habits shaped by discipline, his words measured with wisdom, and his actions rooted in integrity. A man who refuses to confront himself will eventually mislead those entrusted to him. True leadership is built on consistency and character forged in private. What a man practices daily will ultimately define how he leads publicly. Strength is not proven by how many people a man can command, but by how well he can master his own spirit. It is easy to give orders; it is far harder to live them. A disciplined man becomes a trustworthy leader because his life speaks before his voice ever does. When he conquers pride, tempers his anger, guards his tongue, and walks in humility, he creates a foundation others can safely follow. The man who takes responsibility for himself first becomes the kind of leader who inspires others to rise up with faith and determination to fulfill God's plan for their lives.

Responsibility marks the end of casual living. No longer does a man drift through life chasing comfort but begins to live with intention, knowing that every decision carries consequence. His words shape atmospheres, his actions set direction, and his habits build either strength or weakness not only within himself, but in everyone connected to him. What he tolerates, others will normalize. What he pursues, others may follow. Responsibility, then, is a calling where your life is planting seeds in soil you may never fully see. A true leader understands that those seeds will bear fruit and chooses carefully with that future in mind. He disciplines his thoughts, guards his character, and walks with purpose because he knows others will one day eat from what he has sown. He doesn't choose what is easy, but what is right. And in doing so, he becomes a source of strength, stability, and life for those entrusted to him. Live in such a way that your life feeds others with courage, truth, and unwavering faith.

In God's kingdom, leadership is not about climbing higher - it is about bowing lower. A true leader does not seek to be served, but chooses to serve, even when it costs something. He understands that leadership is not a platform for self-glory, but a calling to reflect the heart of Christ who carried the weight of others, washed feet instead of demanding honor, and gave His life as the ultimate act of love. Kingdom leadership requires a man to take responsibility not only for his own life, but for the lives entrusted to him. He becomes a shield for the weak, a guide for the uncertain, and a steady hand in times of chaos. He does not run from burdens - he carries them. He does not shift blame - he owns it. And in doing so, he becomes a living example of God's strength expressed through humility. This is the leader who leaves a lasting impact not because he demanded respect, but because he earned it through faithful service, quiet strength, and a heart fully surrendered to God.

A strong leader does not run from pressure - he leans into it knowing that God often does His deepest work in the place of greatest tension. When situations grow difficult, he does not hide behind excuses or shift the blame; instead, he steps forward with courage, trusting that the same God who called him will also sustain him. He understands that leadership is not proven in comfort, but in the fire. Just as steel is refined under intense heat, so a man of God is strengthened when he chooses obedience over ease and faith over fear. Responsibility may feel heavy, but it is within that weight that true strength is formed. Pressure does not come to destroy a godly man - it comes to reveal what is within him. It exposes his character and deepens his dependence on God. Where others break, he stands. Where others retreat, he advances. He knows God does not place pressure on a man to crush him, but to shape him into a leader who reflects His power, His endurance, and His unwavering strength.

Leading your life begins with setting a standard that is rooted in truth, shaped by purpose, and upheld with consistency. You cannot drift and expect to arrive somewhere meaningful; drifting only leads to wasted time and missed calling. A man of God chooses direction before the day begins. He aligns his thoughts, his actions, and his priorities with something higher than comfort. Where there is no standard, there is no structure, and where there is no structure, there is no strength. A leader lives with intention. He wakes up with purpose, directs his energy wisely, and refuses to be ruled by distractions that pull him away from what matters most. He understands that greatness is built in quiet, consistent obedience. While others react, he responds with clarity. While others wander, he walks with focus. And over time, that intentional life produces something powerful - a life that is not just lived, but led, guided by conviction, anchored in purpose, and aligned with the will of God.

Leading your home is one of the greatest callings a man can have, and it is a responsibility that reaches far beyond providing or protecting - it is about setting direction. A godly man seeks God first, then leads his family with a steady hand and a clear vision. In a world full of noise and confusion, he becomes a voice of wisdom and consistency. His decisions are rooted in truth, not emotion, and his life reflects the path he desires his family to follow. A strong leader creates an atmosphere where peace can live and growth can flourish. His presence brings stability because his heart is anchored in God. When challenges arise, he responds with strength and clarity. He builds up his wife, encourages his children, and cultivates an environment where love, discipline, and faith work together. In every moment, he understands that his influence is shaping lives. So he chooses to lead with intention, knowing that the home he builds today becomes the legacy that speaks long after he is gone.

Your family is not primarily shaped by your words - they are formed by your example. You can speak truth, quote scripture, and give instruction all day long, but if your life tells a different story, your influence begins to erode. Your children, your spouse, and those closest to you are watching how you respond under pressure and how faithfully you live what you claim to believe. What you model becomes the standard they internalize. True leadership begins in the unseen moments, where integrity is forged and consistency is proven. It is lived out in daily choices and steady obedience to what is right. You don't have to be perfect, but you must be genuine because authenticity builds trust, and trust builds influence. When your life consistently reflects truth, your example becomes a living sermon your family cannot ignore. Over time, your actions will echo louder than anything you could ever say. Lead with your life first and let your words simply confirm what they already see.

A strong leader understands that everything entrusted to him is both a gift and a responsibility. His home, his relationships, and his integrity are guarded with intention. He watches what enters his life and is mindful of the influences that shape his family, the tone he sets in his relationships, and the standards he upholds in private. Because he knows that small compromises today can become great losses tomorrow, he chooses vigilance over passivity. Protection is an active, courageous calling. It requires the strength to confront what is wrong, the wisdom to discern what is harmful, and the discipline to remain consistent when it would be easier to relax. A true leader creates an environment where truth, safety, and growth can flourish because he is willing to fight for what matters most. In doing so, he becomes a man whose presence brings security, whose actions inspire trust, and whose leadership preserves what God has placed in his care.

Leadership is not only measured by strength, but by the humility that governs it. Strength without humility hardens into pride, and pride quietly paves the road to destruction. A true leader understands that no matter how far he has come, there is always more to learn and room to grow. He does not elevate himself above correction but welcomes it as a tool that sharpens his character. He listens carefully, receives wisdom, and allows truth to shape his decisions. Because he is grounded in humility, his strength becomes steady, not reckless; firm yet guided by wisdom. A teachable leader carries a quiet confidence that does not need to prove itself. He is strong enough to admit when he is wrong and courageous enough to make it right. Instead of defending his pride, he chooses growth. Instead of resisting change, he embraces it when it leads him closer to truth. This kind of humility builds trust, because those around him see a man who is real, accountable, and willing to be refined.

There will be seasons when the weight of responsibility sets you apart and the path ahead is yours to walk alone. Not everyone will understand your decisions, and not everyone will agree with the direction you choose. But leadership was never meant to be a popularity contest; it is a calling to faithfulness. A man of God does not measure his steps by applause, but by obedience. When the noise of opinions rises and affirmation is absent, he anchors himself in truth and continues forward, knowing that doing what is right often requires standing apart. In those quiet, unseen moments, his character is revealed and his resolve is strengthened. He learns to lead without needing approval, to stand firm without constant encouragement, and to trust God even when the path feels uncertain. Loneliness does not weaken him - it refines him. It strips away the need for validation and replaces it with a deeper dependence on purpose. And in time, that unwavering faithfulness becomes the very thing that guides others.

Influence is never established by force - it is cultivated through the quiet power of example. You can demand attention, but you cannot demand respect; that must be earned over time. People are drawn to what is real, steady, and trustworthy. They watch how you live far more than they listen to what you say. When your life consistently reflects truth - when your actions align with your convictions - your influence begins to grow without striving. Integrity becomes your voice, consistency becomes your platform, and authenticity becomes the bridge that connects your life to others. A leader who walks in truth does not need to chase recognition or assert authority. His character speaks before he ever opens his mouth. There is a weight to a life lived with integrity that commands respect naturally, not forcefully. Others begin to follow not because they are pressured, but because they are inspired. This kind of influence is lasting, because it is rooted in who you are, not just what you do.

The strongest leaders do not need to raise their voices to prove their authority - they let their lives speak for them. They lead quietly, but their impact is unmistakable. Their consistency builds a foundation of trust that others can stand on. Day after day they show up with integrity, discipline, and clarity. Because they are not driven by recognition, their leadership carries a deeper weight. People feel it in the way they respond, the way they serve, and the way they remain anchored in truth. Their actions become a steady message that speaks louder than any announcement ever could. In moments of chaos, they become the calm others look toward. In seasons of uncertainty, they stand firm and provide direction. Their presence brings confidence because it is rooted in stability, not emotion. This kind of leadership is not loud, but it is powerful because it is built on consistency, proven over time, and grounded in a character that does not change when circumstances do.

Every decision you make, every standard you uphold, and every act of integrity you choose is planting something in the lives around you. You may not see the growth right away, and you may never witness the full harvest but that does not make the seed any less powerful. The way you live today will echo into tomorrow through the people you've impacted, the values you've modeled, and the truth you've embodied. A leader understands that influence is not always immediate, but it is always meaningful. Because of this, he plants faithfully, even when recognition is absent and results are unseen. He does not need applause to stay committed, because he knows the seeds he sows may rise in another generation, in another season, in ways he may never fully know. Yet he plants with purpose, trusting that what is done with integrity will bear fruit in its time. This is the legacy of a true leader - not what he gains in the present, but what continues to grow long after he is gone.

A man who leads with true strength is anchored in something far greater than himself. His confidence is not built on ego, talent, or personal ability, but on his connection to God. Because of this, his strength is steady and not easily shaken. When challenges arise, he does not panic or strive in his own power; he turns to the One who sustains him. He understands that human strength has limits, but God's strength does not. This anchoring gives him clarity in confusion, peace in pressure, and courage when the path ahead feels uncertain. In every trial, he draws from that deeper source, allowing God to guide his steps and fortify his spirit. While others may falter under the weight of adversity, he stands firm because he is not standing alone. His leadership becomes a reflection of the strength he receives, not the strength he tries to manufacture. And over time, it becomes evident that what sustains him is not his own power, but the unshakable foundation of God working within him.

Leadership is not forged in moments of excitement, but in the quiet, demanding seasons of endurance. It is built in the daily decision to show up, to stand firm, and to choose what is right again and again, especially when no one is watching. Anyone can rise in a moment of inspiration, but it takes a committed leader to remain steady when the emotions fade and the work becomes routine. True leadership is formed in consistency, where discipline replaces impulse and faithfulness outlasts feeling. Endurance is what separates those who start from those who finish. It is the strength to keep going when progress feels slow, when challenges persist, and when the reward is not immediate. A faithful leader does not drift with circumstances - he anchors himself in purpose and presses forward. Over time, those repeated, steady choices shape his character and solidify his influence. Because in the end, leadership is not proven by how powerfully you begin, but by how faithfully you continue.

There will be moments when the weight of responsibility presses in and you question whether you are enough. Leadership has a way of exposing your limits, reminding you that you don't have all the answers and cannot control every outcome. But that is part of the design. Leadership was never meant to rest on your perfection, but on your willingness to step forward anyway, even when you feel unqualified. God does not call perfect men - He calls willing ones. He looks for those who will stand in the gap, who will show up, who will say yes when it would be easier to step back. In your weakness, His strength is revealed; in your uncertainty, His guidance becomes clear. When you choose to stand, even while feeling inadequate, you make room for God to work through you in ways you never could on your own. And over time, you begin to realize that leadership is not about being enough by yourself - it is about trusting the One who is more than enough.

So step up. Take responsibility for the life you've been given and refuse to drift through it without purpose. Lead your home with strength, not through control, but through consistency, integrity, and love that is backed by action. Let your example speak in the quiet moments, in the way you show up, in the standards you refuse to compromise. Because real leadership is not announced - it is demonstrated, day after day, choice after choice. The world does not need more passive men standing on the sidelines - it needs men who will rise, stand firm, and lead with unwavering strength. Men who are not shaken by pressure, not swayed by culture, and not silenced by fear. When you choose to lead this way, you become a pillar others can lean on and a light others can follow. Your life begins to carry weight, not because of what you say, but because of who you are. So rise up, stand your ground, and lead because the impact of your strength will reach farther than you can see.

| 19 |

"EMBRACING RESPONSIBILITY"

Responsibility is not the enemy of a man - it is the instrument God uses to shape him. It presses, it stretches, it exposes what is truly inside. When a man stops running from responsibility and begins to embrace it, his character rises to meet the challenge. Boys make excuses, but men make decisions. Responsibility doesn't crush a man of God - it reveals his strength, his discipline, and his willingness to stand when others step back. It is in carrying what is hard that a man discovers who he really is. While others avoid responsibility, he shoulders it with purpose, knowing that God entrusted it to him for a reason. Responsibility becomes his proving ground, where faith turns into action and conviction becomes consistency. He leads when it's inconvenient, serves when it's unnoticed, and remains steady when it's difficult. The weight he carries today is shaping the man he is becoming tomorrow. And when he runs toward responsibility instead of away from it, he steps into the life God designed him to live.

Too many men today are trained to run from the very thing that would shape them. Responsibility is treated like a burden to escape instead of a calling to embrace. The world teaches men to shift blame, to justify weakness, to choose comfort over conviction but that path leads nowhere. It produces men who are restless, unfulfilled, and easily shaken. A man was not created to hide from weight; he was built to carry it. Responsibility is not what breaks you - it is what builds you.

It forges your character, sharpens your resolve, and anchors your life in purpose. Every time you choose to stand up instead of back down, to own instead of excuse, you are stepping into the man God designed you to be. Responsibility is your assignment. It is the ground where your faith becomes action and your calling becomes visible. How you carry it matters. You can drag it with resentment, or you can shoulder it with strength. You can avoid it and remain stagnant, or you can embrace it and grow into something unshakable.

A man who refuses responsibility will always live beneath what he was created to become. He may carry strength in his body, but without responsibility, that strength has no aim. He may feel passion in his heart, but without responsibility, that passion burns without building anything lasting. Responsibility is the weight that gives meaning to a man's power. It takes raw ability and turns it into direction, discipline, and impact. It calls him to rise above comfort, to think beyond himself, and to invest his life into something greater than temporary desire. Responsibility is not a burden to avoid; it is a calling to embrace. It is the very thing God uses to shape a man into someone who can be trusted with influence, with leadership, with legacy. When a man accepts responsibility, he stops making excuses and starts making progress. He begins to build, to protect, and to provide not just for himself, but for others. When he embraces responsibility, his life gains clarity and his existence begins to echo beyond his own lifetime.

God never designed man to drift through life half-awake, carried by comfort and controlled by convenience. He placed man in the garden to tend what was given, to guard what was sacred, to lead with strength, and to build what would outlast him. There was nothing passive about that assignment. It required awareness, effort, courage, and intentionality. And that same design still echoes in you today. You were not created to sit on the sidelines of your own life, but to step forward, take ground, and bring order, strength, and purpose into the spaces God has entrusted to you. Responsibility is woven into your identity. It is calling you to rise, to act, and to carry what others may avoid. When a man rejects responsibility, he disconnects from purpose. But when he embraces it, he steps into alignment with how he was created to live. Strength awakens. Clarity sharpens. Purpose deepens. So stand firm because in accepting responsibility, you are becoming the man God designed you to be.

Embracing responsibility means stepping into the hard places when others step back. It's the moment where excuses fall silent and conviction speaks louder than comfort. It's choosing to stand when it would be easier to sit, to act when others hesitate, to move forward when fear tells you to wait. A man who embraces responsibility understands that a man's calling often hides in difficulty, and that the weight others avoid is often the very ground where purpose is revealed. It means refusing to let fear, inconvenience, or discomfort dictate your actions. A man anchored in God steps into chaos to bring order, into weakness to bring strength, into uncertainty to bring faith. And while the path may be costly, it is never empty because God meets him in the very places he chooses to stand. That is where courage is formed and your legacy is built. So step forward because when you embrace responsibility, you are walking in the authority and purpose God placed inside you from the very beginning.

Responsibility will cost you. It will demand your time when you'd rather rest, your energy when you feel drained, your comfort when you'd prefer ease, and sometimes even your reputation when standing right is misunderstood. It will call you into places where sacrifice is required and applause is absent. But this is where true men are formed. Every time you embrace responsibility, you are saying yes to growth, yes to purpose, and yes to the calling God has placed on your life. Yet what it gives in return far outweighs what it takes. Responsibility builds strength that cannot be shaken, character that cannot be faked, and a legacy that cannot be erased. It shapes you into someone others can depend on, someone God can trust with more. The weight you carry today becomes the foundation you stand on tomorrow. Don't measure responsibility by what it costs - measure it by who it makes you. Because in the end, the man who embraces responsibility leaves a mark that outlives it.

The weight of responsibility is what strengthens your spiritual backbone. Just as resistance forms muscle through strain and repetition, responsibility forms endurance through pressure and persistence. Every obligation you carry with faith, every burden you refuse to drop, every moment you choose to stand instead of retreat is shaping something deeper within you. God uses the weight to steady you, to make you firm when everything around you is shifting. What feels heavy in the moment is actually producing strength that cannot be easily shaken. Without responsibility, a man grows soft. He'll be easily moved, easily discouraged, easily defeated. But with it, his spirit becomes resilient, grounded, and unyielding. He is no longer tossed by fear or controlled by comfort because he has been trained under pressure. The weight that once felt overwhelming becomes the very thing that stabilizes him. He learns to carry it with confidence, knowing it is forging endurance that will outlast every storm.

A man's role is not just to exist in the present, but to shape the future. Every decision he makes carries weight beyond today, and every responsibility he accepts becomes a seed planted into tomorrow. God has given him influence over the lives he touches, the environments he shapes, and the legacy he leaves behind. The present is the ground where future outcomes are being formed. Every choice is a seed, and seeds always produce. What you plant in discipline will grow into strength. What you plant in faith will grow into stability. What you plant in courage will grow into impact. But what you neglect will also grow - missed opportunities, weakened character, and a future left to chance. A man who understands this lives with awareness and purpose. He doesn't avoid responsibility; he embraces it, knowing that today's obedience becomes tomorrow's harvest. So plant wisely, act boldly, and lead intentionally because the future is not something you stumble into, it is something you build.

You are not just living for yourself. Your life is a bridge; a pathway others will walk because of the choices you make today. Your family, your community, and those who will come after you are all touched by the standards you set. Every act of faith, every moment of discipline, every responsibility you refuse to drop is building something beyond your own lifetime. God designed your life to leave behind strength where there was weakness, clarity where there was confusion, and direction where there was none. What you do today is shaping the world someone else will step into tomorrow. The future is being formed right now by what you choose to carry today. If you carry responsibility, you create stability. If you carry integrity, you create trust. If you carry courage, you create momentum for others to rise. That is why your choices matter so deeply. You are not just managing your life; you are building a legacy. So stand firm, carry what God has placed in your hands, and refuse to live small.

Responsibility requires vision. It calls you to look beyond what is immediate and see what is eternal, to understand that every choice carries consequences far beyond the present moment. A man with vision weighs his decisions not by how they feel now, but by what they will produce later. He sees the future of his family, the direction of his life, the legacy he is building and that vision gives meaning to the weight he carries. Without vision, responsibility feels like a burden. But with vision, it becomes a mission. A man with vision carries the weight with purpose, knowing that what he holds today is shaping what will stand tomorrow. Vision gives endurance to his steps and strength to his spirit. It reminds him that the pressure is not pointless - it is productive. So lift your eyes. See beyond the moment. Let God sharpen your vision so that you can carry what is hard with conviction. Because when you know where you're going, you won't let go of what's necessary to get there.

There will always be things others won't carry - hard conversations that must be spoken, difficult decisions that cannot be avoided, and sacrifices that go unnoticed by everyone but God. When others step back, a man of God steps forward. He doesn't wait for recognition or applause; he moves because it is right. He understands that leadership is often lonely and that obedience is often quiet. The weight may not be visible, but it is real and it is in these unseen battles that strength is forged and character is proven. This is where true manhood is revealed - not when life is smooth, but when it is stretching and demanding more than you feel ready to give. A man becomes who he is in the moments he chooses to stay, to stand, and to carry what others refuse. He endures not because it is easy, but because it is necessary. So lean into the hard places. Say what needs to be said. Do what needs to be done. Because the weight others avoid is often the very place where God forms the strength that defines you.

Carrying what others won't is about purpose. It's not about proving your strength, but about fulfilling your calling. A man who embraces responsibility does it because something in him knows it must be done. He holds the line when others retreat. He understands that God often entrusts the hardest assignments to those willing to be faithful. In those moments, he becomes someone who stands firm when everything else is shifting. It's about becoming dependable in a world full of excuses. When others justify stepping back, he steps forward. When others look for a way out, he becomes the way through. His consistency becomes his credibility, and his faithfulness becomes his strength. Over time, people begin to lean on him not because he is perfect, but because he is present, willing, and steady. And that kind of man doesn't just carry weight - he carries influence. So stand in the gap. Hold the line. Be the one who can be counted on. Because purpose is often found in the places where others choose not to go.

God is not searching for perfection, but for willingness, for hearts that will step forward when others step back, and say, "I'll carry it," even when the cost is unknown. The weight will test you, stretch you, and press you beyond your comfort, but it will also position you to experience God's strength in ways you never could in ease. What feels heavy in your hands is often exactly what God is using to shape you into who you were meant to become. Men who refuse to shrink back learn to lean in, trusting that God does not assign what He will not sustain. When the burden feels beyond you, that is where His power meets your obedience. He supplies strength for the weary, endurance for the strained, and courage for the uncertain. But it is found in the carrying, not the avoiding. So stand when it would be easier to step away. Trust when it would be easier to doubt. Because on the other side of that weight is a man refined by fire, strengthened by faith, and anchored in a trust that cannot be shaken.

Responsibility is not meant to be carried alone. A wise man leans on God in prayer, draws strength from His Word, and anchors his spirit in truth when the weight feels heavy. He knows that his own strength has limits, but God's does not. So instead of striving alone, he stays connected to the One who renews him, guides him, and sustains him. In that connection, he finds clarity for decisions, endurance for challenges, and peace in the midst of pressure. He also surrounds himself with other strong men who sharpen him. Even the strongest men need support - they need voices that challenge them, encourage them, and call them higher. There is strength in unity and wisdom in shared burdens. A man who walks with the right people becomes stronger, steadier, and more refined. So don't carry it alone. Stay rooted in God, stay connected to others, and keep moving forward together because the weight may be great, but it was never meant to be carried by yourself.

Still, the decision to carry it is yours alone. No one can step into that moment for you, no one can choose obedience on your behalf. There comes a point where the excuses fall silent and the question becomes personal. Will you pick it up, or will you walk away? God may call, truth may be clear, and the need may be evident, but the response is yours to give. And in that moment, everything is revealed because calling is not proven by what you feel, but by what you choose. Every man faces that crossroads, where the weight is real and the cost is undeniable. To walk away may feel easier in the moment, but it leaves something unfinished within you. To pick it up requires courage, but it awakens purpose, strength, and direction. The decision you make in that moment will shape who you become. So choose to carry it. Choose to stand. Choose to answer the call, even when it stretches you. Because the man you are meant to become is found on the other side of that decision.

When you choose to embrace responsibility, you stop drifting through your days reacting to whatever comes your way. Your decisions become deliberate, your actions purposeful, and your mindset is anchored in something greater than convenience. You start to see life as opportunities to lead, to build, and to grow. What once felt overwhelming begins to feel meaningful because now you walk with purpose, clarity, and conviction. Purpose directs your steps, clarity sharpens your vision, and conviction steadies your resolve when pressure rises. You are no longer controlled by emotions or circumstances but guided by truth and commitment. There is a quiet strength that forms within you - a confidence that is rooted deep. And as you continue to carry what God has placed in your hands, you become a man who is not easily shaken, not easily distracted, and not easily turned aside. You become intentional in how you live, and that intentionality becomes the foundation of a life that truly matters.

And though the weight may feel heavy at times, it is producing something eternal within you. What feels like pressure is shaping your spirit in ways comfort never could. God is using the very things that stretch you to strengthen you, the very burdens that test you to transform you. Every moment of endurance, every act of faith under pressure, is building something lasting, something unshakable, something that reaches beyond this life. It is shaping you into a man of strength, honor, and faith - one who can be trusted with more. Trust is forged through consistency, proven through perseverance, and established through obedience. As you carry the weight faithfully, you are becoming dependable in the eyes of God - ready for greater responsibility, greater influence, and greater impact. So don't despise the weight. Embrace it. Because what it is producing in you will one day reveal a man refined, strengthened, and ready for whatever God places in his hands next.

So embrace responsibility. Do not run from it but receive it as part of your calling. Pick it up with intention, carry it with faith, and refuse to let it fall when it becomes inconvenient or uncomfortable. The weight you carry is shaping your discipline, sharpening your focus, and strengthening your resolve. Every step you take under that weight is forging something within you that ease could never produce. This is where transformation happens - not in avoiding the load, but in carrying it well. Because in the end, the weight of responsibility is not what breaks a man - it is what builds him. It builds endurance when you feel like quitting, character when no one is watching, and faith when the outcome is uncertain. The man who embraces the weight becomes steady, dependable, and unshakable because he has been strengthened by what he carries. So stand firm, keep moving forward, and let the weight do its work. Because on the other side of it is the man God created you to be - refined, resilient, and ready.

| 20 |

"THE LION AND INTEGRITY"

There is a kind of man who lives like a lion. He is unshaken when others tremble, unmoved when culture shifts, and unafraid when pressure rises. His strength is not built on noise, image, or approval, but on something far deeper and far more enduring. In a world that rewards appearance over substance, he chooses substance every time. He stands firm because his foundation is forged within, in quiet moments of surrender, conviction, and obedience to God. Integrity is the hidden architecture of his soul - the unseen backbone that holds everything together. It is who he is when the spotlight fades, when the crowd disappears, and when no one is watching. This kind of man cannot be easily shaken, because his life is built on consistency between his private and public world. And though the world may never fully see it, heaven does. For it is in the quiet places, the secret choices, and the unseen battles that true strength is revealed and that is where lions are made.

The lion does not wait for a crowd before it becomes what it was created to be. It does not scan the horizon for applause before it releases its roar. It roars because that power is woven into its very nature. In the same way, a man of integrity does not adjust his character based on who is watching. He does not perform righteousness for recognition or bend under the pressure of hidden moments. What he is in the dark is who he is in the light, because his convictions are anchored in truth. This kind of man stands firm and chooses what is right not because it is easy, but because it is who he is. His character does not shift with convenience or crumble under pressure. It is built deep beneath the surface where no eye can see but God's. And from that unseen place flows a life of consistency, strength, and quiet authority. Like the lion, he does not need validation to walk in power. His life speaks for itself, and his integrity becomes a roar that echoes far beyond the moments when anyone is watching.

Character is built in the quiet decisions no one else sees, in the thoughts you entertain when your mind is unguarded, and in the moments where compromise doesn't shout but whispers. The hidden places are where integrity is either strengthened or slowly eroded. When there is no audience to impress and no consequence to fear, your choices uncover the truth of who you are. A man of God understands that heaven sees what the world does not, and he chooses righteousness not for recognition, but because it is right. What you do in secret is the clearest reflection of your true self. Private discipline produces public strength, and unseen obedience lays the foundation for lasting impact. The man who wins in the hidden places will stand unshaken in the open ones. So guard your heart, govern your thoughts, and honor God when no one is watching. Because long before your life is displayed before others, it is already fully known by Him.

Too many men stand tall in public but in the quiet places, where no applause exists and no eyes are watching, they compromise what they claim to be. True strength is not proven on stages but in shadows. It is forged in the unseen moments where choices are made without recognition. God is not impressed by the reputation a man builds before others; He looks at the character a man maintains when he is alone. What you are in the dark will eventually define who you are in the light. Integrity refuses to wear two faces. It calls a man to live with unwavering consistency - to be the same in private as he is in public. Like a lion that does not lose its nature when it steps into the shadows, a man of integrity remains grounded, disciplined, and true because his identity is built on conviction. This kind of man walks with quiet authority, knowing that his strength is rooted in truth, not performance. And when the light shines, he does not need to pretend because he has already proven himself where it matters most.

Integrity is not something you reach for when it's easy - it is something you cling to when it costs you. It is forged in the quiet places where no one is watching, in the unseen decisions that shape who you truly are. It is the steady anchor of a man's soul, refusing to drift with the current of compromise. Even when standing alone, he stands strong because he knows that the approval of God outweighs the applause of men. A man of integrity draws a line deep within his soul and lives by it without negotiation. He has already settled the matter before temptation arrives - there is no debate, no hesitation, no bending. "This far and no further" is more than a statement - it is a standard, a line you refuse to cross. It is the quiet strength that says no when everything around him says yes. And though the path may be lonely at times, it is never empty for God walks with the man who refuses to bow. In the end, integrity builds a life that cannot be shaken, because it is rooted not in convenience, but in unyielding conviction.

There will always be opportunities to compromise. A small decision here, a subtle shortcut there, a tiny concession that no one else will ever see. But a man of God understands that character is forged in the unseen moments. Every private choice is a brick in the foundation of his life. When he chooses integrity in the quiet places, he strengthens what cannot be shaken. But when he allows even the smallest cracks, he invites weakness into the very structure meant to sustain him. What begins as a whisper of compromise can grow into a collapse of character if left unchecked. The enemy never needs a dramatic fall - he only needs a series of small agreements. That is why a strong man guards his heart with vigilance. He does not negotiate with compromise; he confronts it. He chooses conviction over comfort and obedience over approval. He knows a life built on integrity will stand when the storms come. And while compromise may offer momentary relief, only righteousness provides lasting strength.

The lion stands in its authority, unmoved and unshaken. In the same way, a man of integrity does not sit at the table with compromise hoping to manage it. He recognizes it for what it is: a quiet thief that erodes strength, dulls conviction, and slowly robs him of who God called him to be. He does not entertain it in private, excuse it in small doses, or justify it in difficult moments. Instead, he confronts it immediately, knowing that what is tolerated today will rule tomorrow. A man of integrity sets a boundary at the door of his life and stands guard with unwavering resolve. He understands that compromise rarely storms in - it whispers, it suggests, it negotiates. But he does not negotiate. He shuts it down before it takes root, before it gains a foothold, before it becomes a habit. Like a lion protecting its territory, he defends his character with strength and clarity. He chooses truth when it costs, righteousness when it's difficult, and obedience when it's inconvenient.

Integrity is not cheap. It may cost you the deal everyone else is willing to compromise for, the relationship that thrives on dishonesty, or the promotion that demands silence when you should speak truth. There will be moments when standing upright feels like standing alone, when others misunderstand your restraint or even resist your convictions. But integrity is not about winning approval; it is about honoring what is right before God. What you refuse to sacrifice defines who you truly are. Guard your inner life with fierce devotion, because what is preserved within you becomes the foundation for everything you build around you. A man can gain influence, success, and recognition but without integrity, he cannot sustain any of it. When storms come - and they will - it is not talent, charisma, or opportunity that keeps you standing, but the strength of what you protected in private.

Integrity may cost you now, but it will pay you back with a life that does not collapse under pressure.

There is a strength that rises from a life kept clean before God. It is the quiet confidence of a heart that is not divided, a spirit that is not weighed down by hidden compromise. When you walk in truth, boldness becomes natural. Your steps are steady because your conscience is clear. You don't have to manipulate outcomes or defend appearances, because you are anchored in something deeper than approval. This kind of strength carries the weight of heaven's approval rather than the applause of men. When your life is aligned with truth, your words carry conviction because they come from integrity. Your presence holds authority because it is rooted in honesty. There is a freedom in having nothing to hide - a release from the exhausting burden of maintaining a false image. This is the strength of a man who walks in the light, who answers to God before he answers to anyone else. And in that place, he becomes unshakable not because he is perfect, but because he is real and firmly grounded in truth.

A lion walks with confidence because its identity is settled. It knows what it was made to be. In the same way, a man anchored in integrity is not tossed by every voice or threatened by every challenge. His strength comes from alignment with truth, not from the absence of opposition. When your life is built on what is right before God, you don't need to prove yourself to others or bend under pressure. You move with a steady assurance, grounded in who you are. Integrity becomes the root system that holds you firm when winds rise. Opinions may shift, pressures may mount, and fears may try to creep in, but a man who lives truthfully is not easily shaken. He is steady because his foundation is unmovable. There is a quiet authority in that kind of life - a calm strength that doesn't panic or perform. Like a lion, he does not need to roar to be powerful; his presence speaks for itself. And when trials come, he stands not because he is untouched by them, but because he is anchored in something deeper than them.

Integrity is forged in the quiet, unseen choices of everyday life. It is built when you choose truth over convenience, obedience over comfort, and conviction over compromise. No one decision seems monumental on its own, but together they shape the core of who you become. Each time you do what is right when it would be easier not to, you are laying another brick in the foundation of your character. Over time, those small acts of faithfulness form a life that is solid, dependable, and unshakable. Every refusal to compromise strengthens you more than you realize. Each act of obedience reinforces the inner structure that will one day carry the weight of greater responsibility, greater influence, and greater testing. What is developed in private will be revealed in public. When pressure comes you will stand on what you have already built. Integrity is a slow, steady work, but it produces a strength that cannot be quickly broken - a life anchored in truth, able to endure whatever comes.

The world often applauds the quick win, the clever shortcut, the path that gets results without regard for the cost. But God is not impressed by speed - He is moved by faithfulness. He sees what others overlook, the quiet decisions made in private, the moments when no one is watching and no reward is guaranteed. And in those hidden places, God is at work shaping something far more valuable than temporary success: a life that reflects His character. There is a strength God builds in the man who refuses to cut corners, who stays true when compromise would be easier and more accepted. It is a deep, enduring strength that cannot be manufactured or taken away, because it is formed in partnership with Him. While others may rise quickly and fall just as fast, the man of integrity is being established on a foundation that will last. In time, what God builds in secret will stand in the open, firm and unshaken. Faithfulness may seem slow, but it produces a life that carries weight, authority, and lasting impact.

Living above compromise starts with decisions made in advance. A man of integrity does not wait until temptation arrives to figure out what he believes; he settles it beforehand. He defines his standards in the quiet place, where conviction is formed without distraction. If your values are unclear in private, they will collapse under pressure in public. But when they are established ahead of time, they become a shield that guards your steps and steadies your choices. There is strength in pre-decided obedience. It removes hesitation, silences inner debate, and anchors you when emotions try to lead you astray. A man who has already drawn the line does not waver when it is tested. Not because it is easy, but because it is settled. Integrity is not reactive; it is intentional. It is built on a firm resolve that says, "This is who I am before God," regardless of the circumstance. And that kind of man carries a quiet authority, because his life is not shaped by the moment, but by the truth he chose long before the moment arrived.

There is no such thing as harmless compromise. What seems small in the moment carries weight in the shaping of your soul. Every decision leaves a mark, either reinforcing your integrity or quietly eroding it. The choices you make when it feels insignificant are the very ones that determine your direction. With every thought you entertain, every action you take, and every line you choose to cross or refuse, you are forming the man you will be tomorrow. So the question is not just what you are doing but who you are becoming. Are your choices building strength, or creating cracks beneath the surface? Are you becoming a man who can be trusted, who stands firm, who walks clean before God? Or are you slowly trading away your foundation for temporary ease? The weight of your life is not carried in one defining moment, but in the accumulation of daily decisions. Choose well because over time those choices will either shape a man of unshakable character or one who cannot stand when it matters most.

The lion does not follow the herd or reshape its nature to be accepted - it walks with a confidence rooted in identity. In the same way, a man of integrity is not driven by the need to fit in, but by the call to stand right before God. He understands that truth will often place him on a different path, one that may be lonelier but is far stronger. He is not swayed by the crowd because he is anchored in something greater than the crowd. Integrity will often require separation. It will call you to distance yourself from corrupt environments and to silence voices that try to pull you into compromise. Why? Because what surrounds you will shape you, and what you tolerate will eventually define you. A man who chooses integrity is willing to walk alone if necessary, knowing that it is better to stand apart in truth than to blend in with what is wrong. And in that separation, he discovers a deeper strength - a life that is not diluted, but refined, and a path that leads not just to acceptance, but to lasting impact.

You were not created to blend in with compromise or lower your standards to match a drifting world. You were designed to stand out - to live with conviction, to walk in truth, and to reflect a life that is set apart. Righteousness is a deliberate choice to live differently, to speak differently, and to carry yourself with purpose. When your life is rooted in truth, you become a visible contrast to the world around you, a light that cannot be hidden, a standard that does not shift with culture. To live this way requires courage. It means choosing conviction over comfort, truth over popularity, and obedience over ease. But this is where real strength is found - not in blending in, but in standing firm. You were created to reflect something higher, something eternal. A man who walks in righteousness carries a quiet authority, because his life points beyond himself. And though the world may not always understand him, it cannot ignore the impact of a life lived with unwavering integrity and unshakable truth.

When you live with integrity, you are building a legacy. Every honest decision, every act of obedience, every stand you take for what is right becomes part of a foundation that will outlive you. Your children will learn not just from what you say, but from how you live. Your family will be strengthened by the example you set. And those who come after you will stand on ground that was made firm because you chose truth over compromise. Integrity becomes a testimony that continues to speak long after you are gone. What you protect in your life today becomes a covering for those connected to you tomorrow. A man who walks upright before God creates stability, direction, and strength for others to follow. He breaks cycles of compromise and establishes patterns of righteousness that can be carried forward. You may not always see the full impact of your choices, but heaven does and time will reveal it. A life built on integrity leaves behind a legacy of strength, faithfulness, and unwavering truth.

Rise like the lion and be steady, aware, and unafraid. Guard your heart with vigilance, because it is the wellspring of everything you become. Strengthen your character in the unseen places, where real battles are won long before they are ever visible. Refuse compromise at every level, not just in the obvious moments, but in the subtle ones where it tries to quietly take root. Let your private life match your public life, so that who you are alone is the same man others see. When integrity defines you, it becomes an unshakable force that carries you through every season. There is power in that kind of life, a quiet authority that does not need to announce itself. It stands firm when tested, remains steady under pressure, and endures when others fall away. This is the life you were called to live - not a compromised version shaped by the world, but a resolute, unwavering life built on righteousness. Stand firm and let integrity be the mark that defines you.

| 21 |

"THE FIGHT FOR PURITY"

Every day presents a battlefield where thoughts must be filtered, desires must be disciplined, and boundaries must be reinforced. What you allow into your eyes and ears will eventually take root in your heart, so the fight begins at the gates. A man of purity understands that unchecked thoughts become actions, and repeated actions become chains. So he fights early. He fights consistently. And he fights with conviction, knowing that what he protects today shapes who he becomes tomorrow. It takes strength to turn away, courage to stand alone, and discipline to stay clean when no one else is watching. But this fight is not fought in your own strength; it is won through surrender to God, through renewing your mind, and through staying anchored in truth. The man who commits to purity is sharpening his spirit, strengthening his character, and aligning his life with a higher calling. Purity is not passive - it is a relentless pursuit of what is right, even when everything around you pulls in the opposite direction.

Your heart is not meant to be a dumping ground for whatever the world throws your way. It is a gate, a place of discernment and authority. What you allow through that gate will take root, grow, and eventually bear fruit in your life. Every thought entertained becomes a seed. Given time, those seeds form desires, and those desires move your hands, your words, and your direction. If you entertain compromise, you will eventually walk in it. But if you guard your heart with truth, discipline, and reverence for God, your life will reflect strength, clarity, and conviction. You are a gatekeeper. If you do not choose what enters, the world will choose for you. Guard your heart with intention. Reject what weakens you. Refuse what defiles you. Fill your mind with what is true, honorable, and pure. Because what flows out of your life tomorrow is being decided by what you allow in today. A guarded heart is not a restricted life - it is a powerful one, aligned with God and unshaken by the chaos around it.

Purity begins within the quiet, unseen realm of your thoughts. Before any action is ever taken, a decision has already been made in the mind. What you repeatedly allow to linger in your thoughts will eventually shape your desires, and your desires will direct your steps. A man does not suddenly fall - he drifts there, one tolerated thought at a time. But in the same way, a man does not suddenly become strong - he builds strength by rejecting what is impure the moment it appears and choosing what is right before it takes root. Victory, then, begins with guarding the gateway of your mind. You must become disciplined in what you dwell on, quick to cast down what does not belong, and intentional about filling your thoughts with truth. Purity is not passive - it is a daily act of resistance and renewal. When you win the battle in your mind, you position yourself to walk in strength outwardly. Guard your thoughts, and you guard your life. What you dwell on today will determine who you become tomorrow.

You cannot stop every thought from entering your mind. Temptation may knock loudly, persistently, even convincingly, but you are not obligated to open the door. A man of strength filters every thought the standard of God's Word. What you entertain, you empower. What you dwell on, you become. So stand watch over your inner life with vigilance, because the battle is often won or lost in silence, long before it is ever seen in action. Discipline is the quiet decision to choose truth over impulse, especially when no one is watching. Anyone can appear strong in public, but true strength is revealed in private moments when compromise is easy and no one would know. This is where real men are made. Every time you deny the wrong thought a place to settle, you strengthen your spirit. Every time you choose truth, you sharpen your edge. And over time, those small, unseen victories build a life that stands unshaken, pure, and powerful before God.

Guarding your mind is a deliberate, daily decision. You must choose what deserves access to your thoughts, your eyes, and your attention. Every image, every word, every moment you linger on is either building you up or tearing you down. The world does not filter itself for your holiness, so you must become the gatekeeper of your own soul. What you allow in will eventually take root, and what takes root will shape your desires, your convictions, and ultimately your life. If you continually feed your mind with impurity, you will slowly starve your spirit of strength, clarity, and power. But when you intentionally fill your mind with truth, righteousness, and things that honor God, your spirit begins to thrive. Discipline in what you consume is not restriction - it is protection. It is how you stay sharp in a dull world, clean in a corrupt culture, and strong in a battle that is fought first in the mind. Guard it well, because your mind is not just a place of thought - it is the battlefield where your future is won or lost.

Purity is not built by constantly looking over your shoulder at what you must avoid, but by fixing your eyes on what you are called to become. When a man only fights sin, his strength is drained by endless resistance; but when he pursues righteousness, his strength is renewed by purpose. Light does not struggle to overcome darkness - it simply shines. In the same way, when your life is filled with truth, discipline, integrity, and devotion to God there is less room for what is wrong to take root. So lift your focus higher. Chase after the things that sharpen your spirit and align your life with God's will. Fill your mind with truth, your time with purpose, and your heart with conviction. The man who runs from sin may survive, but the man who runs toward righteousness will thrive. When your life is anchored in pursuit of the right things, temptation loses its grip, and strength becomes your nature. Purity is no longer a burden you carry - it becomes the power by which you live.

Temptation arrives dressed in comfort, convenience, and curiosity. It whispers to your desires, appealing to what feels good in the moment while quietly bypassing your convictions. What seems harmless at first glance often carries hidden consequences, because the enemy of your soul understands that subtle compromise is far more effective than open rebellion. He doesn't need to destroy you in a single blow; he only needs to distract you one small step at a time. That quiet voice that says, "This won't matter," is often the very doorway to something that will. But God has not left you defenseless in this battle. Discernment is your shield, and truth is your anchor. When you train your heart to recognize the difference between what is merely appealing and what is truly righteous, you begin to see temptation for what it is - a counterfeit promise. The fleeting pleasure it offers cannot compare to the lasting peace found in obedience. Stay alert, guard your heart, and fill your mind with what is pure and strong.

Overcoming temptation demands intentional strategy. You must learn where you are most vulnerable and guard those places like a watchman on the wall. Be honest about your weaknesses and put boundaries in place before the battle ever begins. If certain environments weaken you, remove yourself from them. If certain influences pull your thoughts in the wrong direction, cut them off without hesitation. Wisdom is not just knowing what is right - it is structuring your life so that righteousness becomes the natural path you walk. You are not called to flirt with what can destroy you - you are called to flee from it. Every step you take away from a trigger is a step toward strength. Surround yourself with what builds you up - truth, accountability, and the presence of God. Fill your mind with what is pure, and your heart will follow. Victory is not found in a single moment of resistance, but in a lifestyle of preparation. When you live guarded, you live strong. When you live intentional, you live free.

Accountability is wisdom forged in humility and truth. True strength is found in the man who invites truth into his life, even when it challenges him. He understands that growth requires exposure, and that iron only sharpens iron through contact. When a man surrounds himself with godly voices - brothers who speak truth, not comfort - he gains clarity, stability, and strength for the battles he cannot win alone. Isolation, on the other hand, is the breeding ground of compromise. In the shadows, small cracks become deep fractures, and unchecked thoughts become destructive actions. But in the light of accountability, those same struggles lose their power. A man who walks in connection walks in strength. He is reminded of who he is, what he stands for, and who he serves. His conviction is reinforced, his vision stays clear, and his fight remains strong. Brotherhood is not optional - it is a safeguard. And the man who embraces it does not fall easily, because he does not stand alone.

When you fall the battle is not finished. The enemy wants you to believe that one failure defines you, that one misstep disqualifies you, that one moment of weakness erases all progress. But that is a lie. A man of God is not marked by never falling, but by refusing to stay down. Gace calls you out of the dust, reminding you that your identity is not in your failure but in your redemption. The same God who called you to purity also empowers you to rise again. Purity is not about flawless performance - it is about relentless pursuit. It is choosing, again and again, to turn back toward what is right, even after you've drifted. It is persistence in the face of weakness, courage in the face of failure, and faith that God is still at work in you. Every time you get back up, you weaken the grip of sin and strengthen the muscle of obedience. So rise. Shake off the weight of shame. Step back into the fight with renewed resolve. Because a man who keeps getting back up is a man who cannot be defeated.

Repentance is more than feeling sorrow over what was - it is the courageous decision to turn toward what should be. Regret looks backward and lingers in guilt, but repentance looks forward and moves in obedience. It is a realignment of the heart, a recalibration of desire, a surrender of will. When you repent, you are choosing God again, and in that choice, your direction begins to change. Every act of repentance weakens the chains that once held you. Sin loses its authority when you refuse to agree with it, and your spirit grows stronger every time you say "yes" to righteousness. The path may not always be easy, but it becomes clearer with each step of obedience. God does not despise the one who returns - He receives him, restores him, and renews him. So do not stay where you fell. Rise, turn, and walk a different way. Because every return to God is a step into freedom, and every step into freedom is a step toward the man you were created to be.

Living clean in a corrupt world requires the kind of courage that doesn't just resist evil but refuses to be shaped by it. When compromise is celebrated and conviction is questioned, the man who chooses righteousness will stand out. He will feel the weight of being different. But that difference is evidence of transformation. You were never called to mirror the culture around you; you were called to reflect the character of Christ within you. Light does not apologize for shining in darkness - it simply shines. So do not shrink back when your values set you apart. Do not dilute your convictions to gain acceptance from a world that is constantly shifting. Stand firm. Honor the calling on your life. The same God who called you to live clean has empowered you to do so. Your life becomes a testimony, your choices become a witness, and your steadfastness becomes a beacon for others who are searching for truth. In a world desperate for something real, your integrity is not just resistance - it is leadership.

The world calls compromise "freedom," redefines sin as "self-expression," and labels conviction as "judgment." A man who follows the crowd will eventually lose his way, because the crowd is not led by truth - it is led by desire. God's standards are unchanging. What He has spoken is not subject to trends, opinions, or approval ratings. Right is not determined by popularity - it is established by truth. A man of God must learn to stand firm when everything around him shifts. He cannot afford to let culture disciple him - he must let truth define him. There will be moments when conviction makes him stand alone, when doing what is right costs him comfort, approval, or opportunity. But standing with God will always outweigh standing with the crowd. Truth does not bend, and neither should the man who lives by it. In a world that celebrates compromise, be the man who walks in conviction. Because when everything else fades, truth will still be standing and so will the man who chose to stand with it.

Purity sharpens a man from the inside out. When the heart is clean his vision becomes clear - he discerns what matters and what does not. A pure heart gives him the ability to see people rightly, to recognize God's direction more clearly, and to walk forward with confidence instead of confusion. Where impurity clouds judgment, purity brings focus. It aligns his desires with what is good, and in that alignment, he begins to live with intention instead of reaction. And from that clarity flows strength. A man who is not enslaved to hidden struggles carries a quiet authority - his leadership is steady, his love is genuine, and his life is consistent. His words carry weight because his life backs them up. His relationships are deeper because they are not tainted by selfish motives. His decisions are stronger because they are not compromised by secret sin. Purity does not weaken a man - it fortifies him. It frees him to lead boldly, to love sacrificially, and to stand firmly in a world that constantly tries to blur the lines.

When your life is aligned with truth, there is no inner conflict, no hidden weight pressing against your soul. Integrity brings a quiet boldness. You don't have to rehearse your words or manage perceptions, because you are the same in private as you are in public. That kind of life produces confidence, a steady assurance that comes from knowing you are walking upright before God. A clear conscience silences fear and replaces it with peace allowing you to move forward without hesitation. When you choose integrity - when you bring your life into the light - you experience freedom that cannot be manufactured. You stop looking over your shoulder because there is nothing chasing you. You stop living divided because your heart is whole. This is the power of a clean life: it restores your vision, strengthens your spirit, and anchors your soul. A man who walks in integrity walks unburdened, and an unburdened man is a dangerous force for good.

Freedom is the presence of purpose. True freedom is discovered when you step into the design God placed on your life, when your desires are no longer your master but are brought under His authority. Sin will always advertise itself as liberty, but behind its promises are chains - subtle at first, then suffocating. What begins as indulgence becomes dependency, and what feels like control slowly turns into captivity. But purity - though it may feel like restraint in the beginning - is actually the pathway to real life. It clears your mind, strengthens your spirit, and aligns your heart with truth. It doesn't shrink your world; it expands it in the ways that matter most. When you choose purity, you are not losing freedom - you are reclaiming it. You are breaking agreements with what enslaves and stepping into the strength of who you were created to be. Real freedom is not doing whatever you want - it is having the power to live the life God intended, unchained, unburdened, and fully alive.

This fight is not won in a single moment of passion, but in a lifetime of quiet, consistent decisions. Every choice you make is shaping the man you are becoming. Every thought you entertain is either strengthening your spirit or weakening your resolve. The battlefield is within you. In the small, unseen moments, when no one is watching, that is where true victory is forged. Discipline is built in the ordinary. Character is formed in the hidden places. And over time, those daily choices become the foundation of a life that stands strong. Every moment is an opportunity to rise or to settle, to grow or to drift, to walk in purpose or fall into passivity. God has not called you to occasional strength, but to daily faithfulness. The man you become tomorrow is being decided by how you live today. So choose with intention. Guard your mind. Lead your heart. Stand your ground. Because in this daily fight, consistency becomes power, and faithfulness becomes strength.

So guard your heart because what you allow in will eventually shape who you become. Discipline your mind, because your thoughts are the battlefield where victories are first won or lost. Every temptation begins as a whisper, every compromise as a small agreement. But you are not powerless. You have been given authority to choose truth over lies, strength over weakness, and purpose over impulse. You were not created to be mastered by your desires - you were created to master them. You are not a slave to urges, emotions, or fleeting feelings; you are a man called to rule over them with clarity and conviction. This is the path of strength: to stand firm when your flesh demands comfort, to say no when everything in you wants to give in, to rise when it would be easier to stay down. Real power is not found in giving in, but in overcoming. So take your place. Strengthen your resolve. Walk in authority. Because the man who masters himself becomes a force that cannot be easily shaken.

Stand your ground. Every temptation you resist, every thought you take captive, and every compromise you refuse is a declaration of who you truly are. The world may celebrate indulgence, but heaven honors discipline. When you choose purity, you are not just avoiding sin - you are building strength. You are training your spirit to rule over your flesh, aligning your life with a higher calling that demands courage, clarity, and conviction. Fight for purity like a man who knows what is at stake because everything is. Your future, your influence, your relationship with God, and the legacy you will leave behind are all shaped in these hidden battles. And never underestimate the power of small victories. What feels insignificant today is forming unshakable character within you. Brick by brick, choice by choice, you are becoming a man of integrity. So don't back down. Don't negotiate with weakness. Stand firm, fight well, and remember: every victory is transforming you into the man God created you to be.

| 22 |

"THE POWER OF ENDURANCE"

Strength is not revealed in the rush of beginnings, but in the resolve of continuance. Excitement can ignite a man, but it is discipline that sustains him when the fire dims and the road grows long. Anyone can step forward when the moment feels right, but it takes a grounded spirit to keep walking when the emotion is gone and the weight of the journey settles in. True strength is steady, anchored, and unwavering. It chooses obedience over feeling and commitment over convenience. Endurance is the quiet testimony of a man who refuses to quit. It is built in unseen hours, in silent decisions, and in the choice to keep going when no applause follows. When everything feels heavy and progress seems slow, endurance presses forward anyway, trusting that purpose is not proven in speed but in faithfulness. Real strength is forged not in bursts, but in consistency; not in ease, but in perseverance. And the man who endures becomes unshakable, because he has learned how to stand when others fall away.

Time has a way of uncovering what passion alone cannot carry. Emotion can ignite a fire, but it cannot keep it burning when the winds of difficulty begin to blow. Many start with intensity, fueled by excitement and inspiration, but when the feeling fades, so does their movement. Yet what is built slowly through discipline, consistency, and quiet obedience becomes rooted and unshakable. God is not impressed by how fast you begin; He is honored by how faithfully you continue. The strength that lasts is not born in moments of hype, but in seasons of steady commitment. Endurance is the decision to rise again, to keep walking, to stay committed when every easier option is calling your name. It is choosing faithfulness over feelings, purpose over comfort, and obedience over convenience. Real strength is formed not in the spotlight, but in the daily grind of persistence. And in time, what seemed ordinary becomes powerful, what seemed slow becomes strong, and what seemed small becomes a legacy.

God does not measure strength by how loudly a man begins, but by how faithfully he continues. Man celebrates the start - the bold declarations, the visible passion, the early momentum - but God watches the quiet places where consistency is tested. He sees the moments when the fire is no longer emotional but intentional, when obedience replaces excitement, and when commitment carries a man farther than feelings ever could. True strength, in His eyes, is not proven in the spotlight, but in the unseen decisions to keep going, to keep believing, and to keep standing when no one else is watching. He honors the man who stays at his post when others walk away - the one who refuses to abandon his calling when the road stretches long and the weight grows heavy. This is the strength that heaven recognizes: not the strength to start, but the strength to endure. It is the man who remains, who presses forward through weariness, who chooses faithfulness over ease, that God calls strong.

There is a difference between starting strong and staying strong. Many begin their journey with passion, excitement, and fresh motivation, but those things are often temporary. Inspiration can ignite a fire, but it cannot sustain it. Staying strong requires conviction, the settled decision in your heart that no matter what comes, you will not turn back, slow down, or give up. Conviction anchors you when storms rise and keeps your feet planted when everything around you tries to shake your resolve. Endurance is not built on how you feel in the moment, but on why you started in the first place. When you are rooted in purpose, you can keep going when it's hard, stay faithful when it's quiet, and remain steady when progress feels slow. The man who endures is not the one who burns the brightest at the start of the journey, but the one who refuses to quit when the path gets long. So stay the course. Let your purpose outlast your emotions and let your conviction carry you farther than inspiration ever could.

Every calling is proven in the crucible of time. What God places in your hands is never lightweight - it carries purpose, responsibility, and resistance. There will be seasons where the excitement fades, where doubt whispers louder than faith, and where fatigue presses against your resolve. But calling is not confirmed by how you start - it is revealed by how you endure. The weight you carry is not meant to break you, but to build you into someone strong enough to sustain it. If you cannot endure, you cannot carry what He has entrusted to you. Endurance is the evidence that you truly value what God has given. It is the quiet, daily decision to remain when walking away would be easier. Those who fulfill their calling are not always the most gifted - they are the ones who refuse to quit. So stand your ground. Outlast the resistance. Push through the doubt. Because on the other side of endurance is the fulfillment of everything God placed inside you.

Endurance is forged in the quiet places where no one is watching. It is built in the early mornings when discipline overrides comfort, and in the late nights when commitment refuses to surrender to fatigue. These unseen moments are where real strength is developed. Every silent decision to keep going, to stay faithful, and to honor what God has placed in your hands becomes a brick in the foundation of a life that cannot be shaken. What feels small and unnoticed is where God is shaping your character. When there is no applause and no recognition, endurance grows deeper roots. It learns to stand not on approval, but on conviction. This kind of strength is anchored in purpose and sustained by faith. The man who remains committed in obscurity is the one who will be trusted with influence in the open. So stay steady in the unseen battles. Keep showing up. Keep choosing what is right. Because what you are building in secret, God is preparing to reveal in strength.

Many men carry great potential, but potential alone is only the beginning. Potential is what you could become, but endurance is what determines what you will become. Anyone can start strong when passion is high and vision is clear, but it is endurance that carries a man through the long nights, the silent battles, and the seasons where nothing seems to move. What you start in excitement must be sustained in discipline, because the journey to purpose is not built on moments, but on consistency. Without endurance, potential fades into regret. Dreams sit unfinished, callings remain untouched, and purpose is left unrealized. Endurance is the bridge between what God placed inside you and what He intends to bring out of you. It is forged in perseverance, strengthened in resistance, and proven when quitting feels justified but you choose to continue anyway. So be a man who finishes because in the end, it is not potential that defines your life, but the endurance that carried you all the way through.

Finishing what you start reveals a man who does not abandon his word when it becomes inconvenient, nor walk away when the path grows difficult. Integrity carries a weight that refuses to quit, because it understands that every unfinished assignment weakens trust, but every completed one strengthens it. When you follow through, you are not just completing a task - you are honoring your commitments before God and man. A man who finishes becomes a man others can rely on. He builds a reputation not through words, but through consistency. In a world full of half-done efforts and broken promises, finishing sets you apart. It positions you as someone who can be entrusted with greater responsibility, leadership, and influence. God often measures readiness not by how boldly you begin, but by how faithfully you complete. So stay with it. See it through. Because every time you finish what you start, you are shaping a life marked by trustworthiness and that is the foundation of lasting impact.

Too many begin assignments from God with passion but abandon them at the first sign of resistance. Yet difficulty is often the very evidence that the assignment matters. God does not call men into comfort; He calls them into transformation. What seems like an obstacle is often a tool in God's hand, shaping your strength, refining your character, and deepening your dependence on Him. If you quit when it gets hard, you may walk away from the very growth your calling requires. Endurance is what turns trials into training grounds and obstacles into steppingstones. Every challenge you face carries the potential to elevate you if you choose to remain faithful. The man who endures keeps showing up, keeps trusting, and keeps moving forward, even when the path is unclear. In doing so, he not only completes what God has started in him, but he becomes the kind of man who can carry greater responsibility. Stay the course. What feels heavy now is building something unshakable within you.

When you finish what you start, you silence the voice of doubt that once questioned your strength. Completion becomes a declaration that you are not controlled by shifting emotions, but anchored in discipline and conviction. Feelings may rise and fall, motivation may come and go, but a man who finishes has learned to move beyond both. He answers to a higher standard. In that act of finishing, you build confidence not from empty affirmations, but from proven faithfulness. You become evidence to yourself that you can endure, that you can follow through, and that you are capable of carrying responsibility to its end. Finishing also gives weight to your word. It transforms your commitments from mere intentions into trusted promises. When you consistently complete what you begin, people learn that your yes means yes, and your no means no. But even more importantly, God can entrust you with greater assignments because you have proven faithful in the smaller ones.

Endurance is anchored in discipline that stands firm when everything else fades. When the excitement is gone and the path grows difficult, discipline becomes the strength that carries him forward. Every step taken in obedience, even when it feels heavy, is a declaration that purpose matters more than preference. Choosing purpose over comfort is not a one-time decision - it is a daily surrender. It is waking up and saying yes to what is right, even when everything in you wants to choose ease. This is where endurance is proven: not in the spotlight, but in the unseen battles of consistency. God shapes strength in those who refuse to bow to their desires and instead commit to their calling. The man who endures is the man who has settled the matter - he will not quit, he will not drift, and he will not trade his assignment for temporary relief. In the end, it is not the most talented who finish strong, but the most disciplined - the ones who chose purpose, again and again, until the race was complete.

Legacy is built when you choose obedience over convenience, faith over fear, and commitment over comfort. The life God calls you to will not be sustained by bursts of passion alone, but by a steady walk of faithfulness. Every small act of obedience, every unseen sacrifice, every moment you refuse to quit are the bricks that form a lasting legacy. What you do consistently matters far more than what you do occasionally. Endurance is the bridge that carries you from calling to fulfillment. Without it, purpose remains unfinished and potential unrealized. But when you endure - when you remain steady through hardship, delay, and resistance - you align yourself with God's process. Legacy is not about how loudly you start, but how faithfully you finish. Stay the course. Keep showing up. Because in time, what feels like slow, steady progress will become a powerful testimony that your life was not wasted but was built with purpose, shaped by faith, and carried through by endurance.

What you repeatedly do becomes the signature of your life. It is not the moments of inspiration, but the patterns of obedience that define who you are. Every quiet decision to keep going, every unseen act of faithfulness, every time you refuse to quit when it would be easier to walk away - these are the chisels that shape your legacy. Endurance is built in the daily choice to stand, to believe, and to move forward when emotions waver. Over time, those choices form a life that speaks with consistency, strength, and unwavering trust in God. A life of endurance leaves behind a trail marked by faithfulness, a path others can follow when they face their own battles. Your perseverance becomes proof that it can be done, that a man can remain steady in a shifting world. Long after your voice is silent, your life will still testify. It will whisper courage into the hearts of those who come after you, reminding them that faithfulness over time is never wasted. It becomes more than a memory - it becomes a guiding light.

Men who endure are constructing something far greater than themselves. Every time a man chooses to stand firm instead of walking away, to remain faithful instead of compromising, he lays another stone in a foundation that others will one day stand upon. His consistency becomes a blueprint. His perseverance becomes a testimony. Long after his voice is silent, the strength of his life continues to speak, guiding sons, shaping families, and influencing generations he may never meet. A man who lives with eternity in view understands that his choices echo beyond today, reaching into forever. He refuses to be ruled by fleeting feelings because he is anchored in something eternal. His life becomes intentional, his sacrifices purposeful, and his legacy enduring. While others chase what fades, he builds what lasts. And in doing so, he becomes more than a man who lived - he becomes a man who left behind a path of faith, strength, and unwavering conviction for others to follow.

There will be days when everything in you wants to quit, days when the road feels long, the results feel distant, and the weight you carry presses harder than your strength seems to allow. In those moments, it's easy to believe that stopping would bring relief. But those are the very moments where your faith is tested, where your strength is stretched, and where your commitment is proven without applause. Those hard days are not interruptions to your journey - they are the defining chapters of it. Anyone can move forward when it's easy, but it takes a determined spirit to keep going when nothing seems to be changing. When you choose to stand, to press on, and to trust God anyway, you are becoming the kind of person who finishes what they started. So don't measure your progress by what you can see - measure it by your refusal to quit. Because in the end, it won't be the easy days that shaped you - it will be the days you almost stopped but didn't.

There will be moments when your strength feels drained, your motivation fades, and your progress seems invisible. But those are not the moments that disqualify you; they are the moments that define you. When you choose to stand, to take one more step, to pray one more time, even while feeling empty, you are walking in a strength that is not your own. Weakness becomes the very place where His power rests upon you. Pressing forward in those moments is an act of trust. It declares that you believe God is working even when you cannot see it, that He is strengthening you even when you feel worn down. The ones who endure are not the ones who never struggle - they are the ones who refuse to surrender in the struggle. As you keep going, God meets you in your persistence, breathes strength into your spirit, and builds a resilience that cannot be shaken. Stay in the fight. Your endurance is not wasted - it is being forged into a testimony of unwavering faith.

Anyone can feel the surge of inspiration at the starting line, but heaven looks beyond the excitement of a moment and measures the faithfulness of a lifetime. The race set before you will test your resolve, strip away your comfort, and confront every excuse that tries to slow your pace. But within you is a calling that refuses to quit. You were designed not just to step forward, but to press through resistance, through silence, through seasons where nothing seems to move until what God placed in you is fully carried out. Heaven rejoices most when a man refuses to turn back. Completion is the testimony that you trusted God enough to carry through what He began in you. The reward is not for those who begin with passion, but for those who endure with conviction. So when the road grows long remember this: your finish matters more than your start. Stay the course. Hold your ground. And when you cross the line, you won't just carry the weight of your effort - you will carry the evidence of your faith.

When the road feels long and the results seem distant, remember that faith is not proven in ease but in endurance. Every step forward, no matter how small, is an act of obedience. Every time you refuse to quit, you declare that your calling is greater than your comfort. Progress may be unseen by others, but heaven records every act of faithfulness. Keep moving. Keep building. Keep pressing on, because the man you are becoming is being forged in the decision to continue. Finish what you started. Endurance is not just about surviving the storm; it is about emerging from it transformed, refined, and unshakable. The strength you are developing now will define the legacy you leave behind. One day, you will look back and realize that what felt like resistance was actually preparation. So don't turn back. Don't slow down. Become the man who was strong enough to complete what God began in him. In doing so, you'll reflect the faithfulness of the One who never gave up on you.

| 23 |

"THE ROAR IN ADVERSITY"

There comes a moment in every man's life when adversity bursts in, uninvited and unrestrained, shaking the very foundations he once trusted. In that collision between expectation and reality, comfort is stripped away and what remains is revealed. It is there, in the pressure, that faith is no longer theoretical but proven. A man who has built his life on shallow belief will begin to crumble under the weight, but a man rooted in truth will find something rise up within him that cannot be shaken. Faith that survives the storm is anchored and unyielding. It declares that God is still good when life is not, that His promises are still true when circumstances say otherwise. In that defining moment, you are not just enduring hardship - you are becoming the man who trusts God under pressure, the man whose foundation is proven by fire. And when the storm passes, you will not be the same man who was interrupted - you will be stronger, deeper, and unshakable, because your faith was not built for comfort, but for the fight.

Adversity has a way of cutting through the noise of who we pretend to be and exposing who we truly are. When the storm comes, what is shallow cannot stand but what is rooted in truth, in faith, and in God remains unshaken. Trials do not create weakness; they uncover it so it can be replaced with something real. In those moments when life presses hard, God is refining you, removing what cannot last so that what remains is genuine, tested, and strong. Anyone can stand when the sun is shining, but it takes a man anchored in faith to stand when everything around him is shaking. Your endurance, your refusal to quit, and your decision to trust God in the middle of uncertainty declare what truly lives inside you. Adversity is the proving ground where your faith is strengthened, your character is forged, and your calling is clarified. Stand firm. Let the pressure push you deeper, not drive you away. Because when the storm passes, what remains will not be what was easy - it will be what was real.

When everything in you wants to stay down, there is a deeper voice - God's voice - calling you to rise. It reminds you that you are not defeated, only tested; not abandoned, but being strengthened. In that moment, rising becomes an act of trust, a declaration that what God placed in you is greater than what is pressing against you. To rise again is to gather the scattered pieces of your strength and stand, even if your knees are shaking. It is a quiet but powerful decision, "I will not remain here." You may not feel strong, but strength is not always loud - it is often found in the simple act of getting back up one more time. Every time you rise, you reclaim ground the enemy tried to steal, and you build endurance that cannot be shaken. The storm may still surround you, but it no longer controls you. Because when you decide to stand again, you are not standing alone - God meets you in that moment, lifts your spirit, and steadies your steps, proving that no matter how hard life hits, you were created to rise.

There is a roar that is born in adversity - a sound forged in pressure, shaped in pain, and strengthened in the moments when quitting feels closest. It is the roar of perseverance. It rises from a man who has been tested and found his foundation still standing. When life hits hard, when doors close, when strength feels drained, something deeper awakens within him. It is the Spirit of God reminding him that he was not built to break under pressure, but to be refined by it. Even in the darkest moments, he stands, not because the storm has passed, but because his faith has taken root deeper than the storm can reach. This quiet roar carries authority because it is anchored in truth. It speaks when fear tries to paralyze, declaring that God is still faithful. It rises when doubt whispers defeat, answering with unshakable conviction. Every blow he endures strengthens his resolve, every trial sharpens his faith, and every moment of resistance builds a testimony that cannot be shaken.

Every trial places a decision in your hands. Do you retreat into comfort or rise into your calling? Retreat may feel easier in the moment, but it slowly erodes strength and silences purpose. Rising, on the other hand, requires courage. It demands that you face what's difficult, stand when it would be easier to sit, and trust God when the outcome is uncertain. The man who chooses to rise is not the one without fear, but the one who refuses to let fear dictate his direction. He understands that faith is not proven in ease, but in endurance. Adversity is the proving ground where conviction is tested, character is forged, and identity is clarified. In the fire of trials, what is weak is burned away, and what is true remains. The man who rises begins to see hardship as a doorway into greater strength. He learns that every challenge is an opportunity for God to reveal something deeper within him. And when he stands on the other side, he is stronger and unshakably convinced that what tried to break him actually built him.

Refusing to be silenced by trials is a decision to rise above the pressure and speak truth even when everything around you tries to quiet your voice. Hardship often comes with whispers of doubt - telling you to shrink back, to question what God has said, to believe that your situation has more authority than His promises. But the man of faith does not bow to those lies. He stands in the middle of adversity and declares what is true anyway. He understands that trials are not a signal to retreat, but an opportunity to reinforce what he believes. When the storm intensifies, so does his conviction, because he knows that God's Word is not altered by circumstances. When you choose to speak faith in the face of fear, to proclaim hope in the middle of uncertainty, and to stand firm when everything feels unstable, your voice becomes a weapon. It grows sharper, stronger, and more unshakable. The enemy may try to drown it out, but he cannot overcome a man who refuses to stop declaring truth.

There are voices that rise in difficult seasons - voices of fear, doubt, and discouragement that seem louder when the pressure increases. They whisper lies that try to redefine your identity and redirect your path. But those voices are not sent to guide you - they are allowed to test you. They reveal what you truly believe. Will you agree with the pressure, or will you stand on the promises of God? Because in every trial, there is a battle for your perspective. The enemy wants you to magnify the struggle, but God is calling you to magnify the truth. What feels like the end is often the very place where strength is being formed and faith is being proven. So do not bow to the voices that contradict what God has spoken over your life. Answer them. Replace fear with faith, doubt with truth, and discouragement with declaration. Speak what God says even when your emotions say otherwise. This is how you pass the test. You don't silence the voices by ignoring them; you silence them by overpowering them with truth.

The roar in adversity rises from deep within a man. When everything around him whispers loss, weakness, and surrender, he answers with truth. He speaks life not because circumstances are favorable, but because God is faithful. This roar is the sound of a man who chooses to believe what God said over what he sees, who anchors himself in promises instead of problems. Even when the night feels heavy and the outcome uncertain, he declares life because he knows that God's Word carries more weight than any storm he faces. To roar in adversity is to stand in the middle of contradiction and still proclaim victory. It is declaring healing when pain is present, purpose when confusion surrounds you, and hope when everything looks lost. It takes strength to do this, but it is a strength that comes from trust, not self. When you choose to align your voice with God's truth, something shifts within you. Fear loses its grip, doubt begins to break, and your spirit rises above your situation.

When darkness surrounds you, your words are weapons. The valley is not only a place of testing, but a place of declaring. What you say in those moments reveals what you truly believe. If you allow fear to shape your words, it will begin to shape your reality. Silence may feel safe, but it often gives fear room to grow unchecked. Yet when you choose to speak truth - when you declare God's promises in the middle of uncertainty - you shift the atmosphere of your soul. You remind yourself that darkness is not permanent, that God is still present, and that what feels overwhelming is still under His authority. There is power in refusing to agree with fear. There is strength in opening your mouth and declaring what is true, even when everything around you suggest otherwise. Speak life when your circumstances feel lifeless. Speak faith when doubt tries to take hold. Speak victory before you see it. Because what you declare in the valley doesn't just echo in the moment - it shapes how you rise out of it.

Declaring truth in darkness is a deliberate act of spiritual warfare. When everything around you feels uncertain, when the evidence seems to contradict what God has spoken, choosing to stand and declare His faithfulness becomes a bold defiance against fear. It is the voice of conviction rising above the noise of doubt, the steady anchor in a storm that refuses to drift. In those moments, you are reminding your soul that God's promises are not shaken by your circumstances. Darkness may surround you, but it cannot silence the truth when a man decides to speak it. Trials may press you, but they do not have permission to define you. When you declare truth in the middle of adversity, you are strengthening your spirit, building endurance, and shifting the atmosphere around you. Victory often begins with a voice that refuses to agree with defeat. So stand firm, speak boldly, and let your words echo with faith because when truth is declared in darkness, it becomes the light that leads you through.

Truth becomes your weapon when circumstances try to redefine you because truth is established by what God has spoken. When pressure rises and voices of doubt grow louder, truth reminds you that you are not defined by failure, fear, or temporary setbacks, but by the unchanging Word of God. In moments where everything around you shifts, truth stands firm, declaring that you are chosen, strengthened, and sustained. It is not just something you believe - it is something you stand on, something you fight with, and something that refuses to let you be rewritten by adversity. When everything feels unstable, truth becomes your anchor, holding you steady in the storm. It keeps your feet planted when emotions fluctuate and circumstances seem uncertain. Truth whispers what heaven has already decided about you, even when your situation tries to argue otherwise. It steadies your heart, sharpens your focus, and restores your confidence to move forward.

A man who roars in adversity is a man who sees the storm for what it is. He feels the pressure, the resistance, the weight pressing in from every side. But instead of shrinking back, he rises up within it. He understands that faith is not proven in comfort, but in conflict. So he plants his feet, lifts his head, and refuses to bow to what tries to break him. His roar is not noise - it is conviction. It is the sound of a man who knows that God is with him in the fire, and because of that, the fire cannot consume him. His strength is not found in escaping the battle, but in enduring it with unshakable resolve. While others look for a way out, he becomes the kind of man who stands firm right in the middle of it. Pressure doesn't define him - purpose does. The storm may rage, but it cannot rewrite who he is. He declares truth when fear tries to speak, and he holds his ground when everything around him shifts. This is the man who roars - not because the storm is small, but because his faith is greater.

There is power in persistence because every refusal to quit is a declaration that your faith is stronger than your circumstances. Each time you rise again, even when it would be easier to stay down, something deep within you is being forged - strength, resilience, and unwavering trust in God. The pressure you feel is shaping your character, stretching your endurance, and teaching you to stand when everything around you says fall. Adversity is not merely something you endure; it is something that builds you into the man God is calling you to be. Every challenge carries within it the opportunity for growth, and every setback is a chance to rise with greater strength than before. What tries to break you can actually establish you if you refuse to give up. So keep pressing forward. Keep standing firm. Because in the process of persistence, God is not just bringing you through the storm - He is building you into someone the storm cannot overcome.

The roar within you was never meant to echo in isolation - it carries beyond your own battle and reaches the hearts of those who are quietly watching. When you endure with faith, when you stand when others would fall, your life begins to preach a message louder than words ever could. There are people who may never read scripture, but they will read your perseverance. They will study how you respond under pressure, how you hold your ground when circumstances tighten around you, and how you continue forward when quitting would be easier. In those moments, your endurance becomes a living testimony that strength is not reserved for the extraordinary - it is available to anyone who anchors themselves in God. Your faith under pressure becomes proof that storms do not have the final say. It shows others that a man can be shaken but not broken, pressed but not defeated. What you fight through today may be the very thing that gives someone else the courage to rise tomorrow.

God does not waste adversity. Every hardship, every delay, every moment of pressure carries purpose in His hands. What feels like breaking is often His way of shaping your character, strengthening your resolve, and refining what is within you. Just as fire purifies gold, adversity strips away pride, fear, and self-reliance, leaving behind a deeper faith and a stronger foundation. God is never careless with your pain. He is intentional, using every weight you carry to prepare you for the calling you've been given. What feels like pressure is often preparation. The resistance you face is not there to stop you, but to strengthen you for what lies ahead. God is developing endurance, sharpening your discernment, and teaching you to stand when everything in you wants to quit. The man He is forming through adversity is resilient and anchored in truth. So do not despise the process. What you are walking through today is equipping you for tomorrow. In God's hands, adversity is not your enemy - it is your training ground.

The man who learns to roar in adversity is no longer surprised by the storm, nor intimidated by its force. Trials that once threatened to break him have now become the very tools that built him. He has faced pressure, felt the weight, and endured the moments when quitting seemed easier than continuing but he chose to stand. That choice has produced a strength that cannot be easily shaken. He is no longer discouraged because he has seen what God can do in the middle of difficulty. Every test he passed became a testimony, every hardship a reminder that he is not alone in the fight. His roar is the sound of a man who knows that what tried to destroy him only developed him. He stands now with a quiet boldness, unafraid of what comes next, because he has already proven that he can endure. And when a man reaches that place where trials no longer silence him but strengthen him he becomes a threat to overcome because he has mastered the discipline of standing firm no matter what comes.

There will be more battles. There will be more moments when life hits hard, when the wind knocks the breath out of you and the weight feels heavier than before. But something changes when you discover your roar. It is the sound of faith awakened, the declaration that you will not bow, break, or back down. It is the voice inside you that says, "God is with me, and I am still standing." When that roar rises, fear loses its grip, doubt loses its voice, and the storm no longer defines you. You may still feel the pressure, but you stand differently, you fight differently, and you endure with a strength that is no longer your own. Once you discover your roar, you stop approaching hardship as a victim and start walking into it as a man who knows who he is in God. The same trials that once silenced you will now draw something powerful out of you. You will speak truth in the face of darkness, stand firm when others retreat, and carry a confidence that cannot be shaken by circumstances.

Refuse to be silenced by trials. Refuse to let hardship drown out your calling. Even in the darkness, there is a truth that cannot be shaken: God is still with you, still for you, and still working through you. So speak life when everything around you feels lifeless. Stand firm when everything in you wants to collapse. Let your faith become a voice that breaks through the silence of fear. And as you rise, let your life echo with a roar not of pride, but of perseverance. A declaration that says, "I am still standing, and I am not done." The enemy may have struck, but he has not succeeded. The storm may have raged, but it has not erased you. There is still purpose in your breath, still strength in your spirit, and still a path God has prepared ahead of you. So keep moving. Keep declaring. Keep believing. Because the man who refuses to quit, who clings to truth in the darkest hour, becomes a living reminder that endurance, anchored in faith, will always have the final word.

| 24 |

"THE LION'S FOCUS"

There is a kind of focus that separates the ordinary from the unstoppable. It does not chase every opportunity or react to every noise. Instead, it locks onto what matters most and refuses to be pulled away. Like a lion stalking its prey, it moves with patience, intention, and precision. It is not hurried, yet it is never idle. This kind of focus is born when a man understands his assignment from God and chooses to give it his full attention. Distractions lose their power when purpose becomes greater than comfort. This lion-like focus is quiet, but it is powerful. It does not need validation, applause, or recognition to keep going. It is sustained by conviction and strengthened by obedience. While others are scattered, this focus remains anchored. While others start and stop, it endures until the mission is complete. When you learn to guard your focus, you protect your calling. When you eliminate what pulls you away, you make room for what pushes you forward. So fix your eyes, steady your heart, and move with intention.

A lion does not chase everything that moves. It does not burn strength on distractions, noise, or every passing opportunity. It waits; it watches and moves with purpose. In the same way, a man of God must learn the discipline of focus. Not every door is your assignment. Not every battle is yours to fight. The enemy often works not by stopping you, but by pulling your attention in a hundred directions until your strength is drained and your calling is diluted. But when you are anchored in God, you begin to see clearly. You stop reacting to everything around you and start responding only to what matters. There is power in that kind of focus. It produces clarity, strength, and effectiveness. When your heart is set, your steps become steady. When your eyes are fixed, your life gains direction. Like a lion that locks onto its prey, you must lock onto your God-given mission giving your full strength to what God has called you to do. Purpose is fulfilled not by chasing everything, but by committing fully to the right thing.

A man of God cannot afford to chase every distraction that life throws at him. Every unnecessary pursuit drains strength that was meant for purpose. The enemy does not always destroy a man through open rebellion - often, he simply keeps him busy with things that do not matter. A man who follows every opportunity, every impulse, and every passing desire will find himself scattered, not strong. But a man who fixes his eyes on what God has called him to do begins to walk with clarity and authority. Purpose demands focus. Calling requires discipline. A man of God must learn to say no to good things so he can say yes to the right thing. When he locks in on God's assignment, distractions lose their power, and his life gains direction. Like a runner who refuses to look to the left or right, he presses forward with endurance, knowing that fulfillment is found in finishing what God gave him to do. And when he lives with focus, intention, and resolve, his strength is not misused, and his time is not wasted.

Distractions are not always loud or obviously sinful. They come wrapped in comfort that dulls urgency, entertainment that numbs conviction, and busyness that gives the illusion of purpose without producing eternal fruit. Not every open door is from God, and not every opportunity is an assignment. The enemy rarely needs to destroy a man if he can simply distract him. A life filled with good things can still miss the right thing if it pulls you away from God's calling. Discernment is knowing what matters most in this season of your life. A focused man learns to guard his time, his attention, and his heart with intention. God's assignments require clarity, discipline, and a willingness to say no to things that may feel good or look productive. When you stay anchored in His purpose, distractions lose their power. Your life becomes sharper, your direction becomes clearer, and your impact becomes eternal. Stay focused. What God has called you to is too important to be traded for what merely fills your time.

The enemy rarely comes with a single, devastating strike. Instead, he chips away at a man's strength by pulling his focus from what truly matters and scattering his attention across things that drain, delay, and dilute his purpose. What begins as harmless compromise slowly becomes spiritual erosion. Time once given to God is replaced with noise. Conviction grows quiet and direction becomes blurred. And before a man realizes it, he is drifting not because he lacks strength, but because his focus has been divided. The enemy understands that a distracted man is a weakened man, and a weakened man is far easier to defeat. But a man who guards his focus guards his life. He learns to say no to what pulls him away so he can say yes to what builds him up. The battle is not always about resisting obvious evil but about refusing anything that competes with God's best. Stay focused because the man who refuses distraction will walk in strength, direction, and unshakable purpose.

The lion does not waste its strength chasing every movement in the grass - it locks in on one target and gives its full attention to what matters most. In the same way, a man's power is not proven by how much he can do, but by how well he can focus on what God has called him to do. Distraction is one of the enemy's greatest weapons, because scattered strength produces little impact. But when your heart, mind, and energy are fixed on God's purpose, your strength becomes sharp, intentional, and effective. Scripture reminds us to "run with endurance the race set before us," not every race, but your race. Focus is what turns potential into power. Like the lion, he moves with purpose. He waits, watches, and then acts with precision. Strength is maximized not through constant motion, but through disciplined direction. Stay fixed on what God has placed in front of you because when your focus is aligned with God's mission, your strength becomes a force that cannot be easily stopped.

When a man eliminates distractions, he begins to take back ground that was quietly stolen from him. What once consumed his attention loses its grip. In that clarity, he starts to see again. Time becomes valuable instead of wasted. Energy is preserved instead of drained. And purpose, once blurred and distant, begins to come into sharp focus. A man who removes distraction is leading his life with intention under the direction of God. Distraction is one of the enemy's most subtle weapons, but focus is one of a man's greatest strengths. When a man locks in on what truly matters - his walk with God, his calling, his responsibilities - there is a weight and authority that returns to his life. He becomes dangerous to passivity and resistant to compromise. His steps gain direction, his discipline gains strength, and his life begins to produce fruit. Because when a man fixes his eyes on God's mission for him, everything unnecessary begins to fall away, and what remains is a life marked by clarity, purpose, and power.

God did not design you to wander through life reacting to everything around you, tossed by circumstances and controlled by distractions. He formed you with purpose, placed calling within you, and gave you the ability to choose direction over drift. A man who lives intentionally aligns himself with God's will and moves forward with clarity and conviction. Every step becomes meaningful when it is guided by purpose. Drifting leads to wasted years, but intention leads to fulfillment. The enemy thrives on distraction because distraction dulls purpose and weakens resolve. But when you lock your focus on what God has called you to do, everything changes. You begin to walk with discipline, speak with authority, and act with courage. You no longer chase what is easy - you pursue what is right. And as you move with intention, you become a man who is not easily shaken, not easily swayed, and not easily stopped because your life is anchored in purpose, and your steps are ordered by God.

You were never created to drift through life, reacting to whatever comes your way. God designed you with intention, and that intention calls you to live with purpose and direction. Each day is meant to begin with clarity because when your eyes are fixed on Him, your path becomes steady. You are not here by accident, and your life is not random. There is a calling on you that demands focus, a direction that requires conviction. When you align your heart with God's will, you stop wandering and start walking with confidence, knowing that every step has meaning and every decision carries eternal weight. To live this way is to reject passivity and embrace responsibility. It means choosing to act with purpose even when it's difficult, and to move forward even when the path isn't fully revealed. Conviction gives you the strength to stand firm, and clarity keeps you from being pulled in every direction. And as you live with meaning, your life begins to point others to the God who gave you direction in the first place.

When a man knows why he is here, he no longer chases every opportunity. Knowing your purpose causes you to recognize that not every open door is meant for you, and not every good thing is a God thing. With purpose, your time becomes sacred, your energy becomes intentional, and your steps become directed. You stop drifting and start building because you are no longer led by what is urgent - you are led by what is eternal. Without purpose, everything competes for your attention, and confusion becomes the norm. You say yes too quickly, walk into things you were never assigned to, and carry weights you were never meant to bear. But when purpose is clear, clarity follows. You gain the courage to walk away from distractions, even when they look appealing. Purpose simplifies life. It sharpens your direction and keeps your focus fixed on what truly matters. And a focused man is a dangerous man to the kingdom of darkness, because he cannot be easily pulled off course.

Life is not just shaped by what you pursue, but by what you permit. Every distraction you entertain, every compromise you tolerate, and every misaligned opportunity you accept slowly pulls you away from your divine assignment. The enemy rarely needs to destroy a man outright - he only needs to redirect him. But a man of purpose guards his time, his energy, and his attention with conviction. When your heart is anchored in God's calling, you begin to see clearly that not everything good is God, and not every open door is meant for you. The man who fulfills his calling is not the one who does the most, but the one who stays aligned with what matters most. He wakes up with direction, walks with clarity, and refuses to be pulled into lesser pursuits. He remembers who he is and what he has been assigned to do. And in that focus, there is power. In that alignment, there is peace. Because when a man gives his life fully to God, he will not miss what was meant for him - he will walk straight into it.

The lion does not apologize for ignoring what does not matter and neither should you. God never called you to give equal attention to everything; He called you to be faithful to what He assigned you. Too many men are drained not because they lack strength, but because they are scattered. Every distraction you entertain steals focus from your calling. Jesus Himself walked away from crowds, noise, and even good opportunities because He was anchored to the Father's will. You cannot carry purpose and distraction at the same time. One will always suffocate the other. Discipline requires the courage to walk away from conversations that dilute you, habits that weaken you, and paths that lead nowhere. A lion does not chase every movement in the grass; he moves with intention, conserving strength for what truly matters. In the same way, a focused man guards his time, his energy, and his attention with conviction. Stay locked in. Stay disciplined. And move only when it aligns with your purpose.

The enemy rarely needs to destroy a man outright if he can simply distract him long enough to dilute his purpose. A man without focus becomes divided, and a divided man cannot stand strong in his calling. But the man with a lion's focus learns to filter everything through the lens of God's mission. If it doesn't align, it doesn't get access. He becomes disciplined in what he listens to, what he entertains, and where he invests his energy. Like a lion locked onto its target, he refuses to be pulled away by lesser pursuits. This kind of focus is not passive - it is intentional and guarded. It requires the courage to disappoint people, to walk away from distractions, and to say no to things that may be good but are not God's best. The man with lion's focus is not easily shaken because his direction is clear. He knows who he is, whose he is, and what he has been called to do. While others scatter their attention and lose momentum, he moves forward with purpose, steady and unwavering.

Staying locked on God's mission requires daily surrender because your flesh will constantly try to reclaim control. Surrender is the deliberate choice to lay down your plans, your timing, and your preferences, and say, "Lord, not my will, but Yours be done." A man who walks in this posture doesn't drift aimlessly - he moves with clarity, because his life is anchored to something greater than himself. This kind of alignment is not sustained by emotion, but by discipline. It is built in the quiet moment through prayer, obedience, and a heart that continually returns to God when it wanders. Some days it will feel like a battle just to stay focused, but that battle is where transformation happens. As you surrender daily, your desires begin to match His, your focus sharpens, and your life gains direction. Over time, what once required effort becomes conviction, and you become a man who is not easily pulled off course because your heart has learned to stay locked on the mission of God.

A focused man is a dangerous man to the kingdom of darkness, because he cannot be easily pulled off course. Purpose clarifies decisions. It gives strength to say no to what doesn't matter and courage to pursue what does. When you remember your calling, you stop negotiating with comfort and start advancing with conviction. Ask yourself again, "What has God called me to build, to fight for, to become?" Then live like the answer matters. Build with diligence, even when no one sees. Fight with faith, even when resistance is strong. Become the man God envisioned, even when the process is slow and refining. You were not created to wander - you were created to walk with direction. Every day is an opportunity to align your life with heaven's assignment. So don't wait for motivation. Remind yourself until it burns in your spirit. Because when a man is clear on his calling, he stops living accidentally and starts living intentionally and that is where power, purpose, and impact are found.

When your focus is anchored in God, your life gains a steady center that the chaos around you cannot shake. Like a ship secured by a deep anchor, you may feel the pull of the waves, yet you are not carried away by them. Your decisions are no longer ruled by impulse, but by purpose. Your time is no longer consumed by what is loud, but by what is eternal. In God's presence, clarity replaces confusion, and you begin to see that many of the things that once demanded your attention were never worthy of your calling. This kind of focus is cultivated through daily surrender. It is choosing to fix your eyes on God's voice above every competing noise. And as you do, distractions lose their grip because your desire for God becomes greater than your desire for anything else. You are no longer easily pulled off course, because your heart is set on something higher. You move with intention, live with clarity, and walk with a quiet strength that comes from knowing exactly who you are following and why.

The lion's focus does not chase every movement in the grass or react to every distraction in its path. It waits, it watches, and when the moment comes, it gives everything to the one pursuit that matters. In the same way, a man of God is not called to be busy, but to be purposeful. Many live exhausted not because they are doing too much, but because they are doing too much of what does not matter. True focus is the ability to recognize what God has placed in front of you and to pour your strength, attention, and energy into that assignment without apology. When your life aligns with what matters most, something shifts within you. Distractions lose their grip, lesser priorities fall away, and your effort becomes concentrated instead of divided. This is where power is found - not in scattered effort, but in undivided commitment. God does not anoint everything; He anoints what He has called you to do. And when you give yourself fully to that calling, there is a strength, clarity, and authority that follows.

Fix your eyes on what truly matters, because wherever your focus rests, your life will follow. A man who lives with purpose is not driven by impulse but anchored in calling. He wakes up knowing why he exists, and he orders his life around that truth. He does not chase everything; he chooses what matters most and gives himself fully to it. Stay locked on the mission God has given you, even when it feels slow, unnoticed, or difficult. Purpose is not proven in moments of excitement, but in consistency over time. There will always be distractions competing for your attention, but you must learn to say no without apology. The man who refuses distraction sharpens his focus like a weapon. He is steady, intentional, and unyielding. And when a man becomes that focused, he becomes dangerous to everything that stands against God's plan for his life. He is no longer easily moved, easily swayed, or easily stopped because a man aligned with God's purpose walks with a strength that cannot be shaken.

| 25 |

"BREAKING THE CHAINS"

There comes a moment in a man's life when clarity cuts through the noise, and he realizes the battle is not always ahead of him - it's attached to him. The weight he feels is not just from present resistance, but from past residue. Old wounds whisper lies about his worth. Failures try to rewrite his identity. Words spoken in anger or doubt echo louder than truth. Regret tightens its grip, convincing him he is disqualified from becoming who God called him to be. But those chains only have power when they remain unchallenged. The truth is, God does not define you by your lowest moment - He defines you by His purpose. Christ did not break you out only to watch you walk back into bondage. He calls you forward - unburdened, unashamed, and unafraid. You are not the man you were - you are the man God is forming. Shake off what no longer belongs to you, and step into the freedom that was already paid for. Because when a man finally lets go of what's behind him, nothing in front of him can stop him.

Many men walk through life with the weight of yesterday pressing on their shoulders, but God never intended for your past to become your prison. The enemy thrives in reminding you of who you were, hoping you'll forget who you are becoming. Yet Scripture declares that you are God's workmanship, created with purpose, redeemed with intention, and called forward - not backward. What happened may have shaped parts of your story, but it does not get the final say. God does.

And He is not finished with you. So refuse to wear the labels of your lowest moments. Break agreement with the lies that say you are stuck, disqualified, or defined by failure. In Christ, you are transformed and made new. Your past is a chapter, not your identity. Lift your head, step out of the shadows, and walk in the freedom that has already been paid for. Because a man who understands that he is God's workmanship no longer lives bound to what was - he rises with confidence into what God is still writing.

Wounds that go unhealed quietly shape how a man sees the world, others, and even himself. What is ignored is not erased; it is buried, and what is buried often grows in darkness. Hurt can turn into hardness. Failure can evolve into fear that keeps a man from ever stepping forward again. Without realizing it, he begins to build walls where God intended him to build bridges. Yet God never designed you to carry pain as a permanent identity. The wound may explain where you've been, but it does not have the authority to define where you're going. Healing begins when you stop pretending you're fine and invite God into the very place you've been trying to protect. And where God's light enters, healing follows. The courage to confront what hurt you is the first step toward becoming whole again. So don't hide it and don't let it master you. Lay it before God, let Him speak truth over it, and watch as what once wounded you becomes the very place where strength, wisdom, and freedom are born.

God does not stand at a distance, observing your pain from afar - He steps directly into it. He is not intimidated by your brokenness, nor is He overwhelmed by the weight of what you feel. In fact, He draws near to it. Where you feel the tightest chains, He brings His presence. Where you feel the deepest ache, He brings His peace. You are not abandoned in the battle - you are accompanied by a God who moves toward your pain, not away from it. What feels permanent to you is temporary in His hands. He specializes in breaking what has held you captive, in lifting what has crushed you, in restoring what has been lost. But freedom begins with surrender. When you release what you've been gripping so tightly and place it into His hands, He does what you cannot do. In a moment, He can remove what took years to build. In an instant, He can free what felt unmovable. So stop carrying what He's asking you to surrender because the God who meets you in your pain is also the God who breaks your chains.

A man can carry wounds for years, burying them beneath pride, distraction, or silence, but what is buried does not disappear. The pain he refuses to face becomes the lens through which he sees life, relationships, and even God. But the moment he chooses honesty, when he stops pretending and finally names the hurt, he steps into the light. And in that light, chains begin to loosen not because he fixed himself, but because he invited God into the very places he once tried to hide. It takes courage to stand exposed before God without excuses, but that courage is where transformation begins. The broken places, the regrets, the scars become the very ground where His healing power is revealed. When you come honestly, you give Him access. And where God has access, He brings restoration. Freedom is not found in hiding your past, but in surrendering it. And the man who dares to be honest before God will discover that what once held him captive no longer has the power to define him.

The cross of Christ is not just where your sins were forgiven - it is where your chains were broken. When Jesus stretched out His hands and gave His life, He didn't just cover your past; He crushed its authority over you. Too many men live as if forgiveness is the finish line, still dragging guilt, shame, and old identities behind them. But the cross declares that what once controlled you no longer has the right to define you. In Christ, the weight of yesterday loses its grip, and the accusations that once held you captive are silenced by His sacrifice. This means your past is no longer your prison but a testimony of what God has brought you out of. You are not just forgiven in theory; you are released in reality. So stop walking like a man still bound when Christ has already declared you free. Step forward in that freedom. Live like a man who has been redeemed, restored, and released because through Jesus, you are no longer held by what was, you are propelled by who you have become.

When Jesus sets a man free, He does not merely adjust his behavior; He breaks the authority of what once held him captive. The chains of sin, shame, fear, and failure lose their grip, not because you are strong enough to escape them, but because Christ is strong enough to shatter them. This kind of freedom speaks empowers you to move forward with confidence, no longer dragged back into old patterns, no longer defined by what you used to be. In Him, your past becomes a testimony, not a prison. This is the difference between self-effort and supernatural transformation. Self-help tries to manage the old man, but Christ creates a new one. He gives you the strength to walk forward without being pulled backward, to remember where you've been without being ruled by it. His power works within you, renewing your mind, restoring your identity, and reshaping your desires. You can now live with a bold, unshakable confidence: the past is behind you, the chains are broken, and through Christ, you are truly free.

Freedom is something you must step into. God can break every chain, lift every weight, and open every prison door, but He will not force you to walk it out. The habits, the mindsets, the wounds, the identities that once defined you no longer have authority unless you give it back to them. Freedom requires courage. It means choosing obedience over comfort and forward movement over backward attachment. With freedom comes responsibility. You cannot carry yesterday's chains and still claim today's liberty. A free man guards his mind, disciplines his thoughts, and refuses to revisit the prison God brought him out of. He understands that returning is a choice, just as walking forward is a choice. So he fixes his eyes ahead, not behind. He builds new patterns, speaks new truth, and lives in the reality that what once bound him no longer owns him. Because true freedom is not just about what God has done for you - it is about what you now choose to do with it.

Some chains are not wrapped around your hands - they are wrapped around your memory. A man who once stepped out boldly begins to shrink back, not because he lacks strength, but because he remembers the pain of falling. What you walked through was not meant to trap you; it was meant to teach you. Every setback carries a lesson, every fall reveals something that can make you wiser, stronger, and more grounded in Him. The enemy wants you to see failure as a final verdict, but God sees it as a refining process. What didn't work is not proof that you can't succeed - it's preparation for how to move forward with greater clarity and dependence on Him. The very place where you stumbled can become the place where you stand stronger than before. If you will bring your failure to God instead of running from it, He will turn it into wisdom, resilience, and renewed courage. You are not disqualified because you fell - you are being equipped because you did.

Other chains are forged in shame, in the quiet, suffocating weight that tells you to hide your past, to shrink back from purpose, to disqualify yourself before you ever step forward. Shame convinces you that what you've done defines who you are, and that your failures have the final word. But that voice is not from God. It is a lie designed to keep you bound to a version of yourself that Christ already died to redeem. Where shame pushes you into darkness, God calls you into the light. Christ does not speak the language of shame - He speaks redemption. His grace does not demand that you earn your freedom - He offers it as a gift. You are not called to carry what He has already carried for you. You are called to receive what He has already finished. So lift your head. Step out of hiding. And walk forward in the freedom that grace has made available because the voice of shame may accuse, but the voice of Christ declares you redeemed, restored, and released.

Unforgiveness is a chain that doesn't always feel heavy at first, but over time it tightens around the heart. It replays the offense and keeps wounds open. The pain may have been real and undeserved but holding onto it does not heal it. God never asked you to pretend it didn't hurt; He invites you to release its grip. Forgiveness is not approval of the wrong - it is a refusal to let that wrong continue to define you. When you cling to bitterness, you stay connected to the injury, but when you forgive, you step out of its shadow and into freedom. Forgiveness is an act of strength, not weakness. It is a decision to trust God with justice while you walk forward in peace. You may not be able to change what was done, but through Christ, you can break its power over you. When you release others from the debt you feel they owe, you are not excusing them - you are freeing yourself. Chains fall when grace rises. And the moment you let go, you make room for healing, for clarity, and for the life God is calling you to live.

Breaking chains is a daily surrender, a steady renewal of the mind. The battle is not just around you; it is within you, where old thoughts try to reclaim ground that God has already redeemed. Every day, you must make the intentional choice to tear down the lies that once defined you and replace them with truth that sets you free. When your past whispers accusations, you confront it with the Word of God, with the identity He has given you, and with the finished work of Christ. Freedom is not found in ignoring the battle, but in winning it one thought at a time. And as you continue in this process, what once felt like effort becomes instinct. The voice of condemnation grows quieter while the voice of God grows stronger. When guilt tries to rise, you remind yourself that the price has already been paid in full, and there is nothing left for you to carry. You begin to walk differently, think differently, and live differently not because everything changed overnight, but because you stayed committed to the truth.

You were not created to live trapped in repetition - walking the same worn paths of failure, returning to the same struggles, and carrying weights God never intended you to keep. What repeats without change eventually becomes a prison. Yet God interrupts patterns with truth, exposes lies that keep you bound and invites you into a new way of living. Forward movement begins when you refuse to accept "this is just how I am" and instead believe, "this is who God is calling me to become." When God sets you free, He doesn't leave you wandering; He leads you forward with purpose. The same power that breaks cycles also builds new paths. You are not destined to circle the same ground - you are called to advance, to grow, and to become. Every step of obedience breaks another link, every act of faith moves you further ahead. So don't go back to what God has already brought you out of. Keep moving forward. Because chains keep you going in circles but freedom always takes you somewhere new.

Refusing to stay bound requires the courage to walk away from what feels familiar, even when it once felt like home. Bondage has a way of becoming comfortable not because it is good, but because you learn its patterns, its limits, its false sense of security. But God did not design you to live confined by what is easy or predictable. He calls you beyond the borders of your past into a life that reflects His truth. What is familiar may feel safe, but it can quietly keep you from becoming who you were created to be. Freedom, on the other hand, may feel uncertain at first. It stretches you, challenges you, and calls you to trust God in ways you never had to before. But that discomfort means you are stepping into something greater than what you've known. You were not created to remain where you are -you were created to move forward, to live unbound, and to walk in the fullness of what Christ has already secured for you. Don't return to what held you but step boldly into the freedom that was always meant to be yours.

There is a holy strength that awakens in a man the moment he declares, "This ends with me." It is the strength of conviction - the kind that refuses to keep negotiating with what God has already broken off his life. In that moment, he recognizes that through Christ, he has been given authority to move forward. That decision becomes a line drawn in the sand of his soul. And once that line is drawn, he cannot unknow it. He has seen what freedom looks like, and he knows he was created for more. From that point on, everything begins to shift. Old patterns lose their grip because he refuses to give them attention. A new direction forms - one marked by purpose, clarity, and obedience. He steps forward not because everything feels easy, but because everything has been settled within him. This is where transformation begins. And when a man truly decides that the cycle ends with him, he doesn't just change his own life - he alters the trajectory of everything connected to him.

God does not simply remove what bound you - He restores what was taken while you were bound. The years that felt stolen, the confidence that was shaken, the identity that was blurred, and the purpose that seemed delayed are not beyond His reach. He is not limited to setting you free; He is committed to making you whole. What looked like loss in your life becomes the very ground where His redemption is revealed. He brings you back stronger, clearer, and more rooted in who you were created to be. What you surrendered to God was never wasted - it was transformed. The time you thought was gone becomes wisdom. The pain becomes perspective. The struggle becomes strength. And the story you once wanted to hide becomes a testimony that points to His power. God is a restorer, not just a rescuer. He takes what the enemy meant for harm and rebuilds it into something that carries purpose, meaning, and impact. In His hands, nothing is lost - everything is redeemed.

You were never called to build your future while dragging the weight of your past behind you. The chains of yesterday may have shaped parts of your story, but they were never meant to define your destiny. Christ did not set you free so you could continue living as if you were still bound. He broke those chains so you could walk differently, think differently, and live differently. Freedom is not just the absence of bondage - it is the presence of a new identity. God convicts to restore, not to shame. He speaks to lift you, not to hold you down. The limits you've accepted, the ceilings you've believed in, the boundaries you've placed on your own life - those are not the limits He has written over you. God's call is always forward, always upward, always greater than what you've settled for. You are meant to walk unchained, unburdened, and unafraid - not because your past didn't happen, but because it no longer has authority over you. Step forward boldly. What once held you back has no right to hold you now.

Today is an opportunity to step out of everything that has tried to define you, limit you, and hold you in place. But this step forward is not about trying harder or pushing further in your own ability. It is about laying down the weight, the fear, the past, and trusting that God has already done what you could not do for yourself. Freedom is not something you earn through effort; it is something you receive through faith. The chains you feel are not as strong as they seem, because through Christ, they have already been broken. What remains is your decision. Will you stay where you have been, or will you walk into what God has already made available? You don't have to live under what has been lifted. Step forward in confidence, knowing that the man you were created to be was simply waiting for you to believe it. And when you choose to walk in that truth, you will find a strength, a clarity, and a freedom that does not come from striving, but from finally living as who you were always meant to be.

| 26 |

"THE STRENGTH TO BUILD"

There is a strength that goes beyond survival - it is the strength to build. Fighting may win battles and endurance may carry you through storms, but building requires a different kind of resolve. It demands vision when nothing is visible yet, patience when progress feels slow, and faith when results are not immediate. A builder does not wait for perfect conditions; he begins where he is, with what he has, trusting that God will bless what is committed to Him. While others react to circumstances, a builder rises above them, choosing to lay each stone with intention, knowing that what he is constructing today will shape tomorrow. This kind of strength is rooted in purpose. It calls a man to see beyond the present moment and commit to a life that leaves a lasting impact. When a man embraces this calling, he stops drifting and starts directing his life. He becomes a man who doesn't just live day to day, but one who creates, invests, and establishes something that will stand long after he is gone.

A man who builds understands that purpose is not discovered by accident but formed through intention. Each day he rises with clarity knowing that small, consistent choices shape the structure of his life. Every decision becomes a brick, every action a layer, every habit a foundation. He refuses to live by chance or randomness because he knows God has called him to live deliberately. And with that understanding, he becomes careful with what he allows, disciplined in what he pursues, and focused on what truly matters. This kind of man recognizes that construction takes time, pressure, and perseverance. There are no shortcuts to something that will last. He aligns his plans with God's direction, knowing that a life built on truth will stand when storms come. He does not despise the process, because he understands that strength is forged in consistency. And in time, what he has built will reflect a life structured with purpose, anchored in faith, and strong enough to endure.

God has already placed purpose within you, but purpose is not fulfilled automatically; it is revealed and strengthened through alignment. When your thoughts, decisions, and actions begin to agree with what God has spoken - you step into authority over your own direction. You stop reacting to life and start building it, one deliberate choice at a time. Intention is what transforms scattered effort into focused progress. It takes the same energy you once wasted and channels it into something that lasts. Every disciplined decision becomes a brick. Every act of obedience becomes a layer. Every moment of consistency becomes part of a foundation that cannot easily be shaken. This is how a meaningful life is built - not through bursts of inspiration, but through daily, intentional faithfulness. When a man commits to living this way, he no longer wonders who he is becoming - he knows, because he is building it on purpose with God.

Too many men crave outcomes they are unwilling to build foundations for. They want influence without integrity, strength without structure, and impact without the discipline that sustains it. A man who refuses structure will always live in cycles of starting and stopping, rising and falling, hoping and drifting. Real growth is not found in moments of inspiration, but in habits of obedience. Discipline is not restriction; it is alignment. It positions your life to carry the weight of the calling you say you want. Strength is built in the daily choice to show up when it's inconvenient, uncomfortable, and unnoticed. Consistency is forged in repetition, refined through perseverance, and proven over time. Every day you commit, you lay another brick. Every time you follow through, you reinforce the structure of your life. And over time, what once felt difficult becomes who you are. God honors the man who keeps faithfully showing up because in that consistency, He is not just building your results - He is building you.

A strong life is forged in the quiet places where character is shaped and convictions are tested. It is in the unseen moments that a man proves who he truly is. Private obedience becomes the foundation of public strength. Every disciplined decision and every quiet act of faithfulness is laying another stone in the life God is building through you. What feels small in the moment is never insignificant in the process. The strength to build is revealed in consistency, not convenience. It is choosing to stay committed when it would be easier to drift, to remain faithful when results are not immediate, and to keep building when progress feels slow. God sees what others overlook, and He honors what is done in secret. The life that stands firm in the storm is the life that was carefully built when no one else was paying attention. So do not despise the hidden seasons - they are where real strength is formed, where endurance is developed, and where a man becomes unshakable from the inside out.

There will be days when what you're building seems insignificant compared to the vision God placed in your heart. In those moments, the temptation is to question the process, to doubt whether anything is really happening at all. But a builder understands something deeper: foundations are not impressive while they're being laid. They are hidden, quiet, and often unnoticed but they are essential. God does some of His greatest work in the unseen places, where character is formed, discipline is strengthened, and faith is tested. Do not despise the days that seem ordinary or the effort that feels unnoticed. Every act of obedience, every step of consistency, every decision to keep going is adding weight to what you are becoming. There comes a moment when what was built in silence begins to stand in strength. Stay committed to the process because the man who keeps building when nothing seems to be happening is the man who will one day stand in something that cannot be shaken.

You must resist the urge to dismantle what you've begun simply because it isn't unfolding on your timeline. Impatience whispers that slow progress means no progress, but that is a lie designed to pull you away from the very thing God is forming in you. What feels delayed is often being developed. Strength, character, and endurance are built in seasons of steady, unseen work. A man who quits too soon never sees what could have been completed through faithfulness. Don't let frustration cause you to abandon what God has already placed in your hands to build. Impatience destroys more than failure ever could because it convinces you to walk away before the breakthrough arrives. Impatience tears down the structure while it's still under construction. Every day you stay committed, even when progress feels slow, you are laying bricks that will one day stand as something strong, steady, and lasting. Stay the course because what is being built in you is not just for now - it is preparation for what's ahead.

Building also requires wisdom - the kind that sees beyond what is available and discerns what is aligned. Not every opportunity carries purpose, and not every open door is an invitation from God. A wise builder does not move simply because something is possible - he moves because it is purposeful, aligned with God, and worth building for eternity. He filters decisions through purpose, not pressure, and through calling, not convenience. So he chooses carefully. He guards his time, protects his energy, and directs his focus with intention. He knows that every investment is shaping something - either strengthening the foundation or weakening it. Wisdom teaches him to build slowly if necessary, but never carelessly. It reminds him that what is built with clarity will stand, while what is built in haste will eventually collapse. And in that discipline, he finds strength not just to build, but to build something that lasts, something rooted in purpose, and something that reflects the hand of God on his life.

Your foundation determines what your life can carry. It is easy to build something that looks impressive on the surface - strong words, confident appearance, outward success - but if truth is not at the core, it becomes fragile under pressure. Storms do not expose what is visible; they reveal what is hidden. When life shakes you, it is not your image that holds you steady - it is your foundation. A man rooted in God is not easily moved because his strength does not come from performance, but from truth that runs deep beneath everything others can see. When your life is built on God, you gain a strength that time cannot erode and pressure cannot destroy. Trials may come, winds may rise, and seasons may change, but what is anchored in Him will endure. You are not just building for today - you are building for eternity. So invest where it matters most because a life grounded in God may not always look the most impressive at first, but in the end, it will be the one still standing when everything else has fallen.

Jesus made it clear that what you build your life on determines how it will stand. Sand may look solid for a moment, but it cannot endure pressure, storms, or time. In the same way, a life built on shifting priorities, emotions, or worldly approval will eventually collapse under the weight of reality. But when a man anchors his life in Christ, he is building on something unshakable. The winds may come, the rain may fall, and the floods may rise, but a life rooted in Him does not crumble. Building on the rock is not a one-time decision - it is a daily commitment. It is choosing obedience when it's hard, truth when it's uncomfortable, and faith when it's tested. When you build this way, you are establishing something that will last beyond this life. Your choices, your character, and your faithfulness become part of a legacy that echoes into eternity. A man who builds on the rock doesn't just survive the storm - he outlasts it, and what he builds continues to stand long after the storm has passed.

The strength to build is not measured only by what a man can accomplish in his lifetime, but by what continues to stand when he is no longer there to maintain it. A man of God lifts his eyes beyond temporary success and sees the generations that will be impacted by his obedience. He understands that every decision, every sacrifice, and every act of faith is laying bricks into something far greater than himself. His life becomes a foundation that others can stand on, a testimony that speaks long after his voice is silent. When a man embraces this kind of vision, he no longer lives for short-term gain. Instead, he invests in truth, in character, and in faithfulness knowing these are the materials that endure. The strength to build with legacy in mind produces a life that echoes into the future - a life that points others toward God. And in the end, what he leaves behind is not just achievement, but impact - something eternal, something that carries the mark of a life built with purpose and guided by God.

The world measures success by what a man can gather, but God measures it by what a man gives. Possessions fade, titles lose their weight, and accomplishments eventually become memories, but the lives you touch carry forward long after you are gone. Every word of truth you speak, every act of integrity you live out, and every example of faith you model becomes a seed planted in someone else's life. And those seeds grow, multiply, and continue to bear fruit in ways you may never fully see on this side of eternity. A man who understands legacy knows that what he builds in others will echo far beyond his lifetime. Your faith can become someone else's foundation. Your obedience can become someone else's courage. Your consistency can become someone else's direction. When you pour into others with purpose and conviction, you are building something that cannot be destroyed by time. This is the kind of life that leaves a mark on human hearts. And in the end, that is the legacy that truly matters.

You may not stand on a platform or hold a title, but your life is still speaking. In your consistency, your integrity, your discipline, and your faith, you are showing others what matters. Legacy is not built in grand gestures alone - it is formed in the daily decisions that reveal who you truly are. What you tolerate teaches compromise. What you pursue teaches priority. What you honor teaches value. So the question is not whether you are teaching but what you are teaching. Are you modeling faith when it is difficult, or only when it is convenient? Are you showing strength under pressure, or surrendering to it? The life you live is becoming a blueprint for someone else - your family, your friends, those watching from a distance. Make it a blueprint worth following. Let your words align with truth, your standards reflect conviction, and your choices point toward God. Because long after the moment has passed, what you modeled will remain and what you built in others will become the legacy that outlives you.

A man who builds with faith understands that every decision rooted in obedience, every act of integrity, and every moment of trust in God becomes a foundation others can stand on. His faith is not hidden; it is woven into how he leads, how he speaks, and how he endures. And because of that, his life points forward showing others what it looks like to walk with God when it is difficult, to stand firm when it is costly, and to remain faithful when it would be easier to quit. Such a man leaves more than memories - he leaves direction. Long after his voice is gone, his example continues to speak. Those who come after him can look back and find clarity in how he lived, courage in how he stood, and strength in how he trusted God. His life becomes a marker that says, "This is the way. Walk in it." He gives others something solid in a world that often feels uncertain. And in doing so, he fulfills a greater purpose: not just building a life for himself but establishing a legacy that leads others closer to God.

Creating something that lasts demands endurance. There will be resistance that tests your resolve and setbacks that challenge your faith. At times, it may feel like the very thing you are building is being pushed against from every side. But a man who walks with God understands that opposition is often confirmation that what he is building matters. Endurance is forged in those moments when quitting feels easier, yet you choose to remain steady, committed, and anchored in purpose. What is built with God carries a strength that goes beyond human effort. It is not fragile or temporary - it is rooted, reinforced, and sustained by something eternal. When your life, your work, and your calling are aligned with Him, you are not building alone - you are partnering with the One who establishes what cannot be shaken. That kind of durability is not produced overnight, but through faithful obedience over time. Stay the course. What you are building, with God at the center, will outlast the storms sent to destroy it.

You are not building alone. Every step of obedience and every act of discipline is seen and strengthened by God Himself. He steadies your hands when they grow tired, sharpens your vision when distractions try to cloud it, and gives you the wisdom to build with purpose instead of pressure. What feels overwhelming in your own strength becomes possible when His power is at work within you. God is actively involved shaping not only what you are building, but who you are becoming as you build it. When you commit your work to Him, you are no longer building for recognition, approval, or short-term results - you are building something that carries eternal significance. God establishes what is surrendered to Him, anchoring it in truth and purpose so it can stand through time and trials. What you place in His hands is refined, strengthened, and secured. And in the end, you will see what God built through you, something lasting, something meaningful, something eternal.

There are moments when obedience feels costly, when faith requires more than comfort wants to give, and when staying aligned with God demands quiet perseverance. Yet in those very moments, something eternal is being built within you and through you. Every unseen decision to trust Him, every choice to walk in truth instead of ease, and every step forward when it would be easier to stand still is shaping a life that carries weight far beyond the present. What feels like pressure is often the process of strengthening, refining, and preparing you for something greater. You may not always see the results right away, but that does not mean nothing is happening. God is working in layers - forming character, establishing foundation, and aligning your path with His purpose. The seeds you plant in obedience will grow in ways you cannot yet measure. What you build today in faith will become strength tomorrow, not only for you but for others who will be impacted by your life.

Build with intention. Lay each brick on purpose. Every decision, every habit, every act of obedience is shaping the structure of who you are becoming. When you build with faith, you trust that even when you cannot see the full blueprint, God does. He is not only the architect of your purpose, but the strength behind your hands as you work. What feels small today is not insignificant - it is foundational. A man aligned with God is never wasting effort; he is establishing something eternal with every faithful step. Build with endurance. There will be seasons when progress feels slow, when the weight feels heavy, and when the results seem distant. But lasting things are not built quickly - they are built consistently. When you refuse to quit, when you keep showing up, when you stay committed even in silence, you are proving that your foundation is real. A man who builds his life with God is creating something that will stand long after he is gone. His life becomes a legacy of strength, faith, and unwavering obedience.

| 27 |

"THE COURAGE TO PROTECT"

There is a kind of courage that does not announce itself, yet it carries a strength that cannot be shaken. It does not rise for recognition but for responsibility. It is rooted in truth, anchored in God, and unmoved by the opinions of others. When pressure comes, it does not panic or retreat. It steps forward. It holds the line. It understands that protecting what is right is not always celebrated, but it is always necessary. This kind of courage is about being faithful to what God has placed in your care. The courage to protect is seen in the man who guards his family, his integrity, his calling, and his faith without compromise. It is the strength to confront what is wrong, even when it would be easier to stay silent. It is the resolve to stand in the gap when others step back. This courage acts when it matters most. It knows that what is left unprotected will eventually be lost. So it remains alert, disciplined, and unwavering. In doing so, it reflects the heart of one who stands because something sacred is worth defending.

A man who understands protection lives with clarity, not confusion. He does not try to carry every burden or fix every situation, but he refuses to neglect what God has clearly placed in his hands. He recognizes that his faith must be guarded from compromise, his family from neglect, his integrity from corruption, and his calling from distraction. These are sacred assignments and he treats them with seriousness because he understands that what God entrusts is never ordinary. It carries eternal weight, and it demands intentional care. This kind of man sets boundaries, stays alert, and stands firm when pressure comes. He does not wait until something is under attack to take action; he lives watchful and prepared. Because he values what God has given him, he is willing to defend it, nurture it, and remain faithful to it no matter the cost. And in doing so, his life becomes a place of strength and security, not just for himself, but for everyone entrusted to his care.

Defending what matters most begins with clarity. A man must first settle in his heart what is sacred, what is eternal, and what carries weight in the eyes of God. Without that foundation, he becomes reactive instead of intentional, easily pulled into battles that drain him while neglecting the ones that truly matter. But when his values are anchored in God, he recognizes that faith, family, and integrity are worth standing for, guarding, and, if necessary, fighting to preserve. From that place of clarity, his life gains direction and strength. He no longer wastes energy defending pride, comfort, or temporary gain. Instead, he rises with purpose, knowing exactly where to stand and when to act. His decisions carry conviction because they are rooted in alignment with God's will. And when pressure comes, he does not waver because he knows what matters most. And a man who knows what is worth protecting becomes a man who stands firm, unmoved, and unwavering in the face of anything that tries to compromise it.

There will always be forces that attempt to erode what is good, but they rarely come with clear warning signs. Compromise whispers instead of shouts, temptation disguises itself as something reasonable, and deception often feels like truth in its earliest form. This is why a man must remain spiritually alert. Watchfulness is the discipline of examining what enters your mind, your heart, and your life before it has the chance to settle in. A man who walks closely with God develops discernment, and that discernment becomes his defense. Being watchful means you stay rooted in truth, anchored in God's Word, and sensitive to His voice. When something feels off, you bring it into the light. This kind of vigilance keeps your life aligned and your spirit clear. A watchful man lives prepared. He understands that protecting what is good requires intention, consistency, and courage. And because he chooses to stay alert, he preserves not only his own life, but also the lives and values entrusted to him.

Protection requires awareness. A man who is called to protect must be spiritually awake, discerning what is right, what is wrong, and what is trying to quietly take root in his life, his family, and his environment. Awareness is the ability to recognize when something is out of alignment with God and respond before it gains ground. A distracted man is vulnerable, but an alert man is prepared. He stands watch, grounded in truth, anchored in God, and attentive to what truly matters. What a man ignores, he unintentionally allows. What he tolerates, he gives permission to grow whether it is compromise, negativity, temptation, or spiritual weakness. Protection means addressing issues early, standing firm when something is not right, and choosing courage over comfort. A man who walks in awareness does not wait for destruction to appear - he confronts it while it is still small. He guards his heart, his home, and his calling with intention, knowing that vigilance is not optional - it is part of his responsibility.

There are moments when protecting what matters most is not about what you do but what you refuse to allow. Saying no to compromise is the recognition that not everything that presents itself deserves access to your life. When your standards are shaped by God, you begin to see clearly what builds and what breaks, what strengthens and what slowly erodes. The discipline to refuse becomes a shield, guarding your integrity, your purpose, and the people entrusted to your care. This kind of courage is often quiet, but it is powerful. It shows up in private decisions, in unseen boundaries, and in the willingness to walk away even when it costs you something. Saying no to what is easy protects what is eternal. It keeps your heart aligned, your mind clear, and your path steady. A man who refuses the wrong things positions himself to fully embrace the right ones. And over time, those firm, faithful refusals become the very evidence of a life that is guarded, grounded, and led by God.

There are moments in a man's life when conviction must move beyond thought and become action. When what is right is threatened, when truth is being compromised, or when those entrusted to him are at risk, courage steps forward. It speaks when it would be easier to stay quiet. It stands when others shrink back. It refuses to ignore what God has made clear. This kind of courage is driven by a deep, settled conviction that what is right must be defended, no matter the cost. Decisive action is where courage becomes visible. It is the moment when a man chooses to confront instead of avoiding, to correct instead of tolerating, and to protect instead of retreating. These are necessary choices because what goes unchallenged can cause lasting damage. But when a man rises with boldness and clarity, he becomes a barrier against destruction and a force for righteousness. In those defining moments, his actions declare what he truly believes and his courage becomes the protection others depend on.

Standing against evil is always a deliberate choice. It shows up when you refuse to compromise your integrity, when you speak truth instead of staying silent, and when you choose what is right even when it costs you something. Evil often advances through small allowances and unchecked attitudes, but a man of conviction recognizes that every moment is an opportunity to either uphold righteousness or allow darkness to gain ground. His strength is not measured by how much attention he draws, but by how firmly he stands when it matters most. A man who protects responds to what is in front of him. He understands that passivity is not neutrality; it is permission for wrong to continue. So he steps forward with courage. Whether he is defending his family, his values, or his faith, he takes responsibility for the ground God has entrusted to him. And in doing so, he becomes a barrier against what seeks to destroy and a reflection of the strength and righteousness that comes from living aligned with God.

This kind of courage is rooted in conviction. It is steady, anchored, and unwavering because it is built on truth rather than impulse. A man who protects what is right is not reacting to the moment; he is responding from a place of alignment with God. He understands that protecting what matters is not about being seen as strong, but about being faithful to what is right. A true protector moves with discipline and clarity. He does not rush into conflict without direction, nor does he shrink back when it is required. His restraint is just as powerful as his action, because both are guided by truth. He knows when to stand firm, when to speak, and when to act, not out of impulse but out of obedience. This kind of courage reflects the heart of God. It is strong but controlled; bold but wise. And in a world driven by reaction and emotion, a man who is guided by conviction becomes a steady force - one who preserves, defends, and upholds what is right with strength that is both grounded and unshakable.

There will always be resistance when a man chooses to stand for what is right. Not everyone will understand his decisions, and not everyone will agree with the standard he holds. But a man who protects is not driven by the need to be accepted - he is anchored in the call to be faithful. So he stands because he understands that what he is guarding is too valuable to be surrendered for the sake of comfort or agreement. A man who protects measures his choices against God's truth, not public opinion. He is not swayed by pressure, popularity, or fear of rejection. Instead, he listens for the voice of God and aligns his actions with it, even when it places him in the minority. This kind of obedience requires strength, clarity, and unwavering trust but it also produces stability, authority, and peace. Because when a man knows he is walking in obedience, he no longer needs validation from others. He stands firm, not because it is easy, but because it is right and, in that stand, he becomes a protector of what matters most.

Being a protector also means standing watch over the parts of life no one else sees. A man of strength disciplines his thoughts, filters what he allows into his mind, and refuses to entertain lies that weaken his identity. He understands that battles are often won or lost long before they ever become visible. When he guards his mind with truth, his heart with purity, and his spirit with conviction, he builds an inner fortress that cannot easily be shaken. He is not passive with his inner life but is intentional, alert, and anchored in God. What a man allows internally will always find its way outward. Compromise in private becomes weakness in public, but integrity in secret becomes strength in every arena of life. A protector invites God into the hidden places, allowing Him to refine, correct, and strengthen from the inside out. And as his inner life is aligned, his outer life becomes a reflection of that strength - steady, trustworthy, and able to stand firm no matter what comes.

A man cannot stand guard over what matters most if his own spirit is unguarded. When a man neglects his time with God, ignores conviction, or compromises in secret, he weakens the very foundation he is called to stand on. But when he chooses to guard his heart, renew his mind, and stay rooted in truth, something powerful is formed within him. Strength is built in quiet moments of obedience, in unseen decisions to do what is right, and in the discipline to remain faithful when no one is watching. Integrity is forged in the hidden places. It is developed when a man chooses truth over convenience, purity over temptation, and obedience over comfort. The battles fought in private shape his character, sharpen his discernment, and prepare him for the moments when others will depend on his strength. A man who wins in secret will stand with confidence in public. And when the time comes to protect, lead, and stand firm, he will not be shaken because his strength was established long before the battle ever appeared.

Protection is not limited to standing guard against visible threats - it reaches into the unseen areas of life where hearts are shaped, minds are influenced, and character is formed. A man who understands this does not only defend with strength, but leads with wisdom, patience, and discernment. He guards the atmosphere of his home, his relationships, and his influence. He refuses to allow fear, confusion, or compromise to take root where he has been called to lead. Through his words, he brings clarity. Through his actions, he models integrity. Through his faith, he establishes a covering that others can stand under with confidence. When a man walks in this kind of protection, his presence becomes a place of refuge. Those around him are strengthened and built up. His leadership creates room for growth, where mistakes can be corrected without shame and progress can be made with encouragement. And in that environment, people don't just survive - they become who God created them to be.

A man's life speaks louder than his words, setting the tone for those who watch him, follow him, and learn from him. In his home, his consistency builds security. In his workplace, his integrity establishes trust. In his community, his courage inspires strength. When he stands firm in truth, he becomes someone others can lean on when things begin to shake. But when he compromises, even in small ways, it creates cracks that ripple outward. Influence is never neutral; it is either strengthening or weakening what surrounds him. That is why protection is not just about defending oneself - it is about guarding the atmosphere that others live in. A man who understands this knows that his decisions shape more than his own life. He stands against what is wrong, not just for his sake, but for those who depend on his strength. He refuses to normalize compromise because he knows others may follow where he leads. In this way, his life becomes a covering that protects the people entrusted to his influence.

Courage to protect is the quiet resolve to keep standing when the battle does not end, to keep guarding what matters when the pressure does not lift. Endurance transforms courage from an impulse into a lifestyle. When a man commits to protecting what is right, he understands that the assignment will stretch him, test him, and sometimes exhaust him but he does not walk away. His strength is not found in bursts of passion, but in the consistency of his faithfulness. A true protector does not grow weary of doing what is right because his motivation is deeper than convenience - it is rooted in conviction and sustained by God. Even when the threats evolve and the challenges shift, he remains anchored. He shows up again and again, not because it is easy, but because it is necessary. And in that endurance, his character is refined, his faith is strengthened, and his life becomes a steady wall of protection for others. This is the kind of courage that lasts - the kind that does not fade but endures.

There will be moments when doing what is right demands sacrifice, stretches your endurance, and presses against your comfort. In those moments, the easier path will always whisper louder, offering relief without responsibility. But a man anchored in God does not measure decisions by ease - he measures them by purpose. He understands that protecting what matters most may require him to give up what is temporary to preserve what is eternal. The cost is real, but so is the calling. And when his convictions are rooted in truth, he stands not because it is easy, but because it is necessary. A man who understands purpose knows that some battles are worth fighting, even when they come with discomfort or loss. Because in the end, it is not what he avoided that defines him, but what he was willing to stand for. And when he chooses to stand firm, even at a cost, he aligns himself with God's strength proving that what is built on conviction will never be wasted.

A man of faith is not passive in the face of danger, compromise, or spiritual attack; he is alert, grounded, and ready to act. He watches over his home, guards his heart, and stands firm in truth when others shrink back. This kind of courage is fueled by a deep understanding that what God has entrusted to him is worth defending. To live intentionally means he does not wait for problems to escalate; he steps in early, leads with clarity, and refuses to allow what is right to be overtaken by what is wrong. A man who embraces this calling does not abandon his post when it becomes difficult; he leans in, strengthened by God, and remains steady under pressure. This is the kind of man who builds trust, establishes order, and creates safety for others to grow. His life becomes a shield, not because he is perfect, but because he is committed. And through that commitment, God works through him to push back darkness and preserve what matters most.

When a man embraces this responsibility is not easily shaken by emotion, circumstance, or opposition because his strength is rooted in conviction and guided by God. People begin to recognize that he is dependable not because life is easy for him, but because he refuses to abandon what is right when it becomes difficult. His presence brings order into chaos, clarity into confusion, and strength into moments where others might falter. This kind of man stands firm because it is who he has chosen to be. When pressure rises, he leans in with courage and purpose. He understands that what is good, true, and valuable must be protected, even when it costs him something. He refuses to be passive in moments that require action, and he will not allow fear or fatigue to silence his responsibility. His life becomes a barrier against compromise and a shield for those entrusted to him, proving that real strength is not found in dominance, but in faithful, unwavering commitment to what matters most.

The courage to protect is rooted in love. A man who truly loves God will stand for what honors Him. A man who loves truth will refuse to compromise it. And a man who loves the people entrusted to his life will not stand idly by while they are threatened, misled, or harmed. This kind of love creates clarity. It removes hesitation. It replaces fear with conviction. When love is strong, courage becomes steady. It does not waver with circumstances or shrink under pressure. It holds the line when it would be easier to step back. It speaks when silence would be more comfortable. It endures when the cost feels heavy. This is the strength of a man anchored in love. He is not fighting for attention, but for what matters most. And because his foundation is rooted in God, his courage does not depend on how he feels in the moment. It is sustained by something deeper, something unshakable. He knows exactly what he is standing for, and that gives him the power to remain standing.

| 28 |

"THE LION'S LEGACY"

A man's life is not defined solely by his achievements, titles, or the things he builds with his hands - it is revealed in what continues after his voice is silent. Legacy is the echo of a life shaped by obedience to God and lived with intention. It is not found in temporary success, but in eternal impact. The way a man loves, leads, speaks, and stands for truth leaves a mark that outlives him. His character becomes a blueprint. His faith becomes a foundation. And his choices become seeds planted in the lives of others, growing long after he is gone. Whether he realizes it or not, every man is leaving something behind. The question is not if there will be a legacy, but what kind it will be. A life lived carelessly will leave confusion, but a life surrendered to God will leave clarity, strength, and direction. When a man walks faithfully, he becomes a living testimony that points others toward something greater than himself. So live with the end in mind because what you leave behind will speak long after you are gone.

Too many men live measuring success by what they gain instead of what they pass on. They chase moments that fade, recognition that disappears, and comfort that weakens their calling. But a man aligned with God understands that every decision carries weight beyond the present moment. His words shape those who are listening. His actions build patterns others will follow. His faith, lived out consistently, becomes a foundation that outlives him. A lion does not live for the moment. He establishes territory, protects what matters, and creates stability for what comes after him. In the same way, a man of faith recognizes that his life is an assignment, not an accident. He builds with intention, leads with conviction, and stands with endurance because he knows others will walk in what he leaves behind. His legacy is not found in temporary victories but in transformed lives, strengthened families, and unwavering faith that echoes into the next generation.

What you leave behind matters because it reveals the true substance of your life. Titles fade, wealth changes hands, and status is quickly forgotten, but character leaves a mark that time cannot erase. The way you lived becomes a testimony that continues long after you are gone. A man who walks with God does not simply pass through life; he plants seeds in the hearts of others. Those seeds grow into courage, conviction, and truth in the next generation. When your voice is no longer heard, your life will still be speaking through the example you set, the standards you held, and the faith you refused to compromise. So live with eternity in mind. Let your decisions be shaped not by what is temporary, but by what will endure. Choose faith over fear, obedience over convenience, and purpose over comfort. Build a life that directs others toward God, even in your absence. Because in the end, your legacy will not be measured by what you accumulated, but by what you imparted.

Legacy is not something that appears at the end of a man's life - it is something that is being written every single day. Every decision to walk in integrity, every act of obedience, and every quiet sacrifice becomes a brick in the foundation of what you will leave behind. A man's legacy is not built in grand gestures, but in daily faithfulness - showing up, standing firm, and choosing alignment with God again and again. Over time, those small, consistent choices form something powerful. They create a life that speaks long after words are gone. The man who commits to building this way does not chase recognition - he pursues righteousness. And in doing so, he leaves a legacy that carries weight, direction, and impact for generations to come. What you do today matters more than you think, because you are not just living in the moment - you are shaping what will remain when the moment has passed.

Every word you speak is a seed, and every action you take is a blueprint. Whether you realize it or not, you are constantly depositing something into the lives of those who are watching you. Words spoken in truth, patience, and conviction plant strength, clarity, and identity. A man cannot separate what he says from what he lives; the two work together to form the legacy he leaves behind. There is no neutral ground when it comes to legacy. You are either building something that strengthens the next generation or leaving gaps they will have to struggle to fill. Integrity, consistency, and faith are generational investments. When a man chooses to live aligned with God, he creates a pattern others can follow with confidence. But when his life is divided, uncertain, or shifting, it produces uncertainty in those who come after him. So speak with purpose. Live with intention. Because long after you are gone, what you planted through your words and your life will continue to grow in someone else.

The lion does not roam without purpose or restraint. He moves with awareness knowing that his strength carries responsibility. He guards his territory, protects his own, and maintains order with presence and authority. In the same way, a man is not called to live recklessly or be driven by impulse. True strength is revealed in discipline, in the ability to lead with wisdom, and in the willingness to stand as a protector of what matters most. A man who understands this does not waste his strength on selfish pursuits - he channels it into purpose, into stewardship, and into covering those entrusted to him. God did not give you strength for indulgence - He gave it for impact. Your strength is meant to build, to defend, and to lead in alignment with His truth. It is not about dominance for the sake of ego, but about responsibility for the sake of others. When a man embraces this, hie becomes a source of stability in uncertain times, a shield in moments of danger, and a guide for those who follow.

Impacting future generations requires a willingness to look beyond what is immediate and see what is eternal. A man of vision understands that his life is not confined to the present moment. The way he walks with God today becomes a blueprint for tomorrow. His faith sets a standard, his discipline builds a pattern, and his character establishes a foundation that others will stand on long after he is gone. Even when no one seems to be watching, heaven is recording a legacy in motion. The quiet decisions, the unseen obedience, and the consistent pursuit of truth are shaping something far greater than a single lifetime. You may never meet the people your life will influence, but they will feel the impact of how you chose to live. Generations are strengthened or weakened by the examples set before them. When you choose integrity over compromise, faith over fear, and purpose over comfort, you are sending a message forward in time. Your life becomes a testimony that echoes beyond your reach.

There are eyes on your life that are studying your responses, your attitudes, and your decisions. The way you handle failure, the way you recover from setbacks, and the way you carry yourself when no one is applauding becomes a living message. Without saying a word, you are showing others what strength looks like, what faith looks like, and what it means to remain grounded when everything around you is shaking. Your life is teaching, even when you are not speaking. Every reaction is a lesson. Every decision is a demonstration. You are either modeling resilience or retreat, faith or fear, discipline or compromise. The next generation is becoming what you consistently show. So live with awareness. Live with intention. Let your life reflect a steady trust in God, a refusal to quit, and a commitment to walk in integrity no matter the circumstance. Because long after your words fade, the example you set will continue to speak and it will shape lives in ways you may never fully see.

A lion's legacy is not carved out by flawless moments, but by faithful ones. It is built in the quiet return after failure and in the courage to stand back up when it would be easier to stay down. Consistency forms a life that is steady, trustworthy, and real. It shows that strength is not the absence of weakness, but the refusal to let weakness define the end of your story. When a man chooses to keep walking with God, he becomes a living testimony that growth is always possible. That kind of life gives others permission to keep going. It removes the pressure of perfection and replaces it with the power of perseverance. People are not inspired by someone who never falls - they are strengthened by someone who rises again with greater clarity and deeper faith. A lion's legacy says you can get back up, you can change, and you can keep moving forward. And in doing so, it creates a ripple effect of courage, where others find the strength to grow, to endure, and to finish strong without quitting.

If a man lives only for himself, his reach will always be small. Self-centered living creates shallow impact because it is disconnected from purpose that extends beyond the moment. But when a man begins to invest in others, to lift, to guide, and to stand firmly for what is right his life takes on greater meaning. What he builds is no longer temporary or isolated; it becomes something that carries weight in the lives of those around him. Legacy was never meant to be contained within one person. It grows, strengthens, and multiplies when it is shared. Every life you pour into becomes an extension of your influence. Every act of integrity, every word of truth, and every moment of sacrifice plants seeds that continue long after you are gone. When you live with others in mind, your impact does not end with you - it expands through generations. A man who understands this does not just seek to succeed; he seeks to serve, knowing that true greatness is found in what he leaves behind in others.

Living beyond yourself requires a willingness to embrace sacrifice as an investment into something eternal. It is the daily decision to lay aside comfort in order to pursue purpose, to choose discipline when ease calls your name, and to walk in obedience even when convenience offers an easier road. This kind of life is not driven by fleeting feelings but by a deep conviction that God is shaping something greater than the moment you are in. It is in these costly choices that character is forged, faith is strengthened, and legacy begins to take root. To live this way is to understand that not every seed you plant will be seen in full bloom by your own eyes, yet it will still carry eternal weight. Some prayers you pray, some sacrifices you make, and some paths you walk in obedience will bear fruit in the lives of others long after you are gone. But that is the beauty of a life surrendered to God - it is not about recognition, but about impact. When you live beyond yourself, you become part of a story bigger than your own.

A man who lives beyond himself stops building for comfort and starts building for legacy. His decisions are no longer driven by what is easy, but by what is eternal. He understands that every act of obedience, every moment of discipline, and every stand of faith is laying a foundation that others will one day stand upon. His life becomes steady ground in an unstable world - a place where others can look and see what courage looks like in action, what faith looks like under pressure, and what endurance looks like when quitting would have been easier. He may never fully see the reach of his influence, but heaven records every stone he lays. This is the power of a life lived beyond self - it multiplies. It shapes mindsets, strengthens families, and calls others higher. When a man chooses to live this way, he doesn't just impact his moment - he builds something that outlives him, something that carries forward courage, faith, and endurance into the future.

The enemy of legacy is selfishness - the quiet, subtle voice that convinces a man that comfort is enough, that personal satisfaction is the goal, and that ease is the reward worth chasing. But a life centered on self will always shrink in significance. Satisfaction without purpose feeds the flesh but starves the soul. Legacy is not built in moments of indulgence, but in seasons of sacrifice, obedience, and vision. It is forged when a man lifts his eyes beyond himself and chooses to live for something greater than his own desires. A lion does not rise each day asking what will be easiest, but what he was made to do. In the same way, a man of God must reject the pull of selfish living and embrace the weight of responsibility. Your life was designed to carry purpose, to influence others, and to echo beyond your years. When you lay down selfish ambition and step into divine calling, you begin to build something that will outlive you. And that is legacy - a life that speaks long after you are gone.

Your legacy is forged through the daily decisions you make when no one is watching. Every act of discipline, every moment of obedience, every time you choose conviction over comfort, you are laying another brick in the foundation of what you will leave behind. If you desire to leave strength, then strength must define how you respond to pressure, adversity, and responsibility. If you want to leave faith, then faith must be seen in how you trust God when the outcome is uncertain. Legacy is not built in a moment; it is built in the consistency of a life aligned with purpose. Your habits become your character, and your character becomes your impact. When you choose integrity, perseverance, and faithfulness day after day, you are creating a ripple effect that extends far beyond your lifetime. So live with intention. Walk with clarity. Stand with conviction. Because one day, your life will speak without you and what it says will be the legacy you chose to build.

There will be moments when doing what is right feels costly, lonely, and heavy. In those moments, the easier path will whisper to you, offering comfort without conviction and relief without reward. But a man of purpose understands that true strength is not revealed when things are easy - it is revealed when everything in him wants to quit, yet he chooses to stand. These defining moments are the places where character is tested, faith is proven, and integrity is either strengthened or surrendered. Legacy is not built in comfort - it is forged in the fire of difficult decisions. Every time you choose obedience over convenience, courage over fear, and truth over compromise, you are shaping something that will outlive you. What feels like a private battle today will become a public testimony tomorrow. So stand firm when it's hard. Do what is right when no one is watching. Because in those weighty moments, you are not just making a decision - you are becoming the man your legacy demands.

A man who walks in strength teaches others how to stand. A man who lives with clarity removes confusion from those watching his life. Your example becomes a blueprint. Your consistency becomes a compass. Whether you realize it or not, someone is learning how to live by watching how you endure, how you decide, and how you carry what God has entrusted to you. And when the moment comes - when pressure rises and the cost is real - a lion does not retreat. He stands. Not because it is easy, but because it is necessary. He understands that leadership is proven in the moments where quitting would be justified, but faithfulness is chosen instead. In standing firm, he creates courage in others. In holding the line, he gives others permission to do the same. Your stand today becomes someone else's strength tomorrow. So stand with conviction. Lead with clarity. And live in such a way that what you leave behind is not hesitation, but a legacy of unwavering strength.

Impact is not always immediate, and that can test your faith more than failure ever could. You may sow truth, discipline, and obedience into seasons that seem silent, where nothing appears to be changing and no visible fruit is growing. But God works beneath the surface, in places you cannot see, shaping hearts, preparing moments, and aligning futures. Every act of integrity, every choice to stand firm, every step taken in obedience is a seed planted in eternal soil. Do not measure your effectiveness by what you see today - measure it by your faithfulness to what God has called you to do. A life lived with conviction carries a ripple effect far beyond your reach. What you build today may become the very breakthrough someone else needs tomorrow. Long after the moment has passed, the impact remains. So keep building, keep sowing, and keep standing firm. Because in God's hands, nothing done in faith is ever wasted, and every seed planted in obedience has the power to change a life.

Live with the end in mind. Every decision you make, every stand you take, every act of obedience is shaping the legacy you will leave behind. Build with intention, not impulse. Refuse to drift through life chasing comfort while neglecting purpose. Lead with courage when fear whispers to retreat. Stand firm when compromise looks easier. And above all, walk with God daily, because a life aligned with Him is never wasted. It is forged, refined, and strengthened for something far greater than the moment. When your time here is finished, your words will fade, but your life will echo. The character you built, the faith you carried, and the lives you impacted will speak louder than anything you ever said. A lion's legacy is not quiet - it roars through generations. It inspires strength in the weak, courage in the fearful, and faith in the uncertain. So live in a way that when you are gone, your life still points others to God. Let your legacy be one of power, purpose, and unwavering faith - a roar that refuses to die.

| 29 |

"FULLY AWAKENED"

There comes a moment in a man's life when something shifts deep within him. It is not announced with noise or spectacle, yet everything changes. The fog that once clouded his judgment begins to lift, and he sees clearly for the first time in a long while. The excuses that once felt justified now sound hollow, stripped of their power. When a man sees himself through God's truth, he not only understands who he is, but rises with conviction into the man he has been called to become. This awakening is the realization that drifting is no longer an option, and that his life has purpose far beyond convenience or ease. This is the beginning of being fully awakened. There is a steadiness in him now, a quiet strength that comes from knowing his life matters and that he has a role to fulfill. Though the journey ahead will still require growth, endurance, and faith, he is no longer asleep to it. He is awake - aware of the calling, committed to the process, and determined to become the man God designed him to be.

To be fully awakened is to step into clarity that reshapes everything. Your thoughts and your decisions begin to reflect a deeper understanding that your life carries purpose. You stop waiting for the right moment and realize that the moment is now. With conviction rooted in God, you rise from passivity and begin to lead your life intentionally, no longer moved by confusion but anchored in truth. In this place of awakening, you become a man who does not simply respond to life—you shape it. Your choices carry weight because they are guided by calling, not convenience. You recognize that leadership begins within, and from that inner transformation flows strength, discipline, and direction. Fear loses its grip because clarity has taken its place. Doubt fades because purpose stands firm. You walk forward with a steady resolve, knowing who you are and whose you are. This is the life of a man fully awakened to truth, alive to calling, and committed to walking it out with unwavering conviction.

Walking in full spiritual strength means you are no longer led by what you feel in the moment, but by what you know to be true. Emotions rise and fall like waves, but truth stands firm like a rock beneath your feet. When a man matures in his faith, he stops allowing temporary feelings to make permanent decisions. His confidence is no longer rooted in emotional highs, but in the unchanging nature of God. Discipline becomes his ally, not his enemy, and truth becomes his compass in every season. This kind of strength is steady, grounded, and unwavering. A man walking in spiritual strength is guided by the Spirit, not tossed by circumstances. He has learned to silence the noise of doubt and listen for the voice of God. Even when emotions try to pull him off course, he returns to what is anchored within him. This is the life of a man who is no longer reactive, but intentional - no longer drifting, but directed - no longer fragile, but firmly established in the truth that sustains him.

While the world celebrates loud confidence and outward bravado, true strength is revealed in restraint, endurance, and unwavering faith. It is the man who stands firm when pressure mounts, who refuses to compromise when it would be easier to bend, and who holds his ground when others retreat. This kind of strength is built through prayer, obedience, and a deep, settled conviction that God is faithful no matter what comes. When the storm arrives - and it will - spiritual strength is what keeps you anchored. It is the resolve to remain when everything in you wants to run, to believe when every circumstance argues against hope, and to endure when the weight feels unbearable. This strength does not shout; it stands. It does not boast; it perseveres. The man who cultivates this kind of strength in private will not collapse in public. He will rise, steady and immovable, not because of his own power, but because he has learned to draw from a source far greater than himself.

A fully awakened man sees clearly how passivity quietly steals purpose, how hesitation weakens impact, and how silence in critical moments allows what is wrong to grow unchecked. He no longer deceives himself into thinking delay is harmless. He understands that every moment of inaction carries a cost, not just for himself, but for those he is called to lead, protect, and influence. This awareness ignites within him a conviction that refuses to stay dormant. He realizes that comfort can no longer be his master, and fear can no longer be his excuse. So he rises. Not because it is easy, but because it is necessary. He steps forward when it would be more convenient to step back. He speaks when it would be safer to remain silent. He acts when everything in him feels the weight of resistance. This is the mark of a man who is awake. He does not wait for perfect conditions but moves in obedience and courage. And in that rising, he becomes a man of strength, clarity, and decisive faith.

There was a time when you hesitated, waiting for your emotions to be steady, your circumstances to be favorable, and your confidence to be complete. But awakening changes that. You begin to see that delayed obedience is still disobedience, and that faith was never designed to be passive. True spiritual maturity is not found in waiting for the right feeling - it is found in moving when God speaks, even when everything around you feels uncertain. Conviction rises when you step forward not because it is easy, but because it is right. In that awakening, you no longer negotiate with hesitation or bow to the need for perfect conditions. You become a man who walks by faith, not by sight. Obedience becomes immediate, deliberate, and unwavering. And in that place, power is released. Because God does not anoint hesitation - He moves through surrender. When you stop waiting for comfort and start walking in conviction, you step into alignment with His purpose, and that is where real strength is found.

No longer passive means you refuse to stand on the sidelines while life, responsibility, and purpose pass you by. It is the moment a man wakes up and realizes that silence, hesitation, and avoidance are no longer options. Stepping into responsibility means you take ownership of your choices, your calling, and your influence. It means you lead when it would be easier to follow, speak when it would be more comfortable to stay quiet, and act when others delay. Passivity keeps a man small, but purpose demands that he rise. Embracing leadership is about accepting that your life affects others and choosing to live in a way that reflects God's design. When you reject passivity, you step into alignment with who you were created to be: steady, intentional, and unwavering. You begin to move with conviction, not convenience. And though the weight may feel heavy at times, it is the very weight that forges character, builds endurance, and shapes you into the man God has called you to be.

Hesitation loses its grip when identity is settled in God. When a man knows he is chosen, called, and commissioned he no longer lives in the tension of uncertainty. Decisions become clearer, steps become firmer, and obedience becomes quicker. He is no longer paralyzed by the fear of getting it wrong, because his confidence is rooted in his relationship with God. Identity anchors him, and what once caused delay now becomes a place of decisive action. Out of that clarity flows a quiet, steady assurance that cannot be easily shaken. It is the kind of authority that stands without striving and leads without demanding attention. This man moves forward because he knows he has been sent. He speaks because he knows truth has been placed within him. He acts because he understands that obedience matters more than opinion. When identity is clear, hesitation fades into the background, and a life marked by purpose, courage, and conviction steps forward into the light.

A fully awakened man understands that pressure is not his enemy - it is his proving ground. When challenges rise, he does not shrink back in fear or hesitation because he knows that every moment of resistance carries the potential for transformation. Where others withdraw, he steps forward. Where others doubt, he stands firm. He recognizes that God often uses tension to reveal strength, and opposition to refine purpose. Instead of asking to escape the battle, he asks to be strengthened within it, trusting that the fire he faces is shaping him into the man he was called to become. In the very places where it would be easiest to give up, he chooses to press in, to endure, and to believe. He leans into resistance with faith, knowing that growth is rarely found in ease, but in perseverance. And as he stands his ground, within him awakens a steady, unshakable confidence that God is at work in every challenge, forging resilience, sharpening character, and preparing him for the weight of his purpose.

Living as a man of God requires an inner calibration where your thoughts, actions, words, and choices all come into agreement with His truth. There is a quiet strength that flows from knowing who you are and whose you are. Your mind is no longer ruled by fear or distraction but anchored in conviction. Your actions are no longer reactive, but intentional. Your words carry weight because they are shaped by truth, not emotion. This is the transformation that takes place when a man allows God to shape not just what he does, but who he is at the core. When alignment takes hold, the need for approval begins to fall away. You are no longer performing for validation or bending under the pressure of others' expectations. Instead, you live from an unshakable place that is rooted in calling. A man who lives from purpose walks with authority because he is aligned with something eternal. And in that alignment, his life becomes a reflection of the design God intended all along.

This kind of life is not built on convenience - it is forged through discipline. When your flesh craves comfort, discipline calls you to rise. When weariness whispers that you have done enough, purpose reminds you there is more in you to give. A disciplined life is not about perfection; it is about consistency. It is choosing obedience over emotion, commitment over comfort, and calling over convenience. Every time you get up when it would be easier to stay down, you are training your spirit to lead your life instead of your feelings. This is how a man becomes steady, reliable, and unshaken - by mastering the moments that most people surrender to. Awakening does not just lift you once - it keeps calling you higher. It refuses to let you settle into passivity or drift back into old patterns. It presses on your spirit to speak when silence would be easier, to stand when compromise feels safer, and to act when hesitation tempts you to delay. You are no longer governed by what is easy, but by what is right.

The man who is fully awakened understands that every word he speaks, every decision he makes, and every reaction he displays carries weight beyond himself. His life is not isolated; it echoes into the hearts of his family, shapes the atmosphere of his home, and leaves impressions on those quietly observing from a distance. Because of this, he becomes a builder of people, a stabilizer in chaos, and a reflection of God's character in the everyday moments that others might overlook. He understands that a careless life can break spirits, but a disciplined and surrendered life can build legacies. So he walks with integrity when no one is watching and with humility when everyone is. He speaks life instead of criticism, leads with conviction instead of convenience, and chooses faithfulness over fleeting comfort. In doing so, he becomes the kind of man whose presence brings growth, whose example inspires change, and whose life quietly but powerfully points others toward something greater.

There is a boldness that comes with awakening. It is not loud, reckless, or driven by ego, but grounded, steady, and unshakable. You begin to see clearly who you are, whose you are, and what you are called to walk in. This kind of boldness doesn't need validation from others because it is anchored in something eternal. It stands firm when challenged, speaks when silence would be easier, and moves forward even when the path is uncertain. This awakened courage transforms how you live. You are no longer intimidated by opposition, because you understand that resistance is often confirmation that you are advancing. You stop shrinking back and start stepping into moments that once felt overwhelming. Your decisions are no longer filtered through fear, but through truth. And in that truth, you find a strength that cannot be shaken by circumstance or opinion. This is the boldness of a man who is clear in purpose and unwilling to bow to anything that stands against what God has spoken over his life.

When spiritual clarity begins to take hold, your vision changes before your circumstances do. The walls that once felt immovable start to reveal hidden doors. You realize that obstacles were never sent to destroy you - they were positioned to develop you. Fear loses its voice, and purpose begins to speak louder. The same situations that once caused hesitation now stir a deeper confidence within you, because you understand that growth is often disguised as pressure. You begin to welcome what you once avoided, because you trust that God is working through every challenge. Intimidation gives way to invitation—an invitation to rise, to stretch, and to become more than you were before. Spiritual clarity doesn't remove difficulty, but it redefines it. You start to see every moment as an opportunity to walk in strength, wisdom, and purpose. And as your perspective aligns with truth, your life begins to reflect it. You now move forward not as a man held back by obstacles, but as a man strengthened by them.

A fully awakened man no longer measures himself by flawless performance, but by faithful progress. Each day, he rises with intention, choosing discipline over comfort and truth over convenience. He knows his weaknesses, yet he refuses to be ruled by them. Instead of hiding from his shortcomings, he confronts them with humility and courage, trusting that God is still shaping him. He may stumble, but he does not stay down. He may struggle, but he does not surrender. His life is marked by a steady, determined pursuit of becoming the man God has called him to be. The man he used to be no longer defines him. Old patterns, passive mindsets, and defeated thinking have lost their hold. His focus is no longer on where he failed, but on who he is becoming. Progress fuels his passion, and growth shapes his identity. With every step forward, he builds strength, deepens his faith, and sharpens his resolve. He lives with purpose and walks with a mindset that says, "I am not turning back."

When a man becomes aware of what God has placed within him, he can no longer live casually or passively. What once could be ignored now demands attention. What once felt optional now feels essential. With awakening comes the undeniable truth that you are accountable for what you carry. This responsibility is not meant to overwhelm you, but to focus you. It shifts your mindset from comfort to calling, from maintenance to movement. You begin to steward your time differently, guard your habits more carefully, and pursue growth with intention. You recognize that lives may be impacted by your obedience, and that your faithfulness has a ripple effect far beyond what you can see. So you rise - not perfectly but purposefully committed to becoming the man who does not waste what God has entrusted to him. Because an awakened man understands this: what God placed within him is too valuable to remain unused, and too powerful to remain hidden.

There comes a moment when your eyes are opened and you begin to recognize that every day carries divine potential, that each moment holds an opportunity to move in alignment with God's will. This kind of urgency is not frantic or fearful; it is steady, intentional, and rooted in purpose. You stop delaying what you know you are called to do. You stop excusing inaction. Instead, you lean into obedience, understanding that what you do today is shaping who you become tomorrow. A man who lives with purpose-driven urgency values the present because he understands its impact on the future. He does not assume there will always be another chance, another season, another opportunity. He honors God by acting when prompted, by stepping forward when it would be easier to wait. This urgency fuels discipline, sharpens conviction, and strengthens resolve. It is the quiet fire that keeps him moving, growing, and becoming. Not rushed but resolved. Not pressured but purposeful.

To be fully awakened is to be aware of God's presence, attentive to His voice, and sensitive to the direction He is leading. It is a life where your desires begin to reflect His will, your choices carry eternal weight, and your focus shifts from temporary gain to lasting purpose. You are intentional, anchored, and guided by something greater than emotion or circumstance. To be fully awakened is to live with your spirit actively drawing from the strength God provides rather than relying on your own limitations. It means refusing to settle for mediocrity, compromise, or a lesser version of who you were created to be. You recognize that God's design for your life is your calling, your responsibility, and your privilege to pursue. So you rise each day with resolve, choosing discipline over distraction, purpose over passivity, and faith over fear. You understand that awakening is not a one-time moment, but a daily decision to live fully alive, fully surrendered, and fully committed to becoming the man God intended you to be.

Once a man is fully awakened, something irreversible takes place deep within him. His eyes are opened and there is a holy tension within him now, a fire that refuses to let him settle for less. Conviction replaces complacency. Clarity silences confusion. And even when the road ahead is difficult, he knows too much to turn back. The awakening has marked him. It has separated him from the man he used to be. From that point forward, his life takes on a new direction. He moves with intention, not impulse. He stands with strength, not hesitation. He is anchored in purpose, driven by calling, and sustained by the strength of God within him. This is not a fleeting moment of inspiration; it is a transformation of identity. He walks forward - steady, strong, and unshaken - not because the path is easy, but because retreat is no longer possible. He has seen who he is meant to be, and now he lives with a relentless commitment to become that man, honoring God with every step he takes.

| 30 |

"THE LION RISES"

There comes a moment when a man can no longer pretend he doesn't hear the voice of God calling him out of passivity and into purpose. It is not gentle in the sense of being easy, but it is unmistakably clear. It cuts through excuses, silences fear, and exposes the cost of staying the same. This is the line in the sand where a man decides he will no longer live half-hearted, no longer shrink back, no longer delay obedience. The lion rises within him and he realizes he was not created to drift through life, but to stand, to lead, to fight for what is right, and to walk boldly in the calling God placed on his life. When the lion rises, he embraces the weight of responsibility, the challenge of growth, and the refining fire that shapes him into something unshakable. This is where hesitation is replaced with decisive faith, and where purpose outweighs every excuse. The call of God is alive within him, driving him forward. And from this moment on, he rises, he moves, and he becomes the man he was created to be.

You were not created to tiptoe through life, carefully avoiding every risk and retreating when responsibility calls your name. God did not design you to live small, hidden behind fear, doubt, or endless excuses. He formed you with intention - every gift, every challenge, every moment shaping you into a man capable of standing firm when others fall back. The life you were meant to live is discovered when you step forward in faith, even when the ground beneath you feels uncertain. This is the moment to awaken what has been buried under fear and hesitation. You are not here by accident, and your purpose is not optional. It is a divine assignment that requires your courage, your obedience, and your willingness to move when everything in you wants to stand still. So rise up. Refuse to live beneath what you were created for. Because when you step into who God has called you to be, you don't just change your life - you impact everything and everyone your life was meant to touch.

Too many men walk through life aware deep down that they were created for more yet are unwilling to embrace the cost that greatness requires. They feel the quiet pull of who they could become, but silence it with excuses, delays, and the easy road. But potential is never fulfilled by accident. It is forged through sacrifice, sharpened through pressure, and revealed through obedience. Every day you choose comfort over calling you drift further from the man you were designed to be. But you were never created to drift so rise above passivity, rise above fear, and rise above the lesser version of yourself that settles when it should stand. There is a strength inside you that will not awaken until you decide the cost is worth paying. Step into the fire. Refuse to live half-hearted when you were called to live fully surrendered and fully alive. The moment you choose to rise, everything begins to change because a man who decides to become who God called him to be is a man who cannot be stopped.

The lion within you was never meant to be lulled to sleep by comfort - it was designed to rise at the sound of a calling. Comfort may feel safe, but it dulls the edge of who you are meant to become. Calling, however, stretches you beyond what is easy and pulls you into what is necessary. The strength inside you does not awaken in stillness but in the moments when pressure tightens, when the path narrows, and when quitting seems justified. That is where the lion stirs. That is where identity is forged. You were not built for a life of ease, but for a life of purpose - one that calls you forward, higher, and deeper into the man you were created to be. Every hardship has been shaping your endurance, your resolve, and your faith. What felt like setbacks were actually setups for strength. What looked like resistance was really refinement. The moment you're in right now is the very ground where the lion within you rises, takes its place, and steps boldly into the calling that has been waiting for you all along.

This is your moment. Not a distant someday, not a more convenient season - this is the line drawn in the present where decision becomes destiny. Too many men wait for clarity before they move, but calling is revealed in obedience, not hesitation. The door in front of you will not stay open forever. God has already stirred your heart, already placed the weight of purpose on your shoulders. That tension you feel is not pressure to retreat - it is the signal to advance. Step forward now, even if your voice shakes, even if your path isn't fully clear. Faith was never meant to be comfortable - it was meant to be acted upon. So rise and move. Refuse to let delay steal what courage is trying to awaken in you. The time for overthinking has passed; the time for bold obedience has come. You were not created to circle the edge of your calling - you were created to walk in it with authority. Every step you take in faith breaks chains of fear and builds a life that cannot be shaken. This is your call. Answer it with action.

You already know what God has placed on your heart. That burden you carry is sacred. That vision you cannot shake is revelation. And that conviction that keeps returning, even when you try to ignore it, is the Spirit of God pressing on your life with purpose. God does not speak carelessly. When He entrusts something to you, it is because He has already measured your capacity to carry it through Him. The weight you feel is not meant to crush you, but to call you higher. It is an invitation to step out of comfort and into obedience, to stop circling the idea and start walking in it. But assignments from God always require a response. They demand more than agreement - they demand action. Obedience is where calling becomes reality. The longer you delay, the heavier the burden feels - not because it is too much, but because it was never meant to sit idle. So move. Trust. Act. Because what God placed within you was not given for someday - it was given for now.

To step boldly into your calling requires a deliberate break from the version of yourself that once felt safe but was never meant to last. Growth in God is not comfortable. It stretches, refines, and calls you higher. The excuses that once justified hesitation must be laid down. You cannot carry both your calling and your comfort at the same time; one will always have to be surrendered. When you choose purpose, you are choosing to trust God beyond your feelings, beyond your understanding, and beyond the approval of others. Real faith begins when obedience matters more than ease. There is a cost to becoming who God has called you to be, but there is a greater cost in staying the same. Purpose will often lead you down a narrow path, one that requires courage and conviction, but it is the only path that leads to fulfillment. So take the step. Let go of who you were and embrace who you are becoming. Because on the other side of obedience is a man fully alive in the calling God has placed within him.

The man who walks in boldness feels the same tension, the same uncertainty, the same pounding heartbeat but he chooses to step forward anyway. He understands that courage is forged in movement, not in comfort. Like a lion, he does not wait for the wilderness to become quiet before he advances. He moves because he is called, because he is compelled by purpose, because there is something within him that refuses to shrink back. That inner fire burns hotter than the fear trying to contain him. When you stop bowing to fear, you begin to realize that fear was never meant to lead you - it was meant to be conquered. Every step you take in spite of it strengthens you, sharpens you, and aligns you more closely with the man you were created to be. The lion within you awakens not when fear disappears, but when you decide it will no longer dictate your direction. So rise and move forward because on the other side of that fear is growth, authority, and a life marked by obedience and power.

There will always be resistance when you step toward what God has called you to become. Doubt will speak in subtle tones, trying to convince you that you are not ready, not worthy, or not capable. The past will attempt to redefine you by what you used to be instead of who God says you are now. But those voices only have power if you agree with them. You were not called to live bound by what once was - you were called to walk boldly in what is being formed in you. You must choose which voice you will follow. Will it be the voice of fear that keeps you small, or the voice of faith that calls you higher? Will you listen to the past, or will you stand on the promises of God? When you choose truth, you step into freedom. When you choose faith, you step into purpose. Stand firm in that choice. Silence the lies with truth. Move forward even when resistance rises. Because the man who learns to follow the right voice is the man who becomes unstoppable in the hands of God.

You are not who you used to be. In Christ, the old has passed away, and something entirely new has begun within you. The weight you once carried has been lifted, and the chains that once held you have been broken. You are not called to keep looking back at who you were; you are called to rise into who God has declared you to be. This new man is not weak or defeated but is renewed, restored, and equipped to stand firm. Now is the time to walk in that truth. Stand with confidence, not because of your own perfection, but because of Christ's finished work in you. Lead with conviction, knowing that your life has purpose and direction. Move forward without hesitation, refusing to let yesterday dictate your tomorrow. The new man within you is built to endure, to overcome, and to press ahead no matter the resistance. So step forward boldly. Leave the past where it belongs and embrace the calling in front of you. You are not going back - you are moving forward, stronger, wiser, and unshakable.

Becoming a man who cannot be shaken is not about avoiding storms - it is about refusing to be moved by them. Life will bring pressure, uncertainty, and moments where everything familiar feels like it's slipping through your hands. But strength is not proven in comfort; it is forged in resistance. The winds may howl, the rain may fall, but you remain standing because your life is built on something eternal. Stability comes from trusting the One who stands above it. A man who cannot be shaken has learned where to place his weight. He does not lean on feelings, opinions, or temporary success - he leans on unchanging truth. In the middle of chaos, he chooses faith over fear, conviction over compromise, and obedience over ease. His strength is quiet but unbreakable, steady but powerful. When others panic, he stands. When others retreat, he advances. Not because he is fearless, but because he is anchored. And that anchor holds, no matter how violent the storm becomes.

The unshakable man is forged in the unseen moments where character is tested without applause. Discipline becomes his daily practice, not because it is recognized, but because it is necessary. Integrity becomes his standard, not because it is rewarded, but because it is right. In those hidden hours, when shortcuts are tempting and compromise is easy, he chooses the higher path. When the time comes for him to stand in public, he is not scrambling to become something he is not - he is simply revealing what has already been built within him. The storms do not create his strength; they expose it. The pressure does not define him; it proves him. Because he has been faithful in private, he is unshaken in public. His foundation is not built on the shifting approval of others, but on truth, consistency, and obedience. And when everything around him trembles, he remains standing because of the quiet, daily decisions that made him strong long before anyone ever noticed.

This kind of man is not shaped by the shifting winds of culture or the intensity of the moment. When pressure rises, he leans into the truth that has already been settled in his heart. When challenged, he does not retreat into silence or fear; he responds with conviction, knowing who he is and whose he is. And when tested, he does not fold under the weight because his strength was forged long before the test ever came. His foundation is not built on emotions that change, but on truth that stands. And truth does not move when storms come. Because of that, his life becomes a testimony. While others are shaken, he remains steady. While others compromise, he holds the line. While others give in, he endures. Not because he is perfect, but because he is grounded. He has chosen to build his life on what is eternal, not what is temporary. And in doing so, he becomes unshakable - not by his own power, but by the truth he stands on. When the storm passes, he is still there standing, strengthened, and proven.

God is calling you to become that man - not a reflection of shifting culture, but a life forged in the fire of conviction. Culture will always try to redefine what a man should be, bending truth to fit comfort, applause, or convenience. But conviction anchors you in something unchanging. It calls you higher when it would be easier to stay the same. It shapes your decisions in private before they are ever seen in public. This kind of man is not built overnight. He is formed through surrender, refined through trials, and strengthened through obedience. This is the man marked by strength that is steady, courage that moves forward despite fear, humility that bows before God, and faith that does not waver in the storm. His life becomes a reflection of something greater than himself - a testimony that God can take an ordinary man and shape him into something unshakable. When challenges come, he does not retreat. When the path is unclear, he does not drift. He trusts, he stands, and he presses forward.

The lion rises in a man not when he grips tighter to his own strength, but when he finally lets go and bows before God's authority. It is the moment a man stops striving to be his own source and instead becomes a vessel for divine strength. When a man fully embraces God's calling, he steps out of confusion and into clarity, out of fear and into purpose. His identity is no longer shaped by the opinions of the world, but by the voice of the One who created him. True strength is not forged in self-reliance, but in complete dependence on God. The lion rises because the man has learned where his power truly comes from. He no longer fights alone; no longer carries burdens he was never meant to bear. Instead, he stands firm, rooted in truth, empowered by grace, and led by the Spirit. When trials come, he does not retreat because his strength is not his own. When pressure rises, he does not fold because he is anchored in something eternal. This is the man who cannot be shaken.

You were never created to drift through life, reacting instead of leading, surviving instead of building. There is something placed inside you by God that refuses to stay dormant - a call to rise, to engage, and to take responsibility for the ground you've been given. Passivity may feel safe, but it slowly erodes purpose and dulls conviction. A man who understands his calling does not wait for perfect conditions; he steps forward in obedience, trusting that God strengthens those who move. The world is transformed by men who rise with conviction and lead with purpose. Your voice matters. Your actions matter. Your willingness to stand when others sit down carries weight far beyond what you can see. Leadership is about responsibility. It is choosing to show up, to speak truth, to protect what is right, and to pursue what is good even when it costs you. This is your moment to reject passivity and embrace purpose. Rise up, take your place, and become the man God called you to be.

Rise. Not because everything feels easy, but because you were never called to live beneath fear or bow to doubt. The man God is forming in you is not defined by hesitation, insecurity, or failure - he is built on truth, refined through pressure, and strengthened by obedience. Every time you choose faith over fear, every time you move forward when doubt whispers "stay," you are stepping out of the old and into the calling that has been waiting for you all along. So rise above the version of yourself that once held you back. That man served his purpose, but he is not your destiny. You are called higher - to walk with boldness, to move with clarity, and to live with conviction rooted in God's voice, not your feelings. Step forward with confidence, knowing that the same God who called you is the One who empowers you. This is your moment to stand, to move, and to become the man who does not shrink in the face of challenge, but advances with unwavering faith and unshakable purpose.

The moment you've been waiting for is standing in front of you demanding a response. God has made the call clear, and deep within you, you already know it. The lion is not approaching from a distance; he is rising from the depths of your spirit, awakening courage, conviction, and purpose. This is not the time to hesitate or shrink back. This is the moment to step forward with boldness, trusting that the One who called you has already equipped you. So rise with authority, rise with clarity, rise with unwavering faith. Let the fear that once silenced you be replaced with a voice that speaks truth and power. Let the man you were give way to the man you are becoming. You were not created to live cautiously on the edge of your calling, but to walk fully in it, unshaken and unafraid. The lion within you is a reflection of the strength God has placed in you - a strength that does not break under pressure but is revealed through it. Now is the time to let him rise. Not tomorrow, not someday. Now.

SUMMARY

The journey to awakening the lion within is not a moment - it is a decision you make every day. A decision to rise when it would be easier to remain comfortable. A decision to stand when others sit. A decision to speak truth when silence would be safer. A decision to carry responsibility instead of avoiding it. This is what separates men who drift from men who lead.

You have seen what it means to live with strength, discipline, courage, and conviction. You have been reminded that real manhood is not found in noise, pride, or domination but in steady, unwavering obedience to God. The lion within is not reckless - it is resolute. It is anchored. It is unshakable because it is rooted in truth.

There will still be battles ahead. There will be moments of pressure, resistance, and challenge. But now you understand something you may not have fully embraced before: you are not weak, and you are not without purpose. God has already placed within you what you need to stand firm and move forward.

So do not go back to sleep. Do not return to passivity. Do not shrink when you were created to stand. Rise each day with intention. Lead with strength. Walk with integrity. Endure with faith. And as you do, you will not only change your life you will impact your home, your community, and generations to come. Because when a man awakens to who God created him to be the lion does not go back into hiding.